MEDIA DEBATES

ISSUES IN MASS COMMUNICATION

EVERETTE E. DENNIS
Gannett Center for Media Studies
Columbia University

JOHN C. MERRILL
Louisiana State University

Longman
New York & London

Media Debates: Issues in Mass Communication

Copyright © 1991 by **Longman Publishing Group**
All rights reserved.
No part of this publication may be reproduced,
stored in a retrieval system, or transmitted
in any form or by any means, electronic, mechanical,
photocopying, recording, or otherwise,
without the prior permission of the publisher.

Longman, 95 Church Street, White Plains, N.Y. 10601

Associated companies:
Longman Group Ltd., London
Longman Cheshire Pty., Melbourne
Longman Paul Pty., Auckland
Copp Clark Pitman, Toronto

Executive editor: Gordon T. R. Anderson
Production editor: Linda W. Witzling
Text design: Betty L. Sokol
Cover design: Anne M. Pompeo

Library of Congress Cataloging in Publication Data

Dennis, Everette E.
    Media debates : issues in mass communication / Everette Dennis.
  John C. Merrill
      p.   cm.
    Includes bibliographical references.
    ISBN 0-8013-0436-9
    1. Mass media—United States. 2. Journalism—United States.
  I. Merrill, John Calhoun, 1924–   . II. Title.
  P92.U5D445 1990
  302.23′0973—dc20   90-5748
                                                                                     CIP

2 3 4 5 6 7 8 9 10-AL-9594939291

CONTENTS

Preface	ix
Introduction	1

1 Freedom of the Press — 5

Dennis:	The American press is not free.	6
	Argument Summation	11
Merrill:	The American press is free.	11
	Argument Summation	15
Topics for Discussion		16
Topics for Research		16
Further Reading		17

2 Media-Government Relationship — 20

Merrill:	The media and government should not be adversaries.	21
	Argument Summation	25
Dennis:	The media and government should be adversaries.	26
	Argument Summation	30
Topics for Discussion		30
Topics for Research		31
Further Reading		31

3 Media and the Public Trust — 33

Merrill: The media chiefly desire to make profits. — 34
Argument Summation — 38
Dennis: Media mainly serve the public interest. — 38
Argument Summation — 41
Topics for Discussion — 42
Topics for Research — 42
Further Reading — 43

4 People's Right to Know — 45

Dennis: There is no right to know. — 46
Argument Summation — 50
Merrill: There is a right to know. — 50
Argument Summation — 53
Topics for Discussion — 53
Topics for Research — 54
Further Reading — 54

5 Public Access to the Media — 56

Merrill: The public has no right of access. — 57
Argument Summation — 62
Dennis: The public has a right of access. — 62
Argument Summation — 67
Topics for Discussion — 68
Topics for Research — 68
Further Reading — 69

6 Media Pluralism — 70

Dennis: Media pluralism is not shrinking. — 71
Argument Summation — 75
Merrill: Media pluralism is shrinking. — 76
Argument Summation — 79
Topics for Discussion — 79
Topics for Research — 80
Further Reading — 80

7 Power of the Media — 82

Dennis:	The media are quite powerful.	83
	Argument Summation	88
Merrill:	The media are not so powerful.	88
	Argument Summation	91
Topics for Discussion		92
Topics for Research		92
Further Reading		93

8 Quality of Media Content — 95

Dennis:	Media content is generally of poor quality and getting worse.	95
	Argument Summation	101
Merrill:	Media content is generally of good quality and getting better.	101
	Argument Summation	106
Topics for Discussion		106
Topics for Research		106
Further Reading		107

9 Journalistic Objectivity — 109

Merrill:	Journalistic objectivity is not possible.	110
	Argument Summation	115
Dennis:	Journalistic objectivity is possible.	116
	Argument Summation	122
Topics for Discussion		122
Topics for Research		123
Further Reading		123

10 Deciding What Is News — 125

Dennis:	Market forces, not editors' judgments, should decide what is news.	125
	Argument Summation	130
Merrill:	Editors' judgments, not market forces, should decide what is news.	131
	Argument Summation	134
Topics for Discussion		134

	Topics for Research	134
	Further Reading	135

11 News-Gathering Tactics — 136

Merrill:	Tactics should be situational and relative.	136
	Argument Summation	141
Dennis:	News-gathering tactics should be consistent and universal.	141
	Argument Summation	146
Topics for Discussion		147
Topics for Research		147
Further Reading		148

12 Journalistic Ethics — 150

Merrill:	Journalists are essentially unethical.	151
	Argument Summation	154
Dennis:	Journalists are essentially ethical.	154
	Argument Summation	157
Topics for Discussion		157
Topics for Research		157
Further Reading		158

13 Press Councils and Ethical Codes — 160

Merrill:	Press councils and ethical codes are dangerous control mechanisms.	161
	Argument Summation	164
Dennis:	Press councils and ethical codes are useful instruments of criticism that can improve the media.	164
	Argument Summation	169
Topics for Discussion		169
Topics for Research		170
Further Reading		170

14 Propaganda and the Media — 172

Dennis:	Media are defenses against propaganda.	173
	Argument Summation	175
Merrill:	Media are instruments of propaganda.	176
	Argument Summation	179

Topics for Discussion		180
Topics for Research		180
Further Reading		181

15 Advertising   182

Merrill:	Advertising is a negative social force.	183
	Argument Summation	186
Dennis:	Advertising is a positive social force.	186
	Argument Summation	190
Topics for Discussion		190
Topics for Research		190
Further Reading		191

16 Public Relations   192

Dennis:	Public relations manipulates the news.	193
	Argument Summation	195
Merrill:	Public relations provides an essential news service.	195
	Argument Summation	198
Topics for Discussion		199
Topics for Research		199
Further Reading		200

17 Journalism as a Profession   201

Merrill:	Journalism is not a profession.	201
	Argument Summation	205
Dennis:	Journalism is a profession.	206
	Argument Summation	210
Topics for Discussion		210
Topics for Research		210
Further Reading		211

18 Global Communication Dominance   212

Merrill:	The U.S. media have an unhealthy dominance.	213
	Argument Summation	217

Dennis:	The U.S. media contribute fairly to communication equity.	217
	Argument Summation	220
Topics for Discussion		221
Topics for Research		221
Further Reading		222

Index 223

PREFACE

All authors believe their books are one of a kind, aiming to express or explain specific ideas as no one has before. In reality, though, books, especially textbooks, are likely to have more similarities than differences with what has come before. Certainly this is true in the field of communications where courses, topics, and modes of analysis have changed little in the last twenty years.

The authors of this book, guided by an offhand comment from Yogi Berra's son, Dale, have introduced something distinctive in communication study, an approach which at this writing has no direct competitors. Once when asked to compare himself with his father, Dale Berra said, "Our similarities are different." In this book, we have attempted to take up the major topics and issues that endure in media studies, drawing on the traditional arguments and major literature, but approaching our task in a somewhat different fashion. It is our hope that this distinctive approach, tested out in a previous edition and warmly received, will assist anyone trying to identify, sort out, and understand the great issues that engage individuals and institutions concerned about the media and mass communication in modern society.

This book had its origins in a conversation between the authors several years ago, when both expressed interest in doing a book together; but they recognized that their views were far enough apart so that they would find it difficult to write in a unified voice without compromising greatly. It was then that we decided upon the course which we follow here, one, we believe, that is helpful to students of the media and communication, because it leads them to their own conclusions about often controversial issues.

At first glance this book appears to be a conventional debate: There is a neutral statement, followed by a challenge and a response. As we explain in the introduction, in this process we have attempted to tune into an argument that has long persisted in American society and elsewhere in the world. We have assigned each other the task of challenging and responding without regard to our personal views on the subject. We act as adversaries drawing on the best evidence we can find on the subject, and we invite our readers to engage in the same process. The idea is to move from a neutral definition of the topic under scrutiny to the heart of the debate. We deliberately do not offer conclusions, but instead questions for research and discussion which, we hope, will evoke in readers conclusions of their own. Or, the readers may at that point decide both positions argued here are wrong-headed, needing a new formulation, different evidence, and different conclusions. Readers are encouraged to look for underlying assumptions and "biases" in the authors' views because the issues grappled with here are far too complex to be reduced to a simple analysis. They require textured complexity in a fashion that includes both attributes and liabilities inherent in a given position. In the end, though, most media issues are resolved, whether in the short run or for the long haul, by human decisions made with all the human frailties any of us expect in a world where rationality and hard thought must necessarily accommodate eccentricities, ego, greed, self-interest, and other factors.

It is with such thoughts in mind that futurists sometimes express caution about the "human factors" that always seem to get in the way of technology and invention. What is technically or intellectually possible doesn't always happen because of the bedeviling intervention of consumer habits, social convention, and government idiosyncracies. Most of us are sometimes wont to say that a particular policy or decision "doesn't make sense," and we speculate why this might be the case. This book is designed to assist in the sense-making process by equipping its readers with the tools that help explain why the most rational and reasonable course is not always followed by those in charge of our media, our social institutions, and our governments.

We hope that the readers and users of this book—students and teachers in journalism, communication, and media studies programs—will have as much fun in fashioning their own media debates as we have had in constructing the ones that appear in the pages to follow.

This book is designed for college and university courses that go by several names: "Mass Media and Society," "Contemporary Problems in Journalism and Mass Communication," "Ethics in Communication," and others. We wrote the book mainly for intermediate students—juniors, seniors, or beginning graduate students. It may also be useful for media history and law courses. Of course, we hope that the communications professionals who are actors in the dramas depicted here will also be among our readers. We believe that anyone who cares about mass communication should be acquainted with the main arguments of the field. We hope this book will help.

In preparation of this manuscript, we are grateful to many persons—including several generations of students—who stimulated our thinking about communication issues and problems. We are especially grateful to our editor at Longman, Gordon Anderson, as well as those who critiqued this edition of the book including Carol Reuss, University of North Carolina, Chapel Hill; Gary Pettey, Cleveland State University; and Dominic LaSorsa, University of Texas, Austin.

We continue to be grateful to an earlier cadre of valued critics who helped shape this book in its original edition including Vince P. Norris, Pennsylvania State University, Carol Reuss, University of North Carolina, and Dwight L. Teeter, University of Wisconsin, Milwaukee.

INTRODUCTION

Public communication provokes arguments. When the various elements of our system of communication in the United States are functioning, they are almost always bumping into controversy. Because by definition their work is displayed in full public view, they are vulnerable to criticism of all kinds. People who make up the media audience quite naturally like to talk about the various media messages directed toward them. Sometimes they do so with considerable knowledge and apparent insight; they have a right to express their views, to put forth their impressions and concerns. This book presents some of the many arguments that arise in regard to the process of mass communication—whether in the media generally, in media institutions like newspapers and television, in individual communicators like reporters, producers, photographers, public relations personnel and advertising executives, or in the content of communication, both written and visual.

Although many media issues may seem trendy and ephemeral because they themselves are part of the news, they are really part of a larger mosaic of enduring debates that stretch back decades, even centuries in some cases. A county prosecutor tries to stop a reporter from covering a trial. A grieving parent wants the press to leave the scene of a tragedy. A government blocks publication of a book. A television producer intrudes on the privacy of an individual. A terrorist organization holds an editor hostage. An advertiser cancels sponsorship of a popular television show. A critic decries a media corporation. Minority persons say they are portrayed unfairly in television news. Residents in a Third World country complain that their economy is hampered by their image in the West. These and hundreds of other "media issues" arise daily and are often debated and discussed. At first they seem quite perishable and many are, but all of them are linked to similar controversies that have arisen in the past and that will recur in the future. A text about media does not serve the reader well if, in striving for clarity, it suggests agreement or consensus. Issues are not that settled in this field. We are instead aiming to stir up further debate and reader reaction, feeling that controversy creates interest.

Public communication issues are important because they can effect people's lives both directly and indirectly. The content of communication—for example, the image of black or Hispanic Americans in the media or the coverage of health issues, the economy, or the environment—almost always arouses criticism. The way reporters and other media people perform their jobs, whether or not they are ethical, does too. So too is there concern about the way a given medium such as a radio station, magazine, or newspaper behaves in its community. Since folklore (as well as reality) says that those who "pay the piper call the tune," the ownership and control of communication is always on the agenda of those who care about the media system. Beyond these considerations, the social consequences of communication also attract attention and comment. The system of freedom of expression and its relationship with government and other institutions of society are always worthy of hard thought and public scrutiny.

This book examines some of the persistent arguments that puzzle and perplex editors, broadcasters, critics, educators, and others who are concerned about the purposes and practices of the mass media in America. We have selected eighteen of the most common and recurring themes in debates about journalism, the media, and the press. We hope that this book will stimulate the thinking of students and media professionals alike as they confront these issues that have continued to plague, perplex, and excite others over the years. The subjects presented here are organized to encourage the reader to explore the nature, purpose, and operations of mass communication in America. Some of the issues raised are large with social implications while others border on internal "shop talk." Taken together they help us understand the relationship of the communications media to society, as well as the relationship of social forces to the press and mass communication.

In selecting the issues presented here, we perused scores of books, articles, bibliographies, and other scholarly inventories to assure ourselves that we were choosing both the most prevalent and the most important arguments for analysis. The eighteen issues singled out are developed with more than one hundred subsidiary issues.

Whenever possible, we point up the links between the various professional and scholarly controversies considered here, explaining how and why they are interrelated. We begin with freedom of the press, the most fundamental of all issues in any media system, and move to the closely related relationship between media and government. We follow in quick succession with considerations of the media and the public trust, an essential link between communicators and their audiences. Several connected concepts also considered are the people's right to know, public access to the media, and media pluralism. While these early chapters are philosophical underpinnings for any media system, their importance is determined by ascertaining the power of the media. Two succeeding chapters look at content issues, including the quality of media content and journalistic objectivity. Behavioral considerations—including factors involved in deciding what is news, the nature of news-gathering tactics, and journalistic ethics—continue to define and sharpen our inquiry. Two practical ethical channels are considered in our treatment of press councils and ethical codes. Matters of persuasion and public opinion—propaganda and the media, advertising, and public relations—are addressed in the next three chapters. There is then a sharp focus on journalism as a profession, again a vocational application of earlier and more theoretical discussions. Finally, we take the issue to the world stage by looking at global communication dominance.

In most instances a lively contemporary controversy can be examined in the context of a conventional tenet or "article of faith" about the media in America. It is not uncommon for antagonisms to flare over whether the prevailing thought about the issue is adequate or needs to be reconsidered or replaced. We have tried to recreate that spirit in this book. We present the issues in an adversarial style. While not recreating a conventional debate format, we do argue two positions by assembling evidence.

This book is a departure from standard journalism texts in several ways. Each of the eighteen issues is succinctly defined and explained. The prevailing sentiment on each of them is identified. Then one author challenges the contemporary view and the other offers a response. Though each of us argues a particular position, we are not necessarily presenting our personal viewpoints. We are acting as advocates for the position, trying to marshal the best evidence possible. Indeed, since the last edition we have traded a few of the positions. It is important to identify the central questions at the core of the debate and to demonstrate how and why people legitimately reduce a number of complex subjects to stark pro and con arguments. We do this primarily as a catalyst for discussion. We use this procedure because it is the way two people naturally discuss any debatable subject, trivial or significant. But we also indicate that many complexities ought to be considered before anyone comes to a reasoned conclusion, especially in the area of media. Even though resolved through compromise, such decisions require choices that relate evidence, values, and practical solutions to problems.

In using this book both instructors and students should be cautioned that the authors are doing what they rarely do—making the best adversarial argument for a given position, even though it may not reflect a personal view or approach to scholarship. While we personally recognize that no argument is ever so one-sided, we nevertheless believe that such a process both simplifies and purifies the debate and ought to prove helpful in isolating issues and finding answers to perplexing problems for which there are always rationalizations and tradeoffs.

After the first edition, we received many calls from students and professors in various universities who wanted to argue with us about the views expressed in the book. We explained again and again that the positions we argued were not necessarily our own views. Often they are not. Just as lawyers argue the very best case for their clients, we argued as strongly as we could, based on evidence, for the side of the argument we agreed to take on. And just as the lawyer knows that the client is not always an angel, we know that all issues have many sides and that few of them are resolved in such stark fashion. Most of us, however, when confronted with a media issue, eventually do take sides. We decide whether a given story was of high quality or not; whether a reporter was ethical or unethical; whether public relations is generally good; and so on.

One gratifying response to the first edition of this book was the many letters that reached us from other countries. We were repeatedly told that the book, with its various concepts and issues framed as they are, helped readers "make sense" out of the steady flow of media issues coming out of the United States and other countries. One reader wrote, "Now I understand better why Americans get so agitated about government intrusion in press matters." Said another, "At last issues like professionalism and objectivity came into sharper focus for me." Still another said, "After reading your book, I decided that both of you were wrong and I decided to make up my own mind, drawing on some of your arguments while rejecting others." This, of course, is exactly what we had hoped to accomplish.

Media issues belong to people, not to institutions, governments, scholars, or critics. They are matters that affect all of us as members of the many audiences at which media mesages are directed. Because we are all targeted by advertisers, editorial pages, television entertainment programs, radio news, and much more, it is vital that we become better consumers of the media by being more critical about the various processes that create public communication, as well as the consequences of this communication. Each of us needs to engage in the debate, to argue about communication that affects us, to try to influence it, and to talk back.

We can start by building awareness of the great media debates. In the end, we ought to marshal evidence and confront the arguments in our own way for our own purposes. In doing so we can all reach our own conclusions, recognizing that on the issues here set forth there are no right or wrong positions.

Chapter **1**

FREEDOM OF THE PRESS

Student journalists at Marquette University are told they cannot run an abortion rights (pro-choice) advertisement in their campus newspaper, while students at Marshall University are under fire for publishing an allegedly racist column. Passions run high in both scenarios which occurred in 1989 and 1990, with profound disagreements on both sides. Words like "censorship" and "freedom" fly back and forth, yet all parties on both sides would undoubtedly say they are staunch advocates of freedom of the press, a venerable idea that continues to be locked in combat in every community and most nations of the world.

Freedom of the press is usually defined as the right to communicate ideas, opinions, and information through the printed word without government restraint. A deeply held value in America, press freedom is also legally guaranteed in the free press clause of the First Amendment to the Constitution of the United States:

> Congress shall make no law respecting an establishment of religion, or prohibiting the free exercise thereof; or abridging the freedom of speech, or of the press; or the right of the people peaceably to assemble, and to petition the government for redress of grievances.

A central purpose of freedom of the press is to encourage the existence of an educated and informed electorate that can make decisions about public affairs. For some early commentators, freedom of the press simply meant the absence of government licensing of printing and publishing. Later it came to mean "no prior restraint" of publication. This is the idea that prepublication censorship is out of bounds.

Freedom of the press is said to assure satisfaction of society's need for a maximum flow of information and opinion and the individual's right for self-fulfillment. Freedom of the press is also a promoter and protector of other rights: In America, a free press is regarded as central to the functioning of democratic government and a free citizenry. Of course, freedom of the press also means protection from arbitrary and despotic control.

There is much continuing debate about the essential nature of this concept of freedom, what it actually means, to whom it extends, whether it is an individual or institutional right—that is, does freedom of the press belong to every citizen or only to those organizations that constitute "the press," such as newspapers and television stations. In large part, the contemporary interpretation of freedom of the press depends on legally sanctioned definitions of such terms as Congress, no law, and press. "Press" once meant only the print media, but in an age of broadcast and computer technology, the concept of "the press" has been greatly expanded.

CHALLENGE

Dennis: The American press is not free.

Freedom of the press is one of those noble expressions that slide easily off our tongues, though not always fully understood or documented. There is a persistent, romantic notion that freedom of the press flourishes in America and that it is an essential linchpin of our democratic system of government. Many of us want to believe that, but such a belief eludes the truth. The American press is simply not free in any accurate sense of the word. The press fights for freedom and, from time to time, achieves fragments of freedom, but press freedom is far from full-scale attainment.

I make this argument knowing that the press in America is better off and under fewer restraints than media enterprises in many other countries and cultures. I would still argue that bona fide freedom of the press is a distant dream that will probably never be achieved. Why do I say this? Because when all of the romantic rhetoric of press freedom is pushed aside, the most basic formulation of freedom of the press is what the great constitutional scholar Thomas Cooley called, "the right to publish whatever one may please and to be protected against any responsibility for so doing." Cooley wrote those words in the nineteenth century in one of the earliest treatises on our constitutional law, but he added this important qualification:

> except so far as such publications, from their blasphemy, obscenity, or scandalous character, may be a public offense, or by their falsehood and malice they may injuriously affect the standing, reputation, the pecuniary interests or individuals. (Cooley, 1868, 885–86).

While Judge Cooley's 1868 statement effectively summarizes the battlefield on which many of the fights for press freedom have been waged, it also is a chilling inventory of exceptions that make freedom quite conditional. And all of Cooley's conditions—except blasphemy—are still alive and well in the trial courts, clearly constraining freedom.

In part, confusion over the idea of press freedom stems from the word *freedom* itself. *Freedom* can mean the total absence of restraint. The term *liberty* comes closer to Cooley's meaning, because *liberty* is commonly defined as freedom from all restraints except those justly imposed by law. Liberty of the press assumes a system of rights and duties, while freedom of the press does not. In the United States Constitution, the framers were not simply stating philosophical maxims, but were trying to devise a workable system of government. Thus, freedom under our system had a narrower focus than liberty.

The originators of our legal basis for freedom of the press were the framers of the Constitution, individuals influenced by the Enlightenment philosophers who wrote about the "rights of man" in broad-based, idealized fashion. The framers inserted the words "freedom of speech or of the press," in what is now the First Amendment, but they were doing more than stating a philosophy. Rather, they tried to find practical means of letting the press have considerable latitude, but not unrestrained freedom. Those simple words unleashed a lively, continuing debate. Two factors that have fueled this controversy are:

1. The general lack of agreement about what is meant by freedom of the press.

2. The recognition that freedom of the press does not exist in a vacuum, but instead must coexist with other rights accorded to individuals under the Constitution.

Only the most naive dreamer could look on the history of the American media and think that they have ever been completely free from restraint. From the earliest times laws were enacted, mainly at the state level, to protect citizens from the press, just as the Bill of Rights protects citizens from the government and its police. As Cooley suggested, those restrictions included libel (in police terms, false arrest), invasion of privacy (in police terms, unreasonable search and seizure), and many others. It was generally accepted by society that the press should *not* be free to destroy reputations, undermine the confidence of the community, promote violence, murder, and mayhem, or incite other activities deemed to be harmful. The debate over the extensions (or limits) of press freedom has often centered on whether that freedom is absolute or conditional.

The idea of literal or absolute freedom of the press has found few champions more fierce and steadfast than the late Hugo Lafayette Black, who served on the U.S. Supreme Court from 1937 to 1971. To Justice Black, the First Amendment was a literal command. The First Amendment says that "Congress shall make no law . . . abridging freedom of speech, or of the press" and to Black *no law* meant *no law*. "I am," he wrote, "for the First Amendment from the first word to the last. I believe it means what it says" (Cahn, 1962, 53). Justice Black (and sometimes his colleague Justice William O. Douglas) was often adamant about the absolute nature of the First Amendment. Justice Black's brand of First Amendment absolutism is not limited to the lofty chambers of the Supreme Court. I recall encountering this idea being expressed vehemently by an editor at the *Milwaukee Journal*. I was speaking to the staff and speculating about some of the trade-offs that citizens expect from the press as a result of the First Amendment franchise. The editor exploded, telling me that there was nothing about that in the Constitution. "*No law*, that's what it says," he told me. "Sounds familiar," I replied.

There are many laws made by Congress and by state legislatures that constrain and complicate freedom of the press. They range from libel and privacy statutes to laws governing copyright and the publication of government secrets. Even the resolute Justice Black would sometimes admit that at certain times, under certain circumstances, and in certain places, there could be limits on freedom of expression. So much for the foundations of First Amendment absolutism. It should also be noted that Black's position on this issue, even when unyielding, was never the view of a majority of the Supreme Court.

The philosopher Sidney Hook argues that freedom of the press is not absolute and must yield on occasion to the nation's national security needs or to the rights of individuals that collide with notions of press freedom—for example, the right to a fair trial as guaranteed in the Sixth Amendment or the right of privacy.

There are many complex positions involving facts, values, and policies as they explore the intricacies of the concept of press freedom, and almost all of them agree that press freedom is fragile and volatile, lacking real stability. Critics point out the negative nature of the First Amendment that figuratively slaps the hand of Congress in advance, while saying little about what the powerful executive and judicial branches of the federal government may do. The so-called strong presidency and the "imperial judiciary" could not have been foreseen by the framers. Some critics argue that the First Amendment really means "all government" instead of Congress per se. Even though the Fourteenth Amendment has been interpreted so that it extends the provisions of the Bill of Rights (including press freedom) to the states, it was not until 1925 that the Supreme Court, in *Gitlow* v. *New York*, told the states not to impair these rights with laws of their own. But even this court ruling and many subsequent decisions that have defined the conditions and contours of so-called press freedom have failed to wipe out a complex series of state and federal laws and court rulings that place severe limits on freedom of the press.

Most people who have studied freedom of the press agree that one of its fundamental conditions in America is the doctrine of "no prior restraint" of publication. This doctrine holds that the press must be free to publish what it wishes without interference from the government, while remaining subject to various types of legal scrutiny after the fact. This is, of course, a kind of muted freedom, but even here the record is by no means unsullied.

In *Near v. Minnesota* (1931), the Supreme Court struck down a gag law in that state and established the principle of no prior restraint of the press firmly in American constitutional law. On a number of occasions since, however, there have been government attempts to block publication of controversial material. In 1971, for example, the *New York Times* and *Washington Post* published some material about the Vietnam War from classified government documents two weeks before the Supreme Court conceded their right to do so; in the meantime, the *Times* and *Post* were enjoined from further publication. A similar issue arose in 1979 concerning *The Progressive* magazine, when that publication was prevented for several months from publishing a story about the hydrogen bomb.

While there may have been good reason for the government's actions in both instances, they hardly contributed to a sense of freedom from prior restraint. There are scores of examples where courts have placed restraining orders and other gag rules on reporters attempting to cover the judicial system. These restraints may be fully justifiable, but in any event, their presence is *not* press freedom. Of course, such actions are perfectly permissible under our legal system in spite of the First Amendment.

I believe that constraints on press freedom in the public sector by the judiciary, the executive, and the legislative branches of government are only part of the barrier to freedom of the press in the United States. There are also many restrictions in the private sector. These include aspects of contract and property law that severely restrict the press in carrying out its fullest exercise of freedom. In addition, the law of literary property (copyright) sometimes inhibits republication of particular material.

The noble purposes of press freedom, as envisioned by the Enlightenment philosophers and others since, would clearly elevate society, but in most instances these are still distant goals, not actual accomplishments, not the reality of the situation today or perhaps ever. Some commentators say "the structure is the message" in any consideration of media organizations and their behavior. The structure of the newspaper or broadcast organization dictates rules under which reporters and editors operate. There are conventions against certain kinds of behavior. Some stories get covered; some don't. The written or unwritten rules or newsroom policies, so fully documented in studies of media gatekeepers, are also constraints on freedom. Professionalism itself restrains free will and limits individual choice. Many of us would agree that such private restraints (also called "responsibility" and "ethics") actually limit press freedom, but for the right reasons. There are many forces and factors that have an impact on shaping the performance of the media. They condition and control. They slow and mute freedom.

While there are theorists who believe that freedom of the press has a preferred place in our scheme of individual liberty and freedom, both because of its symbolic primacy* in the Bill of Rights and because of its importance to the functioning of democratic government, the fact remains that freedom of the press, if it exists at all, is engaged in continuous bargaining with other rights and interests, both individual and social. This has been called a process of reconciliation, wherein rights exercised by one person or one group can be reconciled with equal opportunity for others to enjoy them. Thus, we have a complex, interrelated system in which rights, principles, practices, and institutions interact. A local newspaper may severely limit my right of privacy today in the name of press freedom, but I might be able to restrain that freedom tomorrow by arguing that pretrial publicity is impairing my right to a fair trial.

The American press lives with rules and regulations, conventions and constraints. By worldwide standards it is relatively free, even with all of the limitations on its freedom. It enjoys a measure of liberty and has a mechanism which, under most circumstances, allows for the adjudication of disputes that constrain freedom. Freedom of the press presupposes the free flow of information and the free dissemination of a wide spectrum of opinions. In most instances we have a rather muted version of this enlightened view of a free press. Even the most perfunctory surface view of the condition of the press in America tells us that it is not really free. A more penetrating look at the many social and psychological factors that can have a chilling effect on freedom—such as the subtle influences of one's peers, bosses or community—yields a haunting indictment of any claim of press freedom. Finally, as we examine the legal sphere there is a subtle message that ought to be understood: Through the years spokespersons for the press have fought vigorously for greater and greater press freedom. If this is necessary the press is hardly free.

Some of my journalist friends tell me that "nowhere does the Constitution say anything about responsibility; the press has no responsibility to do anything." Perhaps, but the same people are fond of enumerating the rights of the press and the rights of reporters. All rights, as anyone who has studied law knows, usually have corresponding *duties*. And any system of free expression which presupposes that there are rights also assumes that there are duties. Whether these duties are also responsibilities is partly a semantic quibble. However, what appears to be a victory for the press one day, such as the *New York Times* decision rendering it difficult for public officials to sue for libel, later can emerge as a constraint. In a late 1970s

---

*The number one placement of the First Amendment was actually an accident, not the result of calibrated planning by the framers.

Supreme Court case, *Herbert v. Lando,* the *New York Times* standard for defining malice ("reckless disregard or knowing falsehood") was used to force a broadcast producer of "60 Minutes" to account for his private thoughts in planning a story. What had been a new right came back to haunt—and also to restrain—the media. Sometimes the intention of the legislature or court in defining and extending freedom can become the loophole by which it later comes back to check the media.

One thoughtful champion of press freedom, Alexander Bickel of Yale Law School, observed that the more we have to define freedom, the less freedom we have. This is not inconsistent with Justice Black's view that we should not have tampered with the command of the framers in the First Amendment. But the fact remains that we have taken considerable license in interpreting its meaning and reach. What remains is hardly a pristine vessel. The charter of press freedom is now somewhat the worse for wear. It is less than whole. It exists mainly in our minds as a social goal, not as a realistic description of the American press today.

Argument Summation: The American press is not free.

Freedom of the press is a noble social goal, but in reality America does not have the unfettered rights implied by "freedom" of the press. While not as restricted as in some countries, American press freedoms are conditioned on numerous exceptions. The exceptions are necessary because press rights often must yield to other interests, such as libel, defamation, privacy, and national security. In addition to legal limits on the press, there are numerous private restrictions, including civil laws like copyright and contract, concentration of media ownership, public relations manipulation of news, and press policies in editing and publishing news. It should be noted that, although the First Amendment says Congress shall make no law restricting freedom of the press, several restrictive laws exist. The courts have said that only an absolute freedom from prior restraint exists, yet papers have been enjoined from printing certain items. These official and private limitations on the press mean that there are active American media, but they are far from a "free" press.

RESPONSE

Merrill: The American press is free.

When we say that America has a free press, of course we do not mean that the press is completely, totally, absolutely free of any and all restraints. Anyone who thinks, even minimally, about press freedom—or any kind of freedom, for that matter—knows full well that freedoms require some kind and some degree of restriction and responsibility.

It may well be that press freedom is a "romantic notion" and that it really doesn't "flourish" in the United States. But that is true with all objectives or goals of a society, and freedom, like "truth," "law and order," "friendship," and "loyalty," is relative, incomplete, and hedged with inadequacies. And nobody has maintained that press freedom flourishes in the United States. Dennis, I feel, exaggerates when he says that the American press is simply not free in any real sense of the word.

The press is indeed free in the commonly understood sense of the word: In a nonabsolutist, pragmatic, reasonable sense it is free and can be referred to as free. This is, of course, with the implicit understanding that it is not absolutely free of all the extrapress and self-imposed restrictions that can easily be brought up by critics.

Even Justice Black and others, who have taken basically an absolutist view of First Amendment freedoms, have recognized some limitations to press freedom. Obviously, nobody—most of all, the Founding Fathers—has ever considered the press completely free, nor would any responsible and moderate person want the press to be. I am not talking about an anarchistic or nihilistic press; I am referring to a free press—free in the sense of having minimal government restraints placed upon it. I am talking about a press in the real world of social and political frictions and problems; I am not considering some theoretical level of freedom for an unreal press that might exist in the minds of absolutists and sophists. Just as I might say that the United States is a democratic country (knowing full well that it is not really or totally so), I can say with assurance and pragmatic validity that America has a "free press."

Of course, Sidney Hook has been quoted asserting that press freedom must yield on occasion to national security. But note that the term *press freedom* is used; and it is this press freedom that "must yield." Such freedom must obviously be assumed by Hook in order to be yielded. What American would really want an unyielding concept of press freedom? Reasonable persons, and certainly the framers of the Constitution were reasonable, would not want an unyielding freedom in a nation based on law and social cooperation.

A number of factors limit freedom of the press. Some are external to the press, such as considerations of national security, court rulings, libel actions, pressures from advertisers and other groups, and subscriber desires. Some are internal, such as professional codes of ethics, the editorial power structure itself, press councils, and the like.

I maintain that the core of press freedom in the United States is editorial autonomy, and that this country's press system can be considered "free" in the sense that it has editorial autonomy—even in the broadcasting aspects of "the press" (those concerning news and commentary, at least). The American press can make its own editorial decisions and, as a result, can legitimately be considered free. And, certainly, in the context of the press systems of other countries—even those like the United Kingdom and Sweden—it is free. Relatively free, of course, but free in a meaningful and realistic sense.

Essentially in the United States there is no prior restraint on the press by government. This means that the media are free to publish or broadcast what they want to without government interference or prepublication censorship. The press can criticize the government without fear of being shut down. This is a key factor. Although, as Dennis has pointed out in his "Challenge," there have been a few instances where the courts have instituted some prior restraint on publications, these must be considered exceptions and aberrations; they should not be cited to negate press freedom in America. General statements that are valid are not to be invalidated by pointing to occasional exceptions.

As to the argument that newsroom policies restrict freedom of the press, nobody would deny that internal journalistic decision making and management control by the news media's own executives have a restrictive and directive role in journalism. But is this a restriction on the press? No. It is, if it is anything, a restriction by the press. And it is an inevitable result of freedom of the press. Managers of the press must have the freedom to make their own decisions vis-a-vis editorial content; so they make these decisions, and in so doing are not restricting press freedom, but are exercising it.

Freedom does not simply mean "free from." To be free from everything—free from other people, free from laws, free from morality, free from thought, free from emotion—is to be nothing. Unlimited or unrestricted freedom is impossible, in fact, and should not be demanded by reasonable people. The truth is that any freedom that is possible and desirable does and should have some limitation. Realistic freedom must have some base point or ground.

An example of this grounding of freedom can be found in Confucian ethics. Here the ground or limitation to freedom is goodness. A person should choose good, not evil. If evil prevailed, freedom would probably disappear. Hence, from an ethical perspective, we should permit only the freedom to select good and not the freedom to choose evil. Freedom to choose is only freedom to choose good not evil. In Confucian ethics choosing good is the only freedom.

Confucius confirmed this principle in his own life as it related to freedom of speech. He was free to speak as he pleased, and he thus recognized "freedom of speech"; he would oppose only the speaking of bad words or empty words—that is, words without corresponding "right" actions. Incipient authoritarianism? We have seen rationales for limiting freedom in the writings of Plato, Immanuel Kant, Walter Lippmann, and others who have argued that any freedom that harms others or the foundations of society must be curtailed. Certainly one might speak of a degree of authoritarianism in Confucius in the same way, and only in the same way, as one might speak of a degree of authoritarianism in Kant or even Jesus Christ. The Categorical Imperative of Kant or the Golden Rule of Christ carries authority, but this authority is self-realized and is in no way externally imposed.

So we can talk about self-determined restrictions within an environment of freedom. And still we have freedom—of speech or of the press. A contemporary proponent of ethical restraint, very much Confucianist in this respect, has been Professor Walter Berns. In *Freedom, Virtue, and the First Amendment* (1957) he issues an articulate call to public virtue. While disassociating himself from intolerance and censorship, he favors certain censorship from a moral perspective. Salacious and pornographic publications, he maintains, can be censored. American Communists have no claim to free expression since they are disloyal. Like Confucius, Berns contends that "bad" speakers and "bad" speeches deserve no protection. Government, he believes, should be engaged in raising the moral quality of the community and therefore must judge and limit public discussion according to the moral quality of the writer or speaker. For Berns and others there is a set of moral principles which, though hard to state with precision, are obligatory on all reasonable persons.

Walter Lippmann (*The Public Philosophy*, 1955) would restrict the concept of freedom also—or, more precisely, would have it restricted voluntarily by the individual. Essentially he believes as does Berns: As long as they contribute to forming the public mind, speech and writing should be free. Lippmann believes that the criterion of loyalty is "an indubitable commitment to defend and preserve the order of political and civil rights." To Lippmann and Berns, the disloyal have cut themselves out of the basic agreement that supports the process of public discussion. Lippmann maintains, for example, that there can be no right (freedom) to destroy a liberal democratic state—in this he echoes Plato—and Berns points out that we cannot limit disloyal speech or writing which would generate an American Lenin or Hitler.

So we can see that there have been, and are, thoughtful persons who recognize the necessity of limiting freedom or placing certain moral restrictions on certain forms of communication—whether it is falsely shouting fire in a crowded theater or advocating something that will do harm to national security, public morality, or the continued environment of responsible freedom.

There is, indeed, some danger of authoritarianism implicit in the ideas of these persons. Like the much-maligned Commission on Freedom of the Press (Hutchins Commission) of the 1940s, they are often seen to pose a threat to freedom by stressing responsibility or virtue. And perhaps they do. The debate still rages as to the relative benefits of virtue, responsibility, and social stability against the benefits of freedom.

We certainly will not get into that at this point, but the reader might like to reassess the pronouncements of John Stuart Mill and others (Locke, Milton, Burke, Jefferson, and Voltaire), who largely base their belief in free expression on utilitarian principles. There are, of course, a relativity and an incompleteness to press freedom, but I believe that such qualifications are implicit in the term itself, and that, when we think of restrictions on press freedom, we are largely thinking about those restrictions placed there by U.S. journalists themselves. By and large, the American press is free to be about as free as it wishes—recognizing, of course, that along with this exercise of freedom come certain responsibilities and obligations to the society which permits it to exist.

In conclusion, let me reiterate my position. In a realistic sense, there is press freedom in the United States. It is quite legitimate for such a term to be used to describe the American press, in spite of the fact that such press freedom is not absolute. The U.S. Constitution protects "freedom of the press"; so there must be something to protect. Journalists think they have press freedom and what they *think* they have, they have. Basically they are speaking of media self-determinism; they are not thinking about limitations and restrictions imposed on them by the press hierarchy itself.

When I say that America has a free press, I am saying that it has a relatively free press, a freer press than perhaps any other country. I am not saying that it has a *completely* free press, nor is anyone else who talks about freedom of the press in the United States. In addition, I am not saying that the media in the United States use their freedom to the degree they might. The freedom is there, but it is not always used. I agree with Philip Wylie, who said:

> The image of our media turns out . . . to be cowardly and unfree in a very great though not inclusive degree. . . . The media, in their mass-circulation or mass-viewed forms, either foster industry's synthetic image, or remain silent about the rot, mess, lies, human debasement, and the rest of the unfavorable truth hid behind the idol. They go along, too, with the support at least by silence, of pious interference with liberty (Wylie, 1969, 212).

Wylie is right; not that there is no implication in his words that the American press could not do better and be *freer* if it would *will* to be. The freedom is there; the fact is that the press often chooses not to use it. Such self-imposed restriction by the press on its freedom does not negate this freedom. It simply sets it temporarily aside until a stronger will, coupled with more courage, will project the press toward a more forceful and responsible utilization of the freedom that it does, in truth, have.

Argument Summation: The American press is free.

The American press is free in the ordinary sense of that term. This does not mean license or anarchism, but legally controlled, socially responsible freedom. It is a socially moderated freedom permitted by the First Amendment to the Constitution. Naturally, journalistic freedom is not total since there are various social pressures on media managers. But press directors can publish what they wish—without prior restraint by government. And this is what is meant by "press freedom" in the United States. The core meaning has come to approximate "journalistic autonomy." Newsroom policies and directives are not relevant to press freedom, although they do apply to the freedom of individual journalists. The first Amendment protects press freedom (the press's freedom); therefore, there must be "press freedom" in the United States to be thus protected.

TOPICS FOR DISCUSSION

1. Discuss "freedom," giving all the possible meanings for the term relevant to the freedom of the press. Now do the same thing with the term "press."

2. Should the media be able to publish or broadcast anything they wish? If not, what should be forbidden? Where should the press freedom line be drawn? Who should draw it?

3. What is the problem with the concept of "a responsible use of freedom"? For example: Who—or what entity—should define responsibility?

4. Why do many persons feel that press freedom is to be preferred over responsibility or virtue?

5. If there is press freedom in the United States, does it belong only to media managers and owners, or to all journalists? Many say that it belongs to "the people." How could it?

TOPICS FOR RESEARCH

1. Thomas Jefferson and other American presidents have typically made positive and negative statements about press freedom. Write an essay indicating why this is the case. Find examples of idealistic pro-press freedom statements from Jefferson or another president. Also find a negative statement. From studies of this topic or biographies of the president, see if you can find public controversies that might have made the given president "go sour" on the press.

2. Find an example of a press freedom issue either in this country or elsewhere. Put the issue in some historical context and use appropriate

sources to explain why the issue is still unsettled. This might involve book or film censorship, freedom of information, or libel.

3. Do a short paper on your personal freedom of the press. Do you have First Amendment press and speech rights? How can you exercise them? Does the present structure of American media help or hinder you in your exercise of press rights?

4. Read the biography or autobiography of someone who has helped extend and expand freedom of the press. Assess their contribution and indicate how it is relevant to modern media issues.

5. Using the material in this chapter, critique the arguments of the authors and their use of sources. They are quoting sources to document and defend their arguments. If you could question those sources (or the authors) about the down side of the cited material, what would you ask? Prepare your own inquiry into the author's approach and conclusions. Pretend that you are their adversary and you are trying to find coherent middle ground in fashioning a sensible argument.

FURTHER READING

Altschull, J. Herbert. *From Milton to McLuhan: Ideas and American Journalism.* White Plains, NY: Longman, 1989.

Becker, Carl. *Freedom and Responsibility in the American Way of Life.* New York: Vintage Books, 1960.

Berns, Walter. *Freedom, Virtue and the First Amendment.* Baton Rouge, LA: Louisiana State University Press, 1957.

———. *The First Amendment and the Future of American Democracy.* New York: Basic Books, 1976.

Brucker, Herbert. *Freedom of Information.* New York: Macmillan, 1949.

Cahn, Edmond N. "Dimensions of First Amendment 'Absolutes.'" A public interview in Dennis et al.: 41–53; Also see *New York University Law Review* 37, no. 4 (June 1962): 549–63.

Chafee, Zechariah. *Government and Mass Communication.* Chicago: University of Chicago Press, 1947.

Chamberlin, Bill, and Charlene J. Brown. *The First Amendment Reconsidered.* White Plains, NY: Longman, 1982.

Cohen, Jeremy. *Congress Shall Make No Law: Oliver Wendell Holmes, the First Amendment and Judicial Decisionmaking.* Ames, IA: Iowa State University Press, 1989.

Cooley, Thomas. *A Treatice on Constitutional Limitations.* Vol. 2, 2d ed. Chicago: Callaghan, 1888.

Commission on Freedom of the Press. *A Free and Responsible Press.* Chicago: University of Chicago Press, 1947.

Dennis, E. E., D. M. Gillmor, and David Grey, eds. *Justice Hugo Black and the First Amendment.* Ames, IA: Iowa State University Press, 1978.

Emerson, Thomas I. *The System of Freedom of Expression.* New York: Random House, 1970.

Friendly, Fred. *Minnesota Rag.* New York: Random House, 1981.

Haiman, Franklyn S. *Speech and Law in a Free Society.* Chicago: University of Chicago Press, 1981.

Helle, Steven. "The News-Gathering Publication Dichotomy and Government Expression." *Duke Law Journal,* no. 1 (1982): 1–60.

Hocking, William E. *Freedom of the Press.* Chicago: University of Chicago Press, 1947.

Lippmann, Walter. *The Public Philosophy.* Boston: Little, Brown, 1955.

Lowenstein, R. L. "Measuring World Press Freedom as a Political Indicator" Ph.D. dissertation, University of Missouri, 1967. Also see Lowenstein and Merrill, *Macromedia.* White Plains, NY: Longman, 1990.

Luskin, John. *Lippmann, Liberty, and the Press.* University, AL: University of Alabama Press, 1972.

McCord, William. *The Springtime of Freedom: Evolution of Developing Societies.* New York: Oxford, 1965.

Meiklejohn, Alexander. *Political Freedom: The Constitutional Powers of the People.* New York: Harper, 1960.

Meiklejohn, Donald. *Freedom and the Public.* Syracuse, NY: Syracuse University Press, 1963.

Merrill, John C. *The Dialectic in Journalism: Toward a Responsible Use of Press Freedom.* Baton Rouge, LA: Louisiana State University Press, 1989.

Merrill, John C. *The Imperative of Freedom.* 2d ed. New York: Freedom House, 1990.

Mill, John Stuart. *On Liberty.* Many editions.

Nelson, H. L., ed. *Freedom of the Press from Hamilton to the Warren Court.* Indianapolis, IN: Bobbs-Merrill, 1967.

Pember, Donald R. *Mass Media Law.* 2d ed. Dubuque, IA: W. C. Brown, 1981.

Popper, Karl R. *The Open Society and Its Enemies.* Princeton, NJ: Princeton University Press, 1930.

Rubin, Bernard. *Media, Politics, and Democracy.* New York: Oxford University Press, 1977. See especially Chapter 3, "The Struggle for Media Freedom."

Schmidt, Benno C., Jr. *Freedom of the Press vs. Public Access.* New York: Praeger, 1976.

Siebert, Fredrick, Theodore Peterson, and Wilbur Schramm. *Four Theories of the Press*. Urbana, IL: University of Illinois Press, 1963.

Stevens, John D. *Shaping the First Amendment*. Beverly Hills, CA: Sage Publications, 1982.

Tribe, Lawrence. *American Constitutional Law*. Mineola, NY: Foundation Press, 1978. See especially Chapter 7.

Wylie, Philip. *The Magic Animal*. New York: Pocket Books, 1969.

Chapter 2

MEDIA-GOVERNMENT RELATIONSHIP

Name any American president from George Washington to George Bush, and you can find an instance of when he got mad at the press, even though he steadfastly affirmed his belief in freedom of the press. The fact is that governments and the media do not always see eye to eye. Governments and government leaders want public support for their policies and the press is often the prickly critic and irritant.

As we saw in Chapter 1, the role of government in relation to the media is most often stated negatively. For example, government is commanded by the First Amendment not to intrude on press freedom. It is also relevant to note that the press is regarded as a fourth branch of government or as a fourth estate which serves as a check on government.

The media, especially those involved in public affairs, are said to play a "watchdog" role and thus keep the government under surveillance. One of the primary purposes of a free press in a democratic system, it is often said, is keeping the public informed about government activities. However, since the media often run into a resistant government, not eager to disclose all, a natural conflict results.

Press probing and revealing government secrecy and other restraints lead to what has been called, generally by press people, an "adversary relationship" between government and the press. Some critics say this adversarial relationship has a "checking value," wherein the press checks on government and makes certain that it is performing properly. This leads to a related question: Who checks on the press and sees that *it* is performing properly? Whether such an adversarial relationship actually exists—or should exist—is open to debate.

CHALLENGE

Merrill: The media and government should not be adversaries.

It is commonly assumed in the United States that we have an adversarial media or press system—and what is more, that we *should* have one. The press and government existing as adversaries is usually seen, at least in the United States, as a proper and necessary relationship. The concept is embraced especially in the rhetoric of journalists.

This assumption is one that needs to be challenged. Granted, many of the hackneyed expressions of American journalism such as the press is a "fourth branch of government" or a "check on government" or a "watchdog" suggest the validity of the notion of a press-government adversary relationship, but is it really justified? I believe not. In the argument that follows, I shall try to explain, first, why there is no adversarial relationship under American libertarian theory, and secondly, why the communications media would not want such a relationship to exist.

Why should the press and government be adversaries? Why not friends? Why not foes at times and friends at times? Why, then, should not the relationship be ambivalent—especially in a free and pluralistic press system? These are questions which it would seem unnecessary to ask in the United States. But evidently it is necessary, for the press has taken unto itself the role of an adversary to governments, and boasts about it.

I maintain that, theoretically, the relationship is not really adversarial (the laws are on the side of the press) and should not be adversarial—no more than it should be cooperative and harmonious. It should be an ambiguous relationship, a free-wheeling one, a changing one. That relationship would be in line with the nature of independent editorial determination, with the spirit of pluralism, and with press freedom.

Beyond this theoretical problem with the adversarial relationship, I maintain that the press does not really want such a pragmatic relationship. The press wants to be an adversary by itself; it basically desires a helpless and law-bound government forced to provide the press with anything it wants, with no secrecy on the part of the government, with no attempts to influence or control any activities of the press, with no criticism of the press. What kind of adversarial relationship is this?

Does not press freedom imply, in effect, that any unit of the press system can take any stance it likes toward government? If I am the editor of newspaper A, I may want to consistently support all government policies. I am free to do so. Or I may want to oppose some weaknesses. I may want to be ambivalent toward government—sometimes pro and sometimes con.

I may, indeed, want to determine for my newspaper an adversarial role vis-a-vis government, to see my newspaper as a vehicle to fight against government: to check on government, to criticize government, and to make it a policy to root out government excesses and wrongdoing. In short, I may decide to use my newspaper as a "watchdog on government" or as "artillery" with which to bombard government.

In reality, in a libertarian society the relationship between press and government is so varied and splintered that it cannot be expressed in any monolithic way. It cannot be called "adversarial." To call it that is a travesty of rhetoric and reality. It is utterly ridiculous for a press to cast itself as an adversary of government: Such a stance would imply that the government is always wrong and the press is always right; it would also imply that the press sees itself as an institution dedicated to portraying for the public their government as a flawed, negatively disposed one that must be constantly watched lest it do great harm to the people.

The government, of course, is really closer to the people than is the press, for at least portions of the government are elected by the people. Not so with the press. The press, largely a profit-making private enterprise, has simply set itself up as a "representative" of the people and a "check" on government.

In 1982 Kurt Luedtke, formerly executive editor of the *Detroit Free Press* and screenwriter for the film *Absence of Malice*, courageously aimed strong words at the American press in this regard:

> You [the American press] are forever inventing new rights and privileges for yourselves, the assertion of which is so insolent that you apparently feel compelled—as I certainly would—to wrap them in the robe of some imaginary public duty and claim that you are acting on my behalf. If I am indeed involved, then I would like you to do a little less for me. But of course I'm not. Your claims of privilege have nothing to do with any societal obligation, because you have no societal obligation: That is the essence of what the First Amendment is all about (Luedtke, 1982).

Let me follow up this extremely relevant quotation of Luedtke with a brief statement by Paul H. Weaver, associate editor of *Fortune* and *The Public Interest:* "The romantic image of the 'adversary press,' then, is a myth: 'functional' for certain purposes, but wholly inaccurate as a model of what newsmen actually do or can hope to achieve" (1974, 95).

Traditionally, U.S. journalism has been rather close to, dependent on, and cooperative with official sources. Undoubtedly this has caused problems, but it has been one of its strengths. Perhaps at times it has led to some press "cheerleading" for government policies, but it has also maximized the amount of information and disinformation available to the citizens of the country. If I, as a government official, see the press as an adversary, how will I respond to it? With caution, with distrust, with skepticism, with a minimum of openness and frankness, and with a certain hostility. In addition, I certainly will turn my caution and hostility into considerable secrecy and distortion of information that I may give out to my adversary. Solid and balanced information, therefore, is often the victim in this adversarial warfare, with the consumer (the public) receiving the distortions and informational shreds from the battle.

Further, it seems strange that journalists find any comfort in the concept of an adversarial press. They, if they are realistic, should know that they are dependent to a very large extent on government for their news. Virtually all the information published by the journalists about government is derived from (and often validated by) some government-related person. Newspeople know almost nothing about public events and issues except what they obtain from external sources and authorities. If the media want to limit or cut off access to such sources, then they will stress their adversarial role; if they want to expand their sources and their information, then they will stress their cooperative and friendly role. Adversaries, of course, are not friendly.

An adversarial role is often not even a responsible—or ethical—role. There is nothing sacred or intrinsically good about being an adversary. In fact, adversaries are more likely than not to deal in propaganda—to play games of "disinformation" and "misinformation." Adversaries like to "win"—they are not comfortable with even-handed information, with attempts to inform thoroughly and fairly.

Let us not forget that, in a real adversarial relationship, government has the same right to "fight" as does the press. The government can, in such a relationship, try to withhold information, to have secret meetings, to distort information for its advantage, to have its favorite reporters and reward them in various ways, to deal in disinformation and other propagandistic techniques, to subpoena journalists, and restrict their activities in various ways.

In short, the government would be a true adversary.

The press, no doubt, does have the upper hand—or would have one—in a real adversarial relationship, unless the Constitution were changed. The press has the last word in any controversy with government. It not only has the last word, it has the first word. The government really has no word at all—except that provided it by the press. Any government official's voice reaching the public through the media is immediately thereafter subjected to analysis and interpretation by media figures: telling the American people who have just heard the official what the person "really" said and what he "really" meant. Instant analysis, as it is often called, might better be referred to as "instant bias" by which the press makes sure it has the last word.

The government's hands are largely tied. About the only way it can be an adversary of the press is through occasional verbal blasts at media practices. And these blasts themselves are subject to media control and management and to instant analyses and the "final word" technique. The government, to be sure, does have one other weapon, a purely defensive one—secrecy in certain deliberations. Without a doubt, it makes use of this weapon. But, in the process, it opens itself to more problems: the "leak" by disgruntled functionaries, escalated criticism by the press when it learns of such government operations, the felt need to justify government activities at every turn, and the helpless feeling of government people when the press fires its unanswerable barrages at them.

In a true adversarial relationship, there is one thing the government could do (and should do) to help its position: It should involve itself more in the media business. It should cease permitting the press to be the informer of the people; it should itself actively inform the people, circumventing when possible the commercial press. When the government has no real voice, it is an unequal and almost helpless contender in this press-government fray. Perhaps the Hutchins Commission was correct in 1947 when it suggested that government might indeed have to get into the communications business. It is obvious that in any kind of rhetorical battle, the side without control of internal, public channels of communications is at a distinct disadvantage.

If the people are to know the maximum and to be exposed to the widest range of positions and opinions, it would seem logical that government voices would be of help. In fact, the government probably has a responsibility to communicate directly to the people, instead of having its messages filtered through the distorted and often biased lens of the American mass media system. Why should the press, any more than any other institution, be saddled with the awesome responsibility of providing government information to the people?

Surely my coauthor will contend—speaking, I am sure, for the great majority of press people—that the government has no right competing with private media. But why not compete? Is not government competition implicit in an adversarial relationship?

Could not the government through its own publications, broadcast outlets, and other resources fill a multitude of gaps with information and viewpoints? Could not the government then have an instrument to compete with the private media? Could not the government then have a chance to set the record straight—or at least to tell in its own way what it has to say to the people? This would be consistent with the concept of pluralism which free press people pay lip service to. It would also make the adversarial relationship more equal. It would give a virtually voiceless entity (the government) a voice with which it could speak directly to its constituency, the people. It would help make it a real contender in this adversarial relationship which actually does not exist at present. An example of this is in Britain where the British Broadcasting Corporation (BBC) competes with independent (private enterprise) networks and stands for quality, while still government-controlled, however loosely.

But then, as has been noted, the press would not like this. In spite of its talk, the press does not really want an adversarial relationship. It cannot really tolerate the thought of the government being its adversary.

The fact that the press looks at itself as an adversary of government is not only theoretically questionable, but leads to problems with ethics. The belief that the press must be a check on government, a critic of government, or a watchdog on government results in a hyperactive and contentious journalism. The adversarial role causes the press to dig and probe, snipe and snoop; it causes the press to speculate, to deal in gossip and innuendo in its attempt to unearth corruption in high and low places. This press concept is responsible for the press's accentuating the negative in governmental matters, of seldom revealing positive activities. It fosters the idea—or is the creature of the idea—that the government is necessarily and inherently evil and must be checked. And in this little game which the press sees itself playing, the press has appointed itself to keep the government honest.

Today, as an increasing number of voices are asking who checks the checker, the press falls back on its constitutional freedom guarantee, and when all the rhetoric is done, the answer from the press is essentially this: *Nobody* checks the checker.The press is nearly free from being checked. Is this answer consistent with the contention that the press and government are *adversaries?*

In conclusion, let me quote a reputable American journalist, James Reston, who ends his discussion in *The Artillery of the Press* by contradicting his "artillery fire" title: "Clever officials," he says, "cannot 'manipulate' reporters, and clever reporters cannot really 'best' the government. From both sides, they have more to gain by cooperating with one another, and with the rising minority of thoughtful people, than by regarding one another as 'the enemy'."(1967, 108). So Reston recognizes the mythology implicit in his book's title and in the whole concept of the adversary relationship of the press and government.

I repeat my position: In reality there is no adversarial relationship between press and government and there should not be one.

Argument Summation: The media and government should not be adversaries.

The media and government are not adversaries—or at least they shouldn't be. Such a situation would assign a role to the press which would be in conflict with editorial self-determination. An adversarial relationship may well exist from time to time, but in a free and open press system such a relationship should be strictly ad hoc. Why should a free press feel it must be an adversary to government? Why not just as well be a friend? Some media at some times and in some circumstances may want to oppose the government in certain particular matters, but a generally assumed opposition to government is not only irrational, but contrary to the basic tenets of a free and self-determining press.

RESPONSE

Dennis: The media and government should be adversaries.

Granted, *adversarial* may be an overly dramatic term to describe the ideal relationship between press and government, but the concept has come to have legitimate meaning and, in fact, as it is commonly understood, it is quite desirable. Adversarial simply means that the media should be critical, argumentative, and contentious in their relationships with government. The press may be the only organizations that have what Justice Potter Stewart called "structural rights," or rights that belong mostly to institutions—such as the press—as opposed to rights like religious freedom that are both personal and institutional or structural under the Constitution. The primary function of the press under this legal arrangement is to provide the people with a free flow of information.

As anyone who has ever observed governments knows, they try to perpetuate themselves by managing and manipulating information. The press is one of a very few social forces that can challenge them. From the time of the divine right of kings to the present, government has realized that information is power and the control of information (at least to some degree) is essential to public support for its policies and mandates. This was the reason for the original press licensing and sedition laws in Britain that American colonists and patriots such as John Peter Zenger rebelled against. In modern times government secrecy, carried to the extreme, sometimes has deprived the American people of information they needed to be fully knowledgeable citizens. When the White House wanted to cover up the Watergate scandal, the press shouted "foul" and revealed for all to see that seamy chapter in the nation's history. Illegal domestic spying and wiretapping by the Central Intelligence Agency and the Federal Bureau of Investigation have also been uncovered by a vigilant press, wary of government in the best adversarial tradition.

Several of my coauthor's arguments deserve close scrutiny. He maintains, for example that under a libertarian theory of the press, there is no adversary relationship between press and government. Indeed, the libertarian idea (not to be confused with the Libertarian Party) allows multiple voices in the marketplace and keeps the press as free as possible from government involvement. He is correct in saying that this is strictly up to the editor or broadcaster. Although we do not live under a libertarian system today, when we did in the late eighteenth and early nineteenth centuries, the press fought hard against government strictures on information and helped establish the present adversary relationship. At the dawn of the nineteenth century, which journalism historians call "The Dark Ages of American Journalism," the government passed the Alien and Sedition Acts which the press opposed with great fervor. Libertarian journalism brought us highly opinionated, partisan publications. Some were adversaries of government; others were "kept cats," not independent journals, but house organs for political parties. All this ended with the rise of a mass press, which was brought about by a happy mixture of technology, education, advertising, and other factors.

Today, while we no longer have a libertarian press system, we do have a press that shares a common value—a critical (or adversarial) posture toward government. We have a system of "social responsibility," wherein the press assumes certain rights and corresponding responsibilities or duties. One is the full and robust coverage of government. An adversarial posture is helpful if not essential to this arrangement. One of the only American newspapers I can think of that exemplifies the libertarian tradition is the *Manchester* (N.H.) *Union-Leader*, a feisty publication known for its biased reporting and vehement attacks on liberal political figures. This paper, operated for many years by the conservative publisher, William Loeb (and presently run much the same way by his widow), sometimes mixes its editorial and news functions. It is clearly a point-of-view newspaper that rejects notions of social responsibility, fairness, and balance. But even the *Union-Leader* has an adversary stance with government, so much so that it can justly be called "antigovernment." To some extent, the *Washington Times*, owned by the Reverend Sun Myung Moon and his followers, is libertarian in its outlook.

Although it may be somewhat trite, no discussion of the typically American media-government relationship is complete without international comparisons. In many countries there is a controlled press, not just in the Soviet Union and China, but also in many developing and industrialized states. In some places, it is not uncommon to have government ownership of the media. Government press councils and laws also limit press freedom. Even in Britain, the mother of democracies, harsh laws, perpetrated by government, keep the media on a short leash. French journalists rightly complain that they could not do vigorous investigative reporting because of the fear of government reprisal.

A call for greater freedom linked to an ambiguous relationship with government is really quite dangerous, even if well-intentioned. As should be evident from such recurrent issues as book censorship by school boards, wherein freedom to read controversial works is challenged, freedom of expression is not something that is established on marble tablets and enshrined for all time. It must be defended repeatedly and continuously or it will cease to exist. Reporters who cover local government often lament their continuing battles with public officials over open meeting and open records practices. The laws regarding public access to meetings and records are on the books, but many government officials will ignore and thwart them unless challenged by the press. Without an adversarial press, it is unlikely that our "sunshine" laws would be used at all. When it comes to such basic rights as press freedom, we must "use 'em or lose 'em."

Typically, during war or other great national crises, press and government are quite cooperative. The coverage of wars by the press usually supports and does not undermine the government. This accommodation is due both to a conscious practice by the press, as well as government censorship which makes coverage difficult and forbids release of information such as that involving troop movements or air and naval maneuvers.

Within the framework of an adversary relationship, a whole range of strategies and tactics can be employed by the press and, yes, by government. Washington correspondents, for example, are engaged in an adversarial process. They try to get information about a particular policy or agency. Some of the information is freely provided by helpful information officers; some that might be embarrassing to the agency is withheld or not volunteered. The reporter then develops a strategy to get the missing information. This is done through the use of leaks, alternate sources, or jealous politicians. In this adversary posture the press is suspicious of the actions of government and vice versa.

Who, in fact, really represents the public interest? Both press and government claim to do so. The government makes a strong claim since it operates by the "consent of the governed." The press, on the other hand, also has some basis for asserting that it is also a representative of the public. At least the press makes this claim in many lawsuits where its motives are challenged. Thus, through court decisions, terms like "the Fourth Branch of Government" and "The Fourth Estate" have gained real meaning with legal teeth. When the courts, for example, grant the press rights that the rest of us do not have to enter a prison to interview inmates, this special privilege is extended to the press as a "trustee" of the people, since we all cannot wander at will within prison walls to find out for ourselves what is happening there. The press does this for us and is, therefore, our representative. Writing in *Saxbe v. Washington Post Co.*, Justice Lewis Powell agreed, saying:

> The people must therefore depend on the press for information concerning public institutions ... The underlying right is the right of the public generally. The press is the necessary representative of the public's interest ... and the instrumentality which effects the public's right (1974, 417 United States, 843 and 864).

In another case, however, a film producer, Fred Wiseman, was denied access to an institution for the mentally ill.

Professor William L. Rivers of Stanford University has documented in great detail the extent of the adversary relationship between press and government in two books, The Adversaries and The Other Government. He argues forcefully that the press is truly an adversary of government. We need to remember that government is not a single entity, but federal, state, and local units of executive, legislative, and judicial bodies.

The virtues of an adversary relationship between press and government are vividly demonstrated when one compares the news coverage of public affairs with, say, business or sports. While the coverage of government is by no means exhaustive (and it assuredly has many flaws), there is a conscious effort by the press, both nationally and in local communities, to cover important events—happenings and issues in legislative bodies, the courts, and public agencies. At the federal level the presidency is watched by a legion of several hundred reporters. A large contingent is assigned to Capitol Hill while very few cover the Supreme Court and the federal bureaucracy. Look at any local community and you will see the local press carefully watching the city council, the courts, and public agencies. This coverage includes some that is purely descriptive, some that is analytical, and some that tries to ferret out wrongdoing. All of it contributes to an adversary relationship. Generally, relationships between government sources and reporters are quite cordial. This cooperation is fine when government is running smoothly and the press is simply doing routine, descriptive coverage. The more contentious, adversarial stance is appropriate when things are not going so well and when the public ought to know about it.

Compare press coverage of government with that of business or sports. Business coverage has improved markedly in recent years, but for a long time it was a tedious treatment of commercial activity. Much of it was little more than the printing of publicity releases that various businesses and industries provided. The press took little interest in internal conflicts and controversies or in corporate strategies that led to a particular product line. Since the 1970s many news organizations have improved their coverage of business because the private sector has such a profound impact on individuals and their communities.

Another area where the press has traditionally cooperated with sources to the extent of becoming boosters and promoters is sports. Local papers typically support local teams and coaches are lionized by reporters and columnists. Under such coverage many fundamental, yet changing assumptions about sports in American life went undetected. Conflicts within sports teams and organizations were ignored. Sports reporters often did not act like journalists, but more like advocates for teams or players. They ignored embarrassing facts and helped make heroes. Today, the adversarial approach is making inroads on sports pages, but progress has been slow.

Critics the world over agree that the adversarial relationship makes the U.S. media distinctive. For the most part, the press in the United States is low key, but on occasion it can rise to greatness by taking on government with a ferocity that can only come when news sources are treated like enemies of full disclosure and free-flowing information. Of course, most of the time this extreme posture is not necessary, but most reporters would argue in favor of a fundamental distrust of government. They might not go as far as I. F. Stone did when he declared that "government always lies," but would agree that it can obscure, distort, and mislead. The public needs an advocate to challenge, cajole, needle, and inquire. In America this is the job of an adversarial press.

Argument Summation: The media and government should be adversaries.

The fluctuating government-media relationship can be characterized either as disagreement between friends or as occasional agreement between adversaries. The latter relationship is preferable in order to preserve a healthy, fundamental distrust of government among the media which is essential to preserve the checking function of the press. American experience during the libertarian period of the media, when the press became spokesmen for biased views, confirms the power of the press to be used for partisan objectives. A nonadversarial relationship would lead to an erosion of press rights by governmental involvement. While government and media both represent the public interest and can cooperate, an adversary posture is needed to assure a fundamental distrust of government that is critical to democratic society.

TOPICS FOR DISCUSSION

1. Should citizens have more trust in their press than in their government? Why? Discuss.

2. In what ways can the government have an adversarial role against the press? Which of the "adversaries" (government or press) has the advantage? Discuss the reasons for your answer.

3. It is argued that governments manipulate information. Could you say the same thing about the press? Give some examples from actual news stories.

4. Many persons assume that out of an adversarial relationship will emerge truth. Discuss. If the adversarial press makes the U.S. press distinctive in the eyes of the world's journalists, would you consider this to be an approbation or a criticism? Why do you think there are not more nations with such an adversarial press?

5. Discuss the advantages and disadvantages that are likely to accrue in a country by having a press which is an adversary to government.

TOPICS FOR RESEARCH

1. Do a study of a local governmental agency and how it relates to the press. This might be police, mayor, health department, others. How much of the agency's press relations work is reactive? How much is proactive or initiative? What barriers does the press construct for the agency in getting its message to the people? What problems does the agency cause for the press in trying to get information? Is the resulting relationship characterized by conflict or consensus?

2. Find a public official or politician—locally or on the national scene—and research his relationship with the press. Is the relationship organized in a systematic fashion? How does the press treat the individual? If you were giving that person advice about improving or changing his or her image, what would it be?

3. Is there domestic censorship in the United States today? Who, if anyone, are the censors? What is the legacy of censorship of newspapers, books, films, etc. from the past? How much was the result of laws? What is their status today? In assessing who cares about censorship today, you might want to consult library journals and information science publications as well as press and media studies and periodicals.

4. Prepare a comparative analysis of press-government relations in the United States with those of another country, preferably one where the press system is radically different.

5. What does press freedom mean in the following countries: the United Kingdom, the Soviet Union, South Africa, and Singapore? How is the concept defined by laws there? What does government do to impair or enhance press freedom?

FURTHER READING

Anderson, David. "Media Success in the Supreme Court." Working paper. New York: Gannett Center for Media Studies, 1987.

Baker, C. Edwin. "Scope of First Amendment Freedom of Speech." *UCLA Law Review* 25, no. 5 (June 1978): 264–1040.

Blasi, Vince. *The Checking Value in First Amendment Theory*. Samuel

Pool Weaver Constitutional Law Series. Chicago: American Bar Foundation, 1977.

Cater, Douglass. *The Fourth Branch of Government.* Boston: Houghton Mifflin, 1959.

DeFleur, Melvin L., and Everette E. Dennis. *Understanding Mass Communication.* 3d ed. Boston: Houghton Mifflin, 1988. See especially Chapter 7, "The News and the Media," for a discussion of changing styles and standards of reporting, including an analysis of adversarial journalism.

Dennis, Everette E. "The Press and the Public Interest: A Definitional Dilemma." *DePaul Law Review* 23, no.3 (Spring 1974): 937–60.

Dennis, Everette E., et al. *Enduring Issues: Mass Communication.* St. Paul, MN: West, 1978.

Franklin, M. A. *The First Amendment and the Fourth Estate.* New York: Foundation Press, 1977.

Friendly, Fred. *Minnesota Rag.* New York: Random House, 1981.

Kohlmeier, Louis. *The Regulators.* New York: Harper & Row, 1969.

Luedtke, Kurt. "An Ex-Newsman Hands Down His Indictment of the Press." *Bulletin of ASNE* 651(May–June 1982): 16–17.

Merrill, J. C. *The Imperative of Freedom.* 2d ed. New York: Freedom House, 1990.

Merrill, J. C. "The Press, the Government, and the Ethics Vacuum." *Communication* 6(1981): 177–91.

Porter, William E. *Assault on the Media: The Nixon Years.* Ann Arbor, MI: University of Michigan Press, 1976.

Reston, James. *The Artillery of the Press.* New York: Harper & Row, Colophon Books, 1967.

Rivers, William L. *The Adversaries.* Boston: Beacon Press, 1970.

———. *The Other Government: Power and the Washington Media.* New York: Universe, 1982.

Rourke, F. E. *Secrecy and Publicity: Dilemmas of Democracy.* Baltimore, MD: Johns Hopkins University Press, 1966.

Weaver, Paul H. "The New Journalism and the Old Thoughts After Watergate." *The Public Interest* 35(Spring 1974). Also in Dennis, et al.: 167–81.

Chapter **3**

MEDIA AND THE PUBLIC TRUST

As one encounters the procession of speakers in London's famous Hyde Park, it is clear that some know what they are talking about, while others are fanciful, unreliable, even disturbed. We trust and believe some of them, while we are wary of others. The same is true of our media. Unsupported and often abrasive views of some talk show hosts on radio and television or lurid headlines in supermarket tabloids may not inspire our confidence immediately (or ever), while network news, major newspapers and other reliable media usually make an effort to gain public trust.

Discussions of the media and the public trust usually center on the relationship between the media (both individually and collectively) and their audiences. The nature of that relationship is summed up in the term *vox populi* or voice of the people. In a democracy the press or media are said to function as the people's voice—expressing their concerns, providing the information they need, and allowing channels for discussion and debate. Will Rogers once said that a good newspaper was "a nation talking to itself," which expresses very well the idea of public trust. Public trust means that the media are trusted, believed, and relied upon by the public, that they are the necessary representative of the people in much of the public discourse in this nation. In recent years, the concept of public trust is often equated with credibility, believability, and trustworthiness. It is said that a news organization, like a newspaper or a television news program, cannot survive and succeed unless it achieves public trust. This means that most of its audience trusts and believes what it reads, hears, or sees in the content delivered by the newspaper or television station. An idealistic view of the media suggests that this is the main reason why media organizations exist and why people choose to work for them rather than for someone else. In this formulation the media mainly perform a public service in delivering news and information, opinion, and entertainment, and they also serve as a useful marketplace for goods and services. There is another view that says the commercial media in our society, at least, are capitalistic enterprises whose main concern is profits. In such a scheme any public service rendered in establishing a public trust relationship is done strictly for self-serving ends. But whatever the view, the media and the public trust is a much-discussed topic.

CHALLENGE

Merrill: The media chiefly desire to make profits.

Tradition, conventional American wisdom, and oft-expressed idealism combine to suggest that U.S. media are primarily in the business of communication to provide a public service. Certainly, it is said, if the media want to get and retain the "public trust" they will provide such public service.

It is not easy to challenge such a sonorous and idealistic contention, but with profit making and competition being such strong inclinations in a capitalist society and supporting the basic American ideology, such a contention must be challenged. In the United States, regardless of flowery rhetoric at media conventions, the "bottom line" is the machine which drives media policy and is the main concern of media directors.

All we have to do is to consider the expanses of advertising filling our media, spotted here and there with bits and pieces of editorial material, to get a panoramic view of the media's drive toward profit making. Surely the 65–75 percent of the average publication's space given over to advertising is not seriously thought of by media moguls as "serving the public interest." Such exorbitant attention to commercialism that fills the coffers of the media makes a very weak argument for providing the public with a substantial and healthy diet of non-propagandistic content.

Let us agree that, under our media philosophy, profits are desired and necessary. The question, however, is whether the media need to make the exceedingly large profits that they do, while sometimes skimping on the number of staff members and their salaries.

Where is the great concern for the public whenever more media units are gobbled up by big media corporations, multi-media conglomerates proliferate, and national media spew forth the same low-level, common denominator pabulum? Where is concern for the public when media managers—in newspapers as well as in broadcasting—make salaries in the six digits, many in the millions, while editors, reporters, and writers grind out their days with salaries of $30,000 to $50,000—with many getting even less?

Where is the concern of the media for public service when even small weekly newspapers in this country are on the selling block for millions of dollars? Where is the concern for the public when family-owned media, which have served their communities for years, are increasingly bought out for fantastic prices by absentee owners who care little or nothing about the communities? Is it the public these media people are concerned about—or lining their own pockets?

Shirley Biagi presents interesting facts about media ownership: The top ten newspaper groups own one-third of the nation's dailies; twenty corporations control about 60 percent of annual magazine revenues; twenty corporations account for more than 50 percent of radio revenue; 70 percent of all TV stations are network affiliates, and six book publishers receive 30 percent of all book revenue yearly (Biagi, 1988).

Admittedly these figures by themselves do not prove that media have no public concern (sense of responsibility). But they do prove that money and the increase of money through concentration of media power are very powerful in American communications. And they show that growth is what fascinates big media moguls of the United States.

Professor Biagi admits that making money is a goal usually supported by the American people, but it is the way these big media companies make this money that is the debatable question, she says. And she poses three interesting questions: "Does the legacy of First Amendment protection for news-gathering organizations mean that they have a special responsibility to provide the information people need in a democracy? Should entertainment-producing companies provide a diversity of cultural outlets for creativity? Will the adoption of corporate values benefit or harm the mass media industries?"(Biagi, 1988, 277.)

Ben Bagdikian, a leading press critic, notes that "in the face of enormously increased interest in public affairs, newspapers have reduced their average space devoted to news" (Bagdikian, 1974, 9). Bagdikian goes on to question the press's concern for public service: Political coverage is poor; most papers are mediocre and many are wretched; most cities are dominated by one newspaper; advertisements increasingly eat into former news space; live news is decreasing; only about 3 percent of American cities have competing newspapers (in 1910 a majority did); and increasing amounts (probably one-third) of news are supplied by public relations outlets (Bagdikian, 1974, 8–17 passim).

In the world of newspapers the control of content is narrowing. Successful companies are getting bigger and more powerful. Listen to Ray Hiebert and his coauthors of a popular basic media textbook:

" . . . The media, in general, have become more competitive in trying to capture the largest, most valuable audience available, instead of attempting to meet the special needs of all segments of society"(Hiebert, Ungurait, and Bohn, 1988).

If this is true, does it sound like the media are concerned about the public interest?

Hiebert et al. proceed to say that broadcasters also are struggling to reach a mass audience, and that specialized audiences are being neglected. When specialized audiences are considered at all, can they be reached profitably? Hiebert et al. note that media investors are prone to take only mild positions on sensitive issues, and that they seem sensitive only to "demands of the marketplace" (Hiebert, Ungurait, and Bohn, 1988, 594–95).

Perhaps it is not "the public be damned" attitude of a former time, but the average publisher or editor seems to care little about the real informational or intellectual health of the people who read their paper. Editorial prerogative is the watchword. "We will make the decisions we want to make. That's our job. You readers will take what we give you. After all, if you don't read us, who will you read?"

And when asked about responsibility for finding out what the readers want and trying to provide it, the typical editor responds: "We are journalists, and journalists develop the instinct to know what the readers want. In a real sense, what we want is what you want."

So what do readers and television viewers generally get? Snippets of gossip and speculation. Pictures of whales trapped in ice. Stories and pictures of congressional malfeasance. A rundown on the brutal rape-murder in smalltown America, with the grieving mother being asked by the reporter how she feels about her daughter's death. The picture of thousands of university students nihilistically awash in Beijing's main square. And as smoke is shown billowing from a U.S. city, the deep funereal voice of the TV anchor takes us "now to the scene of the devastating explosion that shakes man's faith in technology."

It should be obvious to the American media consumer that most of the messages are trivial, superficial, titillating, sensational, negative, crisis-oriented, and often flippant. Except in certain elite journals like the *New York Times, National Geographic, New Yorker,* or *Commentary,* the reader seldom gets any thoughtful, substantive information and analysis. And the TV viewer drifts about in a desert of crime, sex, and shallow situation "comedies." Programs with depth and insight, such as those found on the Public Broadcasting System, are rare.

But business-oriented media managers will be quick to say: "Such material and such programming aimed at the thoughtful and the educated is not *profitable*. The readership and viewership would be too small. Our nets must be cast wide and into shallow waters so that we may catch as many fish as possible." This is "public service?" Perhaps. But it is a special kind—that which provides desserts and pap for idle minds and lazy souls that undoubtedly inhabit vast expanses of the general public. So the motto of the media manager is generally this: "Give them pap, not what they really need." Or perhaps even better: "Give them what we hope they will accept because of its easy assimilation, so our circulations will increase and our ratings will rise—along with our profits, of course."

The Commission on Freedom of the Press (chaired by Dr. Robert Hutchins) in its 1947 report, *A Free and Responsible Press,* rendered the first large-scale indictment of the American press for not taking the public trust seriously, among other things. According to the Commission, one of the three main dangers facing the press was that the few people who ran the press had not provided a service adequate to the needs of society. Such a criticism, taken seriously even today by many critics, indicates that media are not primarily concerned with public service—but with private interest.

Jerome Barron, lawyer and media critic, has emphasized in *Freedom of the Press for Whom?* that the media do not serve the media interest because of their arrogant exclusiveness. Barron cites sources that indict the American media for normally accentuating the false and the irrational and for excluding small and powerless minorities from a media voice (Barron, 1973, 78–79).

But it can be said that media in the United States are businesses, and businesses are profit-making enterprises, with exclusionary privileges, and with financial growth and the "bottom line" as primary objectives. J. Herbert Altschull notes that, in a commercial media system, "the content reflects the views of the advertisers and their commercial allies, who are usually found among the owners and publishers." Altschull puts in the final nail on the "public interest" question by asserting that "no newspaper, magazine, or broadcasting outlet exceeds the boundaries of autonomy acceptable to the paymasters" (Altschull, 1984, 254–55).

Marketplace theory is usually dragged out to justify the American profit-making system, as a recent volume on media freedom and accountability indicates (Dennis, Gillmor, and Glasser, 1989). In theory the system is supposed to increase message pluralism—as well as owner pluralism and unit pluralism—because of the natural desire of free people to compete and to make money. But is it working that way? Many would argue—many do argue—that pluralism is really shrinking and fewer and fewer voices are being heard throughout the land. Is not the desire to make bigger profits actually causing media directors to take fewer chances, to play it safe, to lower their sights and aim for the lowest common denominator? How does this adequately serve the public interest? It is obvious how it serves the personal financial interest of the media owners.

In this day when every survey shows that Americans are trusting and respecting the media less, the high-sounding shibboleths about the media "recognizing a public trust" is ever more hollow. Perhaps it is time to cease this kind of rhetoric and honestly admit that the main purpose of the media is to make a profit—and that public service comes into the picture only to the degree that it fosters this primary media objective.

Argument Summation: The media chiefly desire to make profits.

The American media mainly desire to make profits. Any thought of public service is secondary. Advertising, dominating all the media, is a key to this emphasis—permitting media to make excessively high profits. Where is the public concern when media corporations are gobbling up increasing numbers of smaller media units? Where is the public concern when media executives earn salaries in the six digits, many in the millions, while staffers who actually produce the product earn salaries between $20,000 and $50,000? Where is the public concern when the lowest common denominator is aimed for by the media, and where local, family-owned grassroots papers are disappearing? Political coverage is poor, most papers are mediocre, most cities have only one newspaper owner, live and hard news is decreasing, and public relations is supplying about one-third of the news we do get.

RESPONSE

Dennis: Media mainly serve the public interest.

In recent years no issue has proved more captivating to the leadership of the American media than credibility and public trust. The terms have often been used interchangeably, although *public trust* is the broader and more inclusive formulation. Beginning in the mid-l980s such organizations as the American Society of Newspaper Editors, Radio and Television News Directors, American Newspaper Publishers Association, American Press Institute, *Times Mirror*, the *Los Angeles Times*, the Poynter Institute, and the Gannett Center for Media Studies have shared a common passion for understanding and improving the relationship between the media and the public. Why? At first, in response to the Grenada crisis during the Reagan administration, it became clear that the government could bar the media from a war zone and get away with it. There was no outcry from the public asking that correspondents be allowed to go to the scene of battle. Instead, the public said (in polls), "Keep 'em out." This shocked many within the U.S. media, and they were intrigued enough to look deeper into the matter. They commissioned studies, organized commissions, sponsored public forums, and engaged in other activities to search for an answer to a question raised by *Time* magazine, "Why does the public hate us?"

For several years there were credibility and public trust studies conducted by respected academic organizations and pollsters. There had been such studies before—indeed there is a fifty-year legacy of media-public attitude research—and the results were mixed. There was good news and bad news. In studies cited in *Reshaping the Media* (1989), I showed that most of the public found the media credible and believable, though a sizable minority did not. A majority also found the press generally accurate and impartial, though, again, there was a worrisome minority that had grave doubts. Happily, most Americans did want their media to be government watchdogs, although there was precious little understanding of the First Amendment and of press freedom.

The reason for all this consternation about the media and the public trust goes to the heart of John Merrill's arguments regarding profits. I believe that it is difficult to have significant media profits or any kind of economic success under our system unless there is first a climate of public trust. After all, the public is buying a communication system, they are paying for public communication, and it stands to reason that they want the resulting information to be competently gathered, accurate, and useful to them. This is public trust at its best. The public also wants access to differing opinions and interpretations of public affairs, as well as entertainment, sports, and advertising. Some will argue about advertising, but many people do find it both entertaining and useful. Those who do not can push the mute button and zap the commercials.

I believe there is ample evidence to support the idea that a passion for journalism and a desire to serve the public come first for most people and organizations that make up the media business in the United States. This is clear both from many studies of American journalists and personal experience. That is why press people react so strongly when their lifeline—the public trust—is challenged or threatened by libel suits, or by the misbehavior of reporters such as Janet Cooke of the *Washington Post* or Foster Winans of the *Wall Street Journal*, who both misused their positions and betrayed the public. The press may be defensive at times, but they will act quickly to correct situations and mistakes that challenge credibility and believability. In fact, it was just such a crisis in the 1980s that made Robert MacNeil suggest that "there is plenty of evidence that [the crisis] is grave, evidence that the public trust at least at the moment, is an ebbing tide"(MacNeil, 1985, 4). MacNeil was one of many leading journalists who joined in a constructive critique of such topics as the blending of news and entertainment, biased reporting, and factual inaccuracies. His concern and that of his colleagues: that public trust is essential if media are to command loyal audiences who find public communication both fair and useful.

It is clear that media people care deeply about the public trust and that they will take steps to see that the quality of their work warrants public support. In recent years, for some of the reasons Professor Merrill mentions, they have been pushed to do this with even more vigor by economic trends. There are today more media outlets seeking public attention and advertiser support than ever before. Cable television has opened up scores of new, competing channels; we have successful national newspapers; new electronic media networks including CNN, Fox, and others have emerged; new magazines emerge faster than we can count them; and the once-declining newspaper has stabilized. In this mix there is enormous competition—in spite of ownership considerations that will be discussed later—and with such competition the need for a credible and respected product is more vital than ever.

The issue raised by Professor Merrill is directed toward motivation of media people—both the working press and the owners. He thinks the worst of them: They are all money-grubbing individuals whose only concern is the bottom line. Certainly, this is not true of most journalists, who are far-removed from profit-making considerations. They are driven more by a love of public affairs, writing, and expression. There is also ego involved in bylines and recognition. A similar case can be made for people who make television entertainment programs, edit magazines or books, or draw cartoons. And most journalists I know see themselves as engaged in a public service. Many could do other things, pursue other careers, but they do not because they find working for the media a compelling challenge.

Many media owners do make large profits, but, for the most part, their investments are in media rather than other enterprises. For most (not all) media companies, information and entertainment are the principal concerns. This generally means that they are not investing in other high yield enterprises or trying to diversify their holdings. They are, in short, committed to the media business, producing a "product" that will find a receptive public. Any argument blaming the owners, people like Katharine Graham of the *Washington Post*, Arthur H. Sulzberger of the *New York Times*, Ted Turner of CNN, Rupert Murdoch of the News World Corporation, for taking advantage of general economic trends needs to be carefully examined. Most of the criticism of the growing concentration of ownership in U.S. media, where there are fewer companies owning the means of communication, suggests that this is somehow a unique condition caused by excessive greed. Not at all. Throughout American business there are fewer small firms and more larger companies. It is a fact of life and the media businesses are following the same trend.

To me there are two important questions that we ought to ask about these trends, both relating to the consequences of ownership. First, have the number of voices in the marketplace seriously decreased in a fashion that threatens diversity in communication? And secondly, has the quality of media fare suffered? To the first question, it can be shown that there are more accessible channels of information today than ever before. Until the 1980s, most American households received only four or five television channels. Today, they get scores of them, all offering diverse fare. At the same time other media enterprises are prospering. While there are more big companies, there are also thousands of newsletters published by individual entrepreneurs, courtesy of desktop publishing and the electronic revolution. The idea that there is not diversity in our media marketplace is questionable. Naturally, it is always healthy to watch these economic trends to see that diversity is not seriously threatened. For this we need thoughtful critics like Ben Bagdikian, although he joins a chorus of commentators, including Oswald Garrison Villard and Upton Sinclair, who since the 1920s have predicted that a handful of greedy owners would one day control all U.S. media. To date it has not happened and I do not think it is likely.

To the second point—quality—the quality of American journalism has been on the rise. While there is always plenty of room for improvement, the quality of American journalism and entertainment is far better today than it was ten or twenty years ago, let alone at the turn of the century when there were 7,000 daily newspapers, compared with under 2,000 today. News coverage has improved enormously, partly helped by technology; writing quality is also up by most accounts, design and graphics have improved a thousandfold in all media. There is more specialist coverage both in the print and electronic media and in data bases. There has been, in fact, a communication revolution in the world, something Professor Merrill and his favorite media-bashing sources seem not to know.

The growth of media and the increased development and use of market research have made the media more responsive to its audiences. Media people know what their readers and viewers say they want. They receive almost continuous feedback in the forms of readership studies, television ratings, and other measures of the relationship between the media and the public. These forms of feedback, made possible by market forces and reinvested profits, keep the public trust vigorous and healthy. Without a trusting relationship between media and public and opportunities for feedback, the tendency would be for media consumers, both individually and collectively, to stop watching some TV programs, cancel the newspaper, and fail to renew the magazine. This is not happening and for good reason—the public trust comes first, the profits follow. The motivations of media people are not as venal as has been suggested, though the media people may not be saints.

Argument Summation: Media mainly serve the public interest.

Journalists seek to serve the public interest, which is why they react adversely when their credibility is threatened. Since the public trust is necessary to sell papers, profit motive takes a secondary role. Besides, the vast majority of journalists are far removed from the ranks in which profits are shared. Owners' profits stem mainly from the media themselves. They seek to diversify ownership of the means of communication, not the message. As a result, centralization has not decreased the number of voices in the marketplace, while the quality of news has improved.

TOPICS FOR DISCUSSION

1. Is the desire for profit a sign that media evade public service? How would you define "public service" and the "public trust"?

2. Groups and organizations like the ANPA, the Gannett Center for Media Studies, and the Poynter Institute are doing much to improve the media-public relationship. What do you think is their prime motivation in doing this?

3. Assuming the argument that we have "enormous competition" in our media system is true, do you think that competition implies public service and concern for the public trust?

4. Are the arguments of Merrill and Dennis, in which they give statistics on media and their audience sizes, in any way related to the question about the public trust and public service? If they are, how do they prove or disprove the contention that profits are the media's main concern?

5. Do you think that most citizens have faith in and admire the media? What leads you to have your opinion? What have surveys said about this?

TOPICS FOR RESEARCH

1. Document the public service activities and programming of a local broadcast station. Interview an official at the station to determine how he or she tries to carry out the FCC's mandate of "public interest, convenience and necessity." Have these activities changed over the past decade? Have they increased or decreased? Has deregulation of broadcasting had any impact?

2. Discuss broadcast ratings. Do they provide an index for the idea of public trust or not? What about newspaper readership studies? What do these kinds of studies tell news decision makers about the public and its attitude toward local media?

3. Do an analysis of media available to you in your local community. What part of their content deals with matters of public service and public trust? How does the content seem to reconcile the difference between journalistic work that informs the public and that aimed more at generating a profit? Can both occur? If so, how?

4. Study the editorial policy of any newspaper or magazine. From the published editorials, determine how many are truly public service statements and how many are more self-serving, perhaps even pandering to a

particular audience or group, such as politicians, sports fans, etc. Characterize the publication's editorial policy in terms of: (1) issues covered; (2) positions taken (pro, con, or neutral); and (3) audience to whom editorial seems directed (e.g., policymakers, the public, specific interest groups).

5. Examine "public service" advertising, that which does not advertise specific products or firms, but which promotes public issues such as the Community Chest, AIDS research, ecology, etc. To whom do these ads appeal? What is the motivation of the media in running them? Do you discern issues or causes that do not get public service support? Document carefully, studying a specific magazine or broadcast organization.

FURTHER READING

Altschull, J. Herbert. *Agents of Power*. White Plains, NY: Longman,1984.

American Press Institute. *The Public Perception of Newspapers: Examining Credibility*. The J. Montgomery Curtis Memorial Seminar. Reston, VA: American Press Institute, 1984.

American Society of Newspaper Editors. *Newspaper Credibility: 206 Practical Approaches to Heighten Reader Trust*. Washington, D.C.: American Society of Newspaper Editors, 1986.

———. *Newspaper Credibility: Building Reader Trust*. Washington, D.C.: American Society of Newspaper Editors, 1985.

Aronson, James. *Packaging the News: A Critical Survey of Radio, TV*. New York: International Publishers, 1971.

Associated Press Managing Editors Association. *Journalists and Readers: Bridging the Credibility Gap*. An APME Credibility Committee Report. San Francisco, 1985.

Bagdikian, Ben H. *The Effete Conspiracy and Other Crimes by the Press*. New York: Harper & Row, 1974.

Barron, Jerome A. *Freedom of the Press for Whom?*. Bloomington, IN: Indiana University Press, 1973.

Biagi, Shirley. *Media Impact*. Belmont, CA: Wadsworth, 1988.

Cirino, Robert. *Don't Blame the People*. New York: Vintage Books, 1971.

Clurman, Richard. *Beyond Malice*. New Brunswick, NJ: Transaction Publishers, 1988.

Commission on Freedom of the Press. *A Free and Responsible Press*. Chicago: University of Chicago Press, 1947.

Dennis, Everette E. *Reshaping the Media*. Newbury Park, CA: Sage Publications, 1989.

Dennis, Everette E., Donald M. Gillmor, and Theodore Glasser, eds. *Media Freedom and Accountability.* Westport, CT: Greenwood Press, 1989.

Fry, Donald, ed. *Believing the News.* Ethics Seminar Series, vol. 3. St. Petersburg, FL: The Poynter Institute for Media Studies, 1985.

Gannett Center for Media Studies. "The Mass Media and the Public Trust: What is Known and Why It Matters." Conference Report. New York: Columbia University, 1987.

Gannett Center for Media Studies. "Media Freedom and Responsibility." Conference Report. New York: Columbia University, 1988.

Ghiglione, Loren. *The American Journalist: Paradox of the Press.* Washington, D.C.: Library of Congress, 1990.

Hiebert, Ray, Donald Ungurait, and Thomas Bohn. *Mass Media V.* White Plains, NY: Longman, 1988.

Lichter, S. Robert, Stanley Rothman, and Linda Lichter. *The Media Elite: America's Powerbrokers.* Bethesda, MD: Adler & Adler, 1986.

MacNeil, Robert. "The Mass Media and the Public Trust." New York: Gannett Center for Media Studies. Occasional Paper No. 1, 1985.

Picard, Robert C. *The Press and the Decline of Democracy.* Westport, CT: Greenwood Press, 1985.

Roper, Burns W. *Public Attitudes toward Television and Other Media in a Time of Change.* New York: Television Information Office, 1985.

Times Mirror Company: "The Press and the People." Los Angeles: Times Mirror Co., January 1986.

Weaver, David H., and G. Cleveland Wilhoit. *The American Journalist: A Portrait of U.S. News People and Their Work.* Bloomington, IN: Indiana University Press, 1986.

Chapter **4**

PEOPLE'S RIGHT TO KNOW

Members of a local school board exclude journalists while they discuss a motion to dismiss a teacher and void her contract. Later, the board chairman urges a newspaper editor not to print the story. Here are two related instances of blocking what is often called "the people's right to know." In the first instance, there is an effort to stop the gathering of information; in the second, its publication and dissemination. As defined by many journalists and some legal scholars, the right to know is the right of the listener to information of public interest and importance. In order for this "right" to be functional, however, information must be acquired and published.

Although it is not specifically stated in the Constitution, there is a widely held belief among journalists and other media personnel that there is a "people's right to know." This "right" is usually defined as the right of the public to have access to information about government policy and decision making. The press sees itself as the conduit for such information, since the average citizen has neither the capacity nor the resources to gather continuing and detailed information about what the government is doing. The people, the argument goes, must have full and robust information about what their government is doing in order to be knowledgeable voters and good citizens. Government secrecy is thought to lead to suspicion and a lack of confidence in public officials and their policies. The people's right to know is transformed, however imperfectly, from an abstract principle to a concrete reality in "sunshine acts" that require government bodies to hold open meetings and to have their records open for public inspection. Theoretically, government should operate in the open and should be accountable to the people and the "right to know" would make that possible.

CHALLENGE

Dennis: There is no right to know.

The right to know is not an inalienable right guaranteed by the Constitution, but is instead something that was invented by journalists. For a number of years journalistic organizations have been badgering the courts and the legislatures in the hope of establishing their right to access to various confidential sources of information. This so-called right now has some modest basis in law, in that on occasion courts have said that under certain circumstances and in very specific areas there is a right to know. But this is something so conditional that it is not a right at all, but a quite limited privilege that depends on the disposition of judges. What they give today, they can take away tomorrow. I believe that the right to know is a badly flawed concept that actually interferes with other rights and may do more to impair than to advance First Amendment freedoms.

The right to know is most often invoked when media people are asking for rights and privileges that the rest of us do not have. It is a justification for a vague category of corporate rights because the right to know is not put forth as an *individual* right, but as an *institutional* right and here is where the argument gets hazy. The First Amendment guarantees a "right to speak" that belongs to individuals. Advocates of the right to know say that this "new right" is derived from the "right to listen." Listeners (or anyone receiving the messages of free speech and press) are entitled to a flow of information; hence the right to know. It is notable that most of the rights enumerated in the Bill of Rights are for individuals, but our friends in the media would change this by adding a little corporate-institutional appendage.

According to Harvard law professor Lawrence Tribe, a leading constitutional scholar, right-to-know advocates would differentiate between the "focused right of an individual to speak" and "the undifferentiated right of the public to know" (Tribe, 1978, 674). Professor Tribe says people who take this position argue that the First Amendment does not confer individual rights but protects a system of freedom of expression. "This view," he says, "unduly flattens the First Amendment's complex role" (Tribe, 1978, 675). Another leading scholar, Edwin Baker, agrees. A right to know, he says, is never more than a right to have the government not interfere with a willing speaker's liberty.

The right to know is something of a journalistic invention. It began in the early 1950s when the press felt increasingly thwarted by bureaucrats who were standing between them and government information. It began as a quest for access to records and meetings, the so-called sunshine laws, short for government operations "in the sunshine" or open. These journalists wanted access to government records, documents, and proceedings at both the state and federal levels. This was called the Freedom of Information (FOI) movement. The bible for this activist effort was a thoughtful, weighty tome called *The People's Right to Know—Legal Access to Public Records and Proceedings* by Harold L. Cross (1953).

The FOI movement had many positive consequences. It brought sunshine laws (open-meeting and open-record legislation) in most of the states, fostered the Federal Freedom of Information Act, and opened up many government meetings from which the press and public had previously been barred. The FOI movement was both necessary and desirable, but the journalists did not stop there. Many excesses followed.

Over the years the press claimed that it should have access to many classified government records and files, including some dealing with national defense and national security. Journalists also asked for greater immunity from libel suits, both those brought by public officials and by private citizens. Some reporters asked for a right to rummage through the private papers of individuals to "pursue the truth" and frequently claimed that the right of privacy was an undue hindrance on the press and public.

So what if journalists argued for these things? If these positions were merely the mutterings of media people at the press club, there would be no problem. But all of these claims and many more were brought to the Supreme Court of the United States. In each case the rationale was the people's right to know. This approach is what Anthony Lewis calls "press exceptionalism": special rights for the press that are not available for the rest of the public. This approach also introduces a conceptual problem because the rest of the Bill of Rights applies to individuals, but the right to know is advanced as an *institutional* right.

Efforts were made to establish a broad constitutional right. And, as good lawyers will tell you, there is always "authoritative support" for any position if lawyers look hard enough. In this instance authoritative support was found in the writings of James Madison, who once said, "A popular government without popular information, or the means of acquiring it, is but a Prologue to a Farce or a Tragedy; or perhaps, both. Knowledge will forever govern ignorance; and a people who mean to be their own Governors, must arm themselves with the power which knowledge gives" (Madison, 1006). Right to know advocates got support from Supreme Court justices Hugo Black and William O. Douglas. Douglas was particularly eloquent:

> The press has a preferred position in our constitutional scheme, not to enable it to make money, not to set newsmen aside as a favored class, but to bring fulfillment to the public's right to know. The right to know is crucial to the governing powers of the people (Douglas, 1972, *Branzburg v. Hayes*, 408, United States, 665 at 713.)

This had a bittersweet ring for a number of publishers and broadcasters who are clearly in the communications business to make money and who have only the vaguest, passing interest in the people's right to know, even though their rhetoric sometimes suggests otherwise.

Although the right-to-know leaders appreciated the support of Justice Douglas, they hankered for something more than mere rhetoric. They thought they had it when, in 1974, Justice Potter Stewart gave a notable speech at Yale Law School. In that now-famous speech Justice Stewart said that the "Free Press Clause extends protection to an institution" (Stewart, 1975, 631). This is what the right-to-know advocates were waiting for: the First Amendment as an institutional right, and mighty support for the idea of a people's right to know. But alas, the "word according to Stewart" seemed to have currency only at Yale. It was not a majority position of the Court (or even a minority view) and thus not the law of the land. The people's right to know was still in the realm of grand theory. Although it has been repeatedly pointed out that the Stewart speech had no standing in the developing law of the First Amendment, it is often invoked as though it were chiseled in stone and blessed by the framers. This position of structural freedom of the press based on a right to know was and remains one person's opinion and has not become law.

The Stewart speech nevertheless gave much fuel to hungry legal and journalistic minds seeking support for the right to know. The next turn in the debate was a position put eloquently by Federal Judge Irving Kauffman, who said that freedom of the press was dependent on protection for three aspects of the communication process: acquiring, processing, and disseminating information. This makes perfect sense, and journalists argued vehemently that it is virtually impossible to disseminate information without acquiring it (through news-gathering methods) and processing it (by editing and preparing for publication). This is logical, of course, but once again journalistic fancy was light-years ahead of legal reality. What Judge Kauffman posited was a theory of freedom of expression and from my point of view a very desirable one, but one without a solid legal foundation. To explain: Most legal scholars agree that there is powerful Constitutional support for the dissemination of information. Most First Amendment law centers on the right of people to speak and publish. There is much less legal basis for acquisition of information and, in fact, much of the press's claim in this area is tied to a case which *denied* the press any special journalist's privilege to withhold names of news sources in court proceedings. In that case Justice Byron White offered a less-than-reassuring statement with a double negative construction, that "news gathering is not without its First Amendment protections" (White, 1972, in *Branzburg v. Hayes*, 406 United States, 655 at 707). He did not say what they were. On the matter of processing news or editing it, the law is quite thin. Rarely have courts been asked to give special protection to this aspect of media work and not surprisingly they have not initiated it themselves. In a few instances when they were asked to grant "news-processing" rights, they declined to do so. The press has been inventive and resourceful in trying to establish the right to know as a provision of constitutional law, but to date it has not done so, and from all appearances this idea will have to percolate for a long time before it is allowed to raise conceptual havoc with the rather specific language of the First Amendment.

The right to know is a very limited privilege with many important exceptions, so many that to call it a right is misleading. One of the strongest advocates of the right to know is communication law scholar Franklyn S. Haiman, who says the public's right to know is a vital element of the First Amendment "because much essential knowledge is in the hands of agencies and officials of government who can thwart the democratic process by keeping relevant material secret" (Haiman, 1981, 368). Haiman says the right to know is based on the need of the public for information to exercise its responsibilities of citizenship and:

> In a fundamental sense, data in the hands of government belongs to the public, having been collected through the use of taxpayers' money and for the exercise of authority derived from the people as a whole (Haiman, 1981, 368–69).

All well and good, but then come the *exceptions* (which Haiman acknowledges and supports) to government disclosures that seriously undermine any "right to know." They are:

1. The need to protect the privacy and other legitimate personal interests of those about whom information is gathered.
2. The need to insure candid deliberative processes.
3. The need to safeguard the public's economic interests.
4. The need to preserve the physical safety of society and its institutions (Haiman, 1981, 369).

These broad and compelling exceptions blow a hole in the people's right to know, which need not be absolute, but certainly must have a broader reach than Haiman and other scholars envision if it is to be a fundamental right and have real meaning. Rights are not "now you see them, now you don't" propositions.

The right to know, then, has a flimsy legal foundation, which is reason enough to question whether it should be accorded the kind of status journalists want to confer upon it. But there are even more compelling reasons for viewing this so-called right with real trepidation. Journalist and screenwriter Kurt Luedtke, quoted elsewhere in this book, put it succinctly in a 1982 speech when he told the American Newspaper Publishers Association that:

> There is no such thing as the public's right to know. You made that up, taking care not to specify what it was the public had a right to know. The public knows whatever you choose to tell it,

no more, no less. If the public did have a right to know, it would then have something to say about what it is you choose to call news (Luedtke, 1982, 4–5).

Luedtke is right. If the public really does have a right to know, it surely has a right to determine what information it truly needs to know and to demand that the press (as its surrogate) deliver that information forthwith. Out the window goes the right of the editor and broadcaster to edit and to decide what is news. And here the nightmare begins. If the press is to become the legal representative of the people under a general principle of a right to know, then it will certainly be told by the courts and legislatures that it has a duty to provide particular information to the public. This definitely would be a shocking intrusion on freedom of the press and is something that I would hope no thinking journalist would advocate. New rights bring new duties and I have serious doubts that the press will want the baggage that will come with the public's right to know, if such a right should be given full and complete constitutional protection. I say let well enough alone, stop making self-serving claims in the name of this public "need."

Argument Summation: There is no right to know.

The right to know is not to be found in the Constitution, which preserves individual rights—not institutional rights. The right to know is, rather, a creation of the law and is therefore a privilege which can be taken away. Before rising to constitutional importance it must take on more breadth than is presently recognizable. Originally the freedom of information movement achieved legitimacy by focusing on the need for access to government records, but has since expanded its aims to include a general "right to know." However, even the right of access to government records is severely limited by exceptions such as privacy, economic interests, social stability, and national security.

RESPONSE

Merrill: There is a right to know.

My coauthor contends that the right to know is not an inalienable right guaranteed by the Constitution, and that it is, rather, something invented by journalists. It is difficult to dispute either of these contentions. Such a "right" is not overtly in the Bill of Rights, and it does seem that only journalists have made much, if anything, of such a right.

Nevertheless, even after saying this, I must insist that a right to know for the citizenry of a libertarian society (free and open) does indeed exist— even if such a right is a philosophical right and not spelled out literally in the First Amendment.

It may well be that a people's right to know is not explicitly stated constitutionally, but journalists did more than "invent" it: They inferred from the "freedom of the press" clause that a people's right to know existed. I suppose that by making such an inference, which seems quite logical to me, they did in a sense invent this right to know. But instead of feeling guilty for such an "invention," if such it was, journalists should be proud of the fact that they have seen this public right standing in the philosophical shadows supporting a free press.

Why, we should ask, should the Founding Fathers provide for a free press? Simply for the sake of having a free press? Just so future citizens could brag about such a provision? Obviously there was a pragmatic reason for the free press (as well as the free speech) provision in the Bill of Rights. And this reason revolves around what we now call the people's right to know. If the people of the republic (the sovereign rulers of the country) do not know about public affairs and government business, they surely cannot be good sovereigns; they cannot govern themselves well. In the philosophical framework they find themselves in, they *must* know. Their government is built upon the assumption that they will know; therefore, certainly it is their "right" to know. They need to know; they have a philosophical mandate to know in order to be consistent with their political purpose. The very reason for a free press is that the people can know.

Someone will ask: If the people have a right to know, then does not the press share responsibility with government in letting them know? My answer is yes. If the press argues for such a right (and I maintain that the press in a free society, with its press freedom, *must* believe in such a fundamental right), then it must take very seriously its responsibility of providing knowledge about public affairs to the people. If there is such a public right to know, and I believe there is, then the press has an important responsibility to fulfill this right—to see to it that the people are able to know.

At this point the government enters the picture, for the press cannot let the people know what the press cannot get from government. So, I maintain that the people do have a right to know public business and that both the press and the government have the responsibility to let the people know. Certainly the people cannot know about their government without the cooperation of both press and government. Just because the press and government both fail, from time to time, to let the people know does not eliminate the people's right.

The concept of "the people's right to know" has mainly been promoted since World War II; books such as Kent Cooper's (1956) *The Right to Know* and Harold Cross's (1953) *The People's Right to Know* and numerous articles have been printed declaring such a right and castigating government for infringing on it. No adherent to a libertarian theory of the press can but admire and applaud such antigovernment broadsides, but the problem is larger than this.

Two other important factors are involved in this business of letting the people know: the people and the press. Too often they are left out of a discussion of this topic.

Frankly, the people either don't know they have a right to know or they don't take it seriously. It appears that they simply don't care. Such a right to know is certainly one of great importance—a civil right if there ever was one. Such a right is at the very foundation of American government, of public discussion, of intelligent voting, of public opinion, of the very fabric and essence of democracy. And yet the people appear to have little or no concern for this right. But—unconcern does not do away with the right.

The only segment of our society that seems really concerned about the people's right to know is the press. Journalists criticize, agitate, and fret about the people's right to know being infringed upon by government. They justify—rightly—their own press freedom by appealing to the public's right to know.

A problem with the press is that it places all the blame on government for denying the people this right. This, of course, is not true. The news media themselves participate in the denial of this right. Persons familiar with the typical news operation must recognize that only a very small portion of government-related information gets to the average citizen's eyes or ears. So, in effect, the news media are themselves guilty of the same sins of omission and commission that they point to in government.

Editors and news directors, while promoting the idea of a people's right to know, are busy selecting and rejecting government information. They leave out this story, that picture, this viewpoint. They play out completely, and on and on. They are, in effect, "censors"—perhaps with the best of motives, but "censors" nevertheless. They manage the news just as government officials do. They also play their parts in the restriction of the people's right to know.

Of course, editors call this practice "exercising their editorial prerogative." They see themselves as "editing"; they see the government "managing" and "restricting" public information. But the people's exercise of the right to know is being limited regardless of these semantic games.

All the while press people are hailing the "right to know" as indispensable for the country.

One who observes the editing operations of a newspaper or magazine is struck by the swiftness with which government news is discarded. When wastebaskets fill with information that the people presumably should be reading, it will be noted that there are few tears and there is little gnashing of teeth in journalistic ranks. It is as if these practitioners of journalism obscure their own coverage of government without even realizing that they, like the government officials they criticize, are keeping back information that, in their own words, "the public has a right to know."

Media people are right, of course. The public does have a right to know. This right has always been in the American journalistic context, even though it has not been traditionally as popular as it has been since World War II. Now the emphasis is shifting from the press to the people, from journalistic freedom to journalistic responsibility, from institutional rights of the press to social rights of the citizenry. It is all part of the shift from "negative freedom" to "positive freedom"—from freedom *from* to freedom *to*. Part of the social responsibility theory of the press is an emphasis on what the press does positively, not what the press might be kept by government from doing.

The people's right to know is a logical outgrowth of this trend. I maintain that the philosophical rationale for press freedom (interpreted until recently as the *press's* freedom) all along has been that the people *need* to know. This need philosophically is translated into a "right" in our type of pluralistic, open, libertarian society where the people theoretically are the sovereigns.

So, in spite of the sophisticated arguments put forward by Dennis and others who deny this people's right, I again propose, in conclusion, that such a right exists. However often it is denied the people—by government and by the press—it is still there serving as the main underpinning of a democratic society of the American type. It is the justification for press freedom and the absolute requirement for the political viability of the United States.

Argument Summation: There is a right to know.

Certainly there is no explicit constitutional "right to know," but there is surely an implied or natural right to know. The concept of press freedom assumes such a right, for obviously the press would not have such freedom for no (or only a selfish) reason. The country's philosophy is based on the people as sovereigns; therefore, there is a need for them to know, and this need is logically translated into a "right." Both the press and the government share in the responsibility to let the people know. The people may not think much about such a right, but they instinctively feel they have it, given their type of government. If they do not have such a right, then they see no real reason for a free press.

TOPICS FOR DISCUSSION

1. Think about the public's need to know, desire to know, curiosity to know—and consider these alongside a "right" to know. What are your conclusions?

2. If such a "right to know" is not in the Bill of Rights, where do we get such a right? Is it any more than a theoretical or idealistic right?

3. If it is a right of the people "to know," why do media themselves withhold information? How can a newspaper editor believe in such a people's right while refraining from giving a quote's source, naming a rape victim, or divulging the source of a government "leak"?

4. Can press freedom, which *is* in the Constitution, be equated with the public's "right to know"? Explain your answer.

5. If the invention of the right to know came about in the early 1950s, why do you think it developed so late in American history if the principle on which it rests is valid?

TOPICS FOR RESEARCH

1. Write a paper about forces for and against the "right to know." Who have the pro right-to-know spokespersons been over the years? Who have been their opponents?

2. Prepare a study of the origins, present status and probably future of the federal Freedom of Information Act.

3. Write a review essay about three or four major books or articles about privacy from the perspective of the right to know. When do privacy rights take precedence over the media's desire to know something?

4. What is "intellectual property"? How is it connected to the law of copyright? Why is copyright law in the U. S. federal law as part of the U. S. Code? How do copyright and protection of an individual or author's rights impair the people's right to know? Should anyone care?

5. Why is there a debate over the right to know? Why is it that journalists believe it exists and lawyers say "no way"?

FURTHER READING

Anderson, Jack. "We the People: Do We Have a Right to Know?" *Parade* January 30, 1966: 4–5.

Boyer, John H. "Supreme Court and the Right to Know." FOI Center Report 272. Columbia, MO: University of Missouri, November 1971.

Cooper, Kent. *The Right to Know*. New York: Farrar, Strauss Cudahy, 1956.

Cross, Harold L. *The People's Right to Know—Legal Access to Public*

Records and Proceedings. New York: Columbia University Press, 1953.

Dennis, Everette E., D. M. Gillmor, and David Grey, eds. *Justice Hugo Black and the First Amendment.* Ames, IA: Iowa State University Press, 1978.

Douglas, William O. *The Right of the People.* New York: Doubleday, 1958.

Haiman, Franklyn S. *Speech and Law in a Free Society.* Chicago: University of Chicago Press, 1981.

Luedtke, Kurt. "The Twin Perils: Arrogance and Irrelevance." Speech at annual meeting, American Newspaper Publishers Assn. Convention. San Francisco, May 1982.

———. "An Ex-Newsman Hands Down His Indictment of the Press." *The Bulletin of ASNE* 65(May–June 1982): 16–17.

Madison, James. *Writings of James Madison.* G. Hunt, ed. 1906.

Merrill, J. C. "Is There a Right to Know?" FOI Center Report 002. Columbia, MO: University of Missouri, January, 1967.

———. "The People's Right to Know Myth." *New York State Bar Journal* 7 (November, 1973): 45.

———. "The Press, the Government, and the Ethics Vacuum." *Communication* (1981): 6.

Rourke, Francis E. *Secrecy and Publicity: Dilemmas of Democracy.* Baltimore, MD: Johns Hopkins University Press, 1966.

Schauerte, Bud. "Yes, There Is the Right to Know." FOI Center Report 003. University of Missouri, May, 1967.

Schwarzlose, Richard A. "For Journalists Only?" *Columbia Journalism Review* 16, no. 2 (July–August 1977): 32–33.

Spangler, Raymond. "You Have a Right to Know—What?" *The Quill* 58, no. 2 (February 1970): 4.

Stewart, Potter. "Or of the Press." *Hastings Law Journal* 26(January 1975): 631–38.

"The People's Right to Know: How Much or How Little?" *Time* (11 January 1971): 16–17.

Tribe, Lawrence H. *American Constitutional Law.* Mineola, NY: Foundation Press, 1978. See especially Chapter 12, "Communication and Expression," 576–736.

Whalen, Charles W., Jr. *Your Right to Know.* New York: Vintage Books, 1973.

Williams, Lord Francis. "The Right to Know." *Twentieth Century* (Spring, 1962): 6–17.

Chapter 5

PUBLIC ACCESS TO THE MEDIA

A woman believes that the local newspaper is essentially sexist, both in its use of news sources (mostly men) and in its trivialization of women's issues. She wants the newspaper to be more sensitive to women and to publish her views critiquing the paper on a regular basis. The paper refuses, and she asserts that she and thousands of like-minded people have been denied "access" to the public through the public media. She may have a point, but to date there is no constitutionally guaranteed "access to the media."

The principle of public access to the media is based on a positive interpretation of the press clause of the First Amendment. The clause ("Congress shall make no law . . . ") is, of course, stated negatively. Under a positive interpretation it is often claimed that the public has a right to freedom of the press through access to the media, that is, through a right to publish opinions and be heard in the printed press and on broadcast stations.

It is maintained that the public has no real freedom of the press without this right of access; only those who own the means of communication have freedom of the press. (The counter argument is that in order to have freedom of religion, speech, or assembly, one need not own a church, a public platform, or a street.) The theory of access posits that the First Amendment grants protection to all persons, not just those who own the mass media. The right of reply to newspaper and broadcast material and the right to buy advertising have been suggested as corollaries to the right of access.

While guaranteed public access to the print media—such as the right of reply to an editorial or the right to run an advertisement—has generally been denied by courts, the electronic media present a different case. Largely because the regulation of broadcasting has been based on a theory of scarcity—that is, there are a limited number of broadcast (not cable) frequencies, so that not everyone can operate a radio or television station—the government has granted a number of privileges to citizens who want to respond to broadcast editorials and other electronic content. With the electronic media the public does have a limited and prescribed right of access; not so with the print media.

CHALLENGE

Merrill: The public has no right of access.

Many critics of the press during the last several decades have proposed that the First Amendment should be reinterpreted to force the mass media to give space and time to individuals and groups wanting to present "minority" points of views. One key leader in this crusade for a "right of access to the press" has been Professor Jerome Barron. He has argued that the First Amendment prohibition of government restraint does not forbid the government from acting to enhance citizens' opportunities to exercise their freedom to the press. He has argued vigorously in favor of a legal right of access to the mass media by citizens.

In the June 1967 *Harvard Law Review* and subsequently in many other articles and speeches, Barron has proclaimed that the main interest of media owners and controllers is to maximize profit, not discussion. Only with a right of access to the press, Barron argues, can the voice of the people be heard. What he and others are advocating is a new interpretation of the First Amendment whereby the courts can mandate use by the press of material from individuals and groups.

This key passage from Barron's original *Harvard Law Review* article provides the thrust of the "access" position:

> Our constitutional theory is in the grip of a romantic conception of free expression, a belief that the "marketplace of ideas" is freely accessible. But if there . . . [ever was] a self-operating marketplace of ideas, it has long ceased to exist. The mass media's development of an antipathy to ideas requires legal intervention if novel and unpopular ideas are to be assured a forum . . . (Barron, 1967, 1641).

The courts have not been impressed with Barron's arguments so far, although the topic has become popular in public and journalistic debates. The firmest rejection of Barron's arguments came in a Florida case called *Tornillo v. The Miami Herald*. In the fall of 1972 Pat Tornillo, Jr., a candidate for the Democratic nomination in a Florida state legislative primary, sought to use a 1918 state law that a newspaper assailing a candidate's character had to give that candidate a chance to reply free of charge. The *Miami Herald*, having carried a critical editorial about Tornillo, nevertheless refused to provide free space to Tornillo to answer. Tornillo and Barron, who was Tornillo's legal counsel, convinced the Florida Supreme Court of their position, but the U. S. Supreme Court took the view that editorial decisions were to be made by editors, not courts.

If an individual citizen (such as Tornillo) should have the right of access to a newspaper, why should not the government have a similar right? Why should not President Bush, for example, have the right to force the *Washington Post* to print his answer to a critical editorial? Why would not any government official have such a right to get his (or his agency's) side into the press? It is hard to imagine the chaos that would result from such a situation, with editorial decisions of this type being made in the already overloaded courts. The editors of the country would find themselves mere figureheads, making no editorial decisions—or feeling the "chilling effect" of such a legal system to a degree that they would fill their columns with material from those they most feared might take them to court.

Barron may have seen his suggestion as a new "interpretation" of the First Amendment. I see it as a perversion or abdication of the First Amendment. It so obviously takes away editorial freedom or determination (by the press) that it should strike any reasonable person as a travesty of the concept of press freedom. In essence, if individuals could force their opinions into newspapers, newspaper editors would lose their freedom to use or reject an article; any editorial determination would obviously be gone.

No one will deny that there are persons in the public who would like to have access to the large audiences reached by the major mass media. Naturally I have opinions; I have certain messages I would like to see made public in a newspaper like the *New York Times* or my local daily. Naturally, a certain limitation is placed on me if I cannot get my opinions published. I still, however, can *speak* my opinions, whether or not my voice reaches all the listeners I might like. My right of free speech is not negated just because I do not have as large an audience as I would like. The fact that there is a freedom of speech clause in the First Amendment, as well as a free press clause, indicates to me that the writers of the Bill of Rights intended to separate the two: that there should be the press's freedom to print *and* the people's freedom to speak. If not, there would have been no need to state both rights in the First Amendment.

It is, in fact, relatively easy for people with something to say today to get their ideas (or some of them) before the public or portions of it. But, say the "access" people, the problem is getting a big audience for the message. The important thing, they say, is getting one's message into the mass media—newspapers, magazines, radio, and television. This, of course, is a natural desire for anyone who thinks he has something important to say. But I agree completely with Ayn Rand in her position on this matter. She is in opposition to those, like Barron, who would "redefine" the First Amendment as giving "the people" some kind of inalienable right to have someone else publish their opinions.

> The right of free speech means that a man has a right to express his ideas without danger of suppression, interference, or punitive action by the government. It does not mean that others must provide him with a lecture hall, a radio station, or a printing press through which to express his ideas (Rand, 1964, 97).

With Rand I believe that there are no "rights" for consumers of journalism if no journalist chooses to produce the particular kinds of journalism that certain consumers want. There is only the right of citizens to be journalists and produce them—or for them to try to get the kind of journalism they desire, or to try to get their ideas into the journalistic media.

"Remember," writes Ayn Rand (1964), "that rights are moral principles which define and protect a man's freedom of action, but impose no obligations on other men. " A case in point would be Rand's own book in which these words appear: She had the freedom to write, but it was a publisher who decided that her views were of sufficient interest to warrant publication.

Let us consider a basic question: Who are the editors or editorial decision makers in the American press system? Who should be? Are they persons working for (or owning) private newspapers—or are they some outside authority? This is a question that cannot be turned aside with idealistic arguments about some theoretical "people's freedom," the desire on the part of individuals to have their opinions published. The concept of "people's freedom" suggests the socialist world's emphasis on a "people's press." Even a cursory knowledge of the press of a country like the Soviet Union exposes what happens to "press freedom" and pluralism when the rhetoric of a "people's press" is actually put into practice.

I fail to see how the Founding Fathers had in mind any concept of "the people" (nonprinters and nonpublishers) having "freedom of the press." The concept is far-fetched when applied to the press, both from philosophical and from linguistic perspectives. When the First Amendment was written, in the post-colonial period, the writers had in mind prohibiting the control and suppression of the press by a government such as that then prevailing in England; they did not want such a situation to exist in the United States. They wanted the press, not the government, not the courts, to make editorial decisions. They were trying to head off any a priori press censorship or control by government.

I believe that when the Founding Fathers spoke of the "press," they meant the press; they did not mean "the people." When they wanted to talk about the people, they spoke of the people. If they had considered the Barron contention that the people should have a right of access to the press, they would have clearly placed that "right" where it belonged—in the Bill of Rights. Certainly they would not have obscured such a right under the free press right; it would have been much too important for such linguistic games. If the people were to have the right to force their messages and opinions into the papers of the states, this would have been a "right" so important that it would have had to be explicated (or at least listed) in the Bill of Rights.

If one looks at this complex issue as having to do only with assuring minority opinions a fair hearing, it is little wonder that a proposal like Professor Barron's would be considered salutary and perhaps even long overdue. This, however, is not where the problem ends. If such a proposal were taken seriously by enough powerful people in the country to bring it into practice, a whole new bag of troubles would be opened to plague the person concerned about protecting a free press. Even as "freedom of the press" implies the freedom to be heard—a freedom for the consumer—we must not forget that it also implies the freedom to print or not to print—a freedom for the publisher.

The First Amendment provides that federal government will not pass any laws which abridge press freedom. Although press freedom is not defined in the Bill of Rights, an explicit concern with not passing laws which might diminish press freedom appears to be quite clear. When any group—even government seeking to remedy certain ills which it believes it detects—tells a publisher what he or she must print, it is taking upon itself an omnipotence not far removed from authoritarianism. It is restricting press freedom in the name of freedom for an individual to have an outlet for his messages and in the name of freedom to read.

This paradox brings up the interesting point that "freedom of the press" should not be used synonymously with "freedom of information." It is obvious that the press can have freedom to print anything it desires without making available to the reader everything it has available to print. Its freedom, in other words, imposes an implicit restriction on the reader's freedom of access to every bit of information or point of view.

Looking at it in this way, it is not difficult to see that press freedom does not imply freedom of information. The latter term refers to the right of the reader to have all material available for reading, while the former term denotes the right of the publisher to publish or not to publish.

Perhaps the problem is that we try to make the term "freedom of the press" cover too much. If we were to understand it narrowly, in the sense clearly indicated by its syntax, we would emphasize the *press* and its *freedom* in the context of information flow. This would mean that "freedom" belongs to "the press." The press alone, in this definition, would be in the position of determining what it would or would not print. The press would have no prior restrictions on its editorial prerogatives; this would be *press freedom*. Those who favor an interpretation of the First Amendment that protects "freedom of information" would hardly agree to a definition that deemphasizes the rights of "the people."

The person who is concerned about what is not in the press does not appear to be concerned primarily about the *freedom of the press* to make editorial decisions. However laudable this concern may be, we must recognize that such a position is potentially authoritarian, just as the existing libertarianism of the press is potentially restrictive.

Those who would compel publication justify their position by using terms such as "the public's inherent right to be heard," and the "public's right to know," and "press responsibility." Such people thus put what they regard as the social good above what individual publishers consider their right of editorial self-determination.

Few thoughtful individuals would quarrel with the position that "the good of society" or "social responsibility" is a laudable concept that should be served by the press. However, trouble comes when these theoretical concepts are applied to the actual workings of the press in society. The *what* of the concept presents considerable difficulty. What, for instance, is the best way to do the most good for society, and what is the best way to be socially responsible? There are many who would feel very strongly that forcing opinions (especially "certain" opinions) into a newspaper would be very harmful to the social good, and that this would be the epitome of social irresponsibility.

The *how* of the concept adds further complications. How would decisions be made about what would or would not be printed? What would be a rational manner of making such determinations if we were to take them out of the hands of individual publishers and editors? A federal court? A federal ombudsman? A Federal Press Agency organized on the lines of the Federal Communications Commission?

Among all the minority positions in a given community or in the nation, which would have a "right" to be published and which would not? Which spokesman for any one "minority" would be published as a representative of the whole minority? Or would all of them—or many of them—be published, since undoubtedly there is a pluralism in minority opinions even on a single issue? These are basic and important questions—questions that would constantly plague the authority that would have to make such decisions.

This would take us back to the same situation that exists when editors or publishers make the decisions about what to use and not to use. Viewpoints that one court (or authoritative body) would deem valuable and thus worthy of publication might, to another authoritative body that is equally perspicacious and dedicated, seem inane, irrational, or otherwise lacking in value. Undoubtedly, even among the staunchest advocates of minority rights there is preference for some minorities over others. How will such a system differ in any substantial way from variances of decisions presently made by editors? One thing is certain: Not every opinion can be used. Somebody has to make the editorial decisions, be it editor or court or other entity. Therefore, always there will be the charge by someone that he is not given the proper exposure for his opinions.

Beyond this, there is another perplexing, closely related problem.

What emphasis should various minority views receive in the press or even in a single newspaper? Would this be decided by the proportion of the total population which the minority under consideration comprises? Would it be decided on the basis of the "worth" or "intrinsic value to society" of the viewpoint espoused? If so, how would such worth be ascertained? Would it be decided on the basis of the economic or political pressure which a particular person or group might bring to bear on the power structure? How would a nonpress decision on what will or will not be printed have any real advantage over pluralistic editorial decisions made by the press itself?

Many persons will reply that these are unimportant and theoretical questions that should not be permitted to interfere with the serious consideration of a forced publishing system. "Sure," they will say, "there will be problems and weaknesses, but we must push on, in spite of obstacles, toward a New Journalism in which all opinions receive equal and just airing, and no minority group or 'aggrieved' individual can feel slighted by the treatment received in the press."

I maintain that proposals for the right of public access or for a legally forced publishing concept, in spite of idealistic objectives, are extremely naive in view of the practicalities of day-to-day journalism and the explicit language of the Bill of Rights.

Argument Summation: The public has no right of access.

A public right of access to the media contradicts both the idea of press freedom and the principle of editorial self-determination. Either the media determine their content or some other group or person does. In a capitalist society, where the press's freedom is constitutionally protected, the idea of a people's right of access is preposterous. Such a "right" has even been rejected by the Supreme Court (*Tornillo* v. *The Miami Herald*, 1972).

It is impossible to imagine the U.S. press being forced (a necessary situation for such a right to exist) to publish the many news items and opinions that would seek exposure in the media. Courts, presumably, would have to turn into editors, and editors—then powerless—would be mere technocrats and functionaries in court-run entities.

RESPONSE

Dennis: The public has a right of access.

On its face this may seem to be a difficult, if not impossible, position. However, it is not. Many opponents of the right of access say the issue has already been decided in the *Tornillo* case. Did the Supreme Court of the

United States demolish access in its 9 to 0 decision striking down the Florida law? No, not quite, but unfortunately for access advocates, Jerome Barron, an attorney for plaintiff Tornillo, used the case, albeit a weak one, to test the theory of access. He lost, but that loss does not forever pull the chain on the right of access.

Public access to the media is based on a quite simple and, I believe, just assumption: that when the framers of the Constitution wrote the First Amendment, they meant that *all* the people have a right to freedom of the press, not just the *owners* of the media. Professor Barron worries that a "romantic and lopsidedly pro-publisher" (Barron, 1973, 12) view of the First Amendment does not necessarily benefit the public. When we look closely at other features of the First Amendment, the interpretation that only the owners of the media can enjoy press freedom seems strange indeed. Press people often forget that the First Amendment also says something about religion, speech, and assembly. Consider freedom of religion, for example. No one would sensibly argue that only organized religious groups or churches have freedom of religion. On the contrary, we understand that both individual and institutional rights (those of churches) to freedom of religion can be accommodated under the First Amendment. The religious rights of individuals have been tested repeatedly in the courts and, over time, a substantial legal basis for them has been developed.

Very few cases involving individual rights to press freedom have gone to the courts, and there is little formal legal foundation for a people's right of access. This should not deter us from pursuing the case for access. After all, there was no legal assurance for a right of privacy in 1890 when Samuel D. Warren and Louis Brandeis wrote a famous law review article proposing it. In time, the right of privacy was articulated in statutes, court decisions, and philosophical treatises. Today few would question that there is such a right. Indeed, there is both a tort(s) of privacy and a constitutional right of privacy. Similarly, Professor Barron is ahead of his time in arguing for a legally protected right of access.

While it is true that the framers did not specify people's rights, it can be argued that they did intend the provisions of the Bill of Rights to apply to individuals. Institutional rights (such as those extended to the press as an institution) are granted because they have responsibilities to individuals, to citizens who can benefit from the activities of the press. The role of the press, then, is to deliver press freedom to individuals, communities, and the country. A country is the sum of its parts and its parts include individuals. The framers expected the press to promote the free flow of information. Is that free flow one-way only or should the press be responsible to its audience? Should it meet people's informational needs? Should it reflect and report on their opinions and ideas? The answers, I think, are a resounding "yes." But just how this should be accomplished and whether a right of access is the best way need considerable analysis and study.

In spite of some harsh things said about him, Professor Barron is hardly a dangerous radical. A law school dean and distinguished legal scholar, he simply believes that all people should have a legal right to buy advertising and be able to reply to editorials which either mention them or affect them directly. This is a modest request and a step toward allowing the public to talk back to the media in an age when mass communication plays a central role in their lives.

Barron and others in the access movement would not turn the news media over to a howling mob and strip editors of their legitimate right to make editorial decisions. Barron's two proposals would require enabling legislation in states and perhaps in Washington. That legislation would then no doubt be tested for constitutionality by media groups opposing it. If it met the test, there would be a guaranteed public right of access.

It has long been assumed that by granting freedom to the *issuer* of communication (the media), quite naturally the *user* (the public) also had press freedom. This was the view of the distinguished philosopher William Ernest Hocking, a member of the Commission on Freedom of the Press. "There are," he wrote, "two distinct interests . . . only one of them needs protection; to protect the issuer is to protect the consumer" (Hocking, 1947, 164). Freedom of the press, he suggested, "has always been a matter of public, as well as individual importance. Inseparable from the right of the press to be free has been the right of the people to have a free press."

It seems to me that this is a specious position. There can be a perfectly free press, but it may be so elitist that it traditionally speaks to and for a limited segment of the population. Indeed, in America today market researchers advise media executives that certain people are not worth communicating with because they have limited ability to buy the products being promoted through advertising. For years minority persons in the United States were "the invisible Americans." Their views, problems, and concerns were simply not covered by major media. This lapse became quite evident during the demonstrations, marches, sit-ins, and riots of the 1960s when many disenfranchised people took to the streets. As a result of the upheavals, American media leaders agreed to provide (a) more complete and extensive coverage of minority communities and (b) jobs in the newsroom for minority persons. During the social upheaval of the 1960s there were several reports on the press that criticized the media for turning their backs on the problems of minorities. In the early 1980s a Brookings Institution report pointed out that some of America's most popular tourist cities—Boston, Philadelphia, and St. Louis—were in worse shape than less glamorous places like Detroit and Newark. How could this be?

Two distinguished researchers, Floyd Mattson and Jim Richstad, assert that not only are people entitled to freedom of the press, but that there is an inherent "right to communicate." Other scholars agree that communication is one of the people's basic needs, and it would follow that there ought to be some mechanism for this in a civilized society. It would also seem that there will be a great benefit to society if people's sense of powerlessness can be reduced and partially satisfied by letting them have a forum for their ideas, complaints, and frustrations. There are some opportunities, of course, in newspaper letter columns and radio and television call-in shows, but they are minimal, given the potential demand. If we can agree that there is a fundamental right to communicate and that the Constitution means everybody should enjoy freedom of the press, then it should not be impossible to develop a regime wherein such freedom of expression could be encouraged. It could occur in at least two ways:

1. Through natural forces of the free marketplace.

2. Through government intervention and mandatory access where appropriate and necessary.

In the first instance, I would see advocates of access in the private sector mobilizing information campaigns to help people use the available channels of expression, those mentioned above and others. In addition, it may take reminders from access leaders to leaders of the media to point up both the commercial and social value of staying in touch with all aspects of the community.

Individuals and institutions or neighborhoods systematically or routinely ignored in news coverage should fight back by competing for their fair share of media attention. This can be done with various strategies and regular information campaigns. The commercial advantage to the media of staying in touch with particular market segments, as well as the social obligation to reach out to all elements of the community, can be emphasized. Many editors would respond affirmatively to such an approach. And they would likely provide space on the editorial page for occasional columns and commentaries. The same could be done with television and radio.

Perhaps the most significant development on the public access front is cable television. As America is wired for cable in the 1980s and 1990s, many local cable operators are providing public access time for use by local citizens. In cities where public access has been tried, it has enjoyed a degree of success. Access in this instance is an umbrella term for free, noncommercial channel time that a cable operator makes available for use by public agencies, nonprofit organizations, and private citizens. Under most franchise agreements the cable operator provides studio facilities, cameras, and editing equipment. Cable public access has existed in New York City since 1970, and there is a track record of high use by individuals, especially persons from the black community, who had a difficult time getting on commercial television. Public access gives ordinary people a chance to participate in the marvels of the electronic age, as well as to be heard by their fellow citizens. Public access channels, however, are not particularly popular with commercial cable television operators, who would rather put revenue-producing fare on the channel, even they admit that strong public access programming can draw an additional clientele to the tube and thus enhance revenues. But cable representatives don't see the two as incompatible at all.

In broadcasting, there is already a strong access tradition, although it can be said that it is not as effective as it ought to be. There is a right of reply to personal attack that permits individual and institutional response to broadcast editorials and news coverage, as well as a right to equal time in political broadcasts. There was formerly a legally required procedure for ascertainment whereby attitudes of community leaders are sought out. These opportunities for access do not, at present, affect a large percentage of the population, but they could be used more judiciously by the access movement people.

Two other mechanisms for access are public opinion polls and two-way television made possible in some cable systems. Polls, if conducted properly, give all citizens an equal possibility of being chosen to have their views aired. Of course, the chance is quite small since sample sizes for national polls are tiny. A better job needs to be done in polling questions that truly concern the American people, rather than those of interest solely to political figures and educators. Alex Edelstein of the University of Washington has been a leader in calling for public opinion studies that emphasize "salience information," that is, information of direct concern to people as ascertained in open-ended personal interviews. This, he says, is superior to having individual citizens rank the five most important issues in the country, based on some preconceived list developed by elitist pollsters in their offices.

There have been experiments with interactive television for a number of years. In some interactive systems viewers can make choices and do such things as home shopping or banking. One experimental system called QUBE in Columbus, Ohio, also unsuccessfully tried a "town meeting" approach to citizen choice on a number of public issues. Some television stations also use 1-900 telephone numbers to get feedback from viewers, but these efforts are quite unscientific and only partly successful. However, the prospect of interactive television still exists and could have an impact on our ability to talk to ourselves while talking back to the media. At present, the most effective interactive communication comes through personal computers.

Attempts to force the print media to provide greater public access will no doubt be thwarted by political forces at the legislative level and by the courts, where the judiciary is wary of prior restraints or special requirements for the press. Still, as the press continues to ask for more and more special privileges based on its social role of "representing the people," imaginative citizens and lawyers will probably look for an opening. (This is, in fact, one of the reasons why I said earlier that it is dangerous for the press to ask for rights that the rest of us do not have.)

Providing a public right of access does not mean a perfect situation where people will be happy and satisfied all the time. It is not feasible to give every citizen in the population air time on television or a guest column in the newspaper. Thus, it may be necessary for the media to try to select representative views and citizens to stand in for the rest of us who cannot be heard. This selection is already done to a limited degree with letters to the editor.

Naturally, no one is required to listen to anyone else's views, and in many instances getting a listener, whether in print or electronic media, will require the speaker to make compelling and persuasive presentations. We live in a real world, and while communication might become an inherent human right, individual voices will need to live within realistic limits. There is nothing inconsistent about this limitation, though. To argue that the right of access might be limited to time, place, and circumstances or offered up to the channel capacity of available resources does not diminish its importance. After all, freedom of the press itself lives with many constraints and barriers. It is not in full flower at every moment, nor need it be to exist.

Professor Barron has done us a favor by making his case in law review articles and in the courts. Just because he did not prevail in a rather weak case is no reason to doubt that access would benefit individuals and society in many ways. Ayn Rand can have her "virtue of selfishness." Selfishness and greed are not the basis for a coherent and successful society, although such a society can tolerate within limits these essentially negative forces. Nor am I persuaded by "red-baiting" references to a "people's press" in the Soviet Union or China. No one in the access movement is suggesting that the people take over the traditional media, wresting control from professional editors and managers. Instead, they are asking for a chance to be heard, to contribute to the community and to national dialogue, to be represented in the media that claim to represent them and to act as public trustees. The question is one of truly participative media wherein all of us have some chance, however small, of being heard.

Argument Summation: The public has a right of access.

The First Amendment must apply to all Americans, not just media owners. The Constitution provides institutional press rights because the media have responsibilities to individuals. Public access does not mean stripping editors of their control; rather it would provide for the right for individuals to buy "advertorial" space to express their views and to respond to editorials that mention them. A right of access is required to give the disenfranchised a means to actualize their right to communicate and to prevent wealthy press owners from ignoring poorer segments of society. Access can be achieved either through more effective utilization of existing mechanisms or through legislative requirements.

TOPICS FOR DISCUSSION

1. Do you think the writers of the First Amendment meant that all people have a right to freedom of the press? What does such an idea mean? Can people have freedom *of* the press, or must they have freedom *to* the press?

2. Do you think the press's role is to deliver freedom to the people—or do you think the press's role is to deliver information and opinion to the people?

3. Consider the possible scenarios if the right of people's access to the press were upheld by the Supreme Court.

4. Explain how such a "right of access" can be logical in a privately owned media system.

5. Can you think of other ways the media can be more representative of people's opinions and news—other than enthroning such a people's legal right to access?

TOPICS FOR RESEARCH

1. Do an analysis of the 1972 Supreme Court case, *Tornillo v. Miami Herald*, relying on periodicals that covered the conflict. To what extent did the press (newsmagazines, newspapers, trade journals, scholarly publications) explain and explicate the "right of access"? How did that case distinguish the "right" from the "law"? Does the right of access have any future?

2. Do a study of letters to the editor of a local newspaper. Who writes such letters? To what extent do they counter the paper's position? Are they an "access channel" for the public or not? Connect your observations and study with published articles about letters to the editor from the scholarly literature of media studies.

3. Prepare a paper on the public's "right of reply" to television and radio stations. Interview local station officials and ask them to discuss how often, if at all, the right of reply has been exercised by local citizens or organizations.

4. If you have a local cable system with a public access channel, do a study of that channel and its use. Who uses it? What kinds of programs do they offer? What positions are put forth? Can you characterize the public access channel?

5. Write a short paper on C-SPAN, the congressional cable service. How does it give the public access to meetings and events not available in full in other news reports or sources? Does C-SPAN accomplish access? If so, how?

FURTHER READING

Barron, Jerome A. "Access to the Press—A New First Amendment Right." *Harvard Law Review* 80, no. 8 (June 1967): 1641–78.

Barron, Jerome A. *Freedom of the Press for Whom? The Right of Access to Mass Media.* (Bloomington, IN: University of Indiana Press, 1973.

Dennis, Everette E. "The Press and the Public Interest: A Definitional Dilemma." *DePaul Law Review* 23(Spring 1974): 937–60.

Dennis, Everette E., Donald M. Gillmor, and Theodore Glasser. *Media Freedom and Responsibility.* Westport, CT: Greenwood Press, 1990.

Gross, Gerald., ed. *The Responsibility of the Press.* New York: Simon and Schuster, Clarion Books, 1971.

Hocking, William Ernest. *Freedom of the Press. A Framework of Principle.* A report from The Commission on Freedom of the Press. Chicago: University of Chicago Press, 1947.

"Media Freedom and Accountability." A Conference Report. New York: Gannett Center for Media Studies, 1986.

Murray, Edward. "The Editor's Right to Decide," *Seminar* (March 1970): 23–26.

Rand, Ayn. *Virtue of Selfishness.* New York: New American Library, 1964.

Rubin, Bernard. *Media, Politics, and Democracy.* New York: Oxford University Press, 1977. See especially Chapter 4, "Popular Participation and Media."

———. *Small Voices and Great Trumpets, Minorities and the Media.* New York: Praeger, 1980.

Schmidt, Benno C., Jr. *Freedom of the Press v. Public Access.* Springfield, MA: Praeger, 1976.

Wicklein, John. *Electronic Nightmare: The New Communications and Freedom.* New York: Viking Press, 1981.

Chapter 6

MEDIA PLURALISM

As late as 1989 in some Eastern European countries like Rumania and Bulgaria, there was little diversity in media, as newspapers and broadcasting stations were controlled by the state and subjected to rigid laws and standards about what could be disseminated to the public. With government changes and relaxation in regulations in the 1990s, the same countries were soon awash in hundreds of new media—newspapers and magazines, as well as more diverse broadcasting messages. Where there had once been a few tightly controlled media and voices, soon there were many. Diversity of media is pluralistic communication.

The value of media pluralism stems from the idea that democracy is best served by diversity in the communication marketplace, that a variety of competing voices can provide the public with a multiplicity of information and opinions on which to base its decisions. The long-standing trend toward the concentration of ownership in the mass media (chains buying chains, fewer and fewer owners), as well as the declining number of competing newspapers and broadcast outlets in many cities, suggests that media pluralism is declining. Further, arguments about the homogenization of media content due to market research, rating services, and other measures suggest that diversity in content and overall pluralism are also down. Media pluralism, then, is usually ascertained by considering the actual number of publications and broadcast outlets in the marketplace, the nature of the ownership of those outlets, and finally, the characteristics of the content (programming and news) which they deliver. Clearly, the prevailing view is that diversity and pluralism are down, regardless of whether one justifies and supports the reasons why this has happened.

Challenge

Dennis: Media pluralism is not shrinking.

The response is predictable. A newspaper dies and editorialists throughout the nation declare that "a voice is lost and we are poorer for it." The decade of the 1980s was devastating for large, afternoon daily newspapers (called PMs), as such papers as the *Philadelphia Bulletin, Cleveland Press, Washington Star, Minneapolis Star, Des Moines Tribune,* and the *Los Angeles Herald-Examiner* either died or were merged into larger, healthier morning dailies. It was a blow to diversity, a blow to media pluralism. Or was it?

The purpose of this discussion is to move beyond the usual knee-jerk reaction to the condition of "our declining dailies" and to get a more substantive understanding of media pluralism. To do that we have to get some things straight.

Debating about media pluralism requires a close look at one of the most curious and complex concepts in the field of mass communication. It is a strange mixture of constitutional history, economic theory, sociology, and good old-fashioned moralizing. To begin with, few would doubt that one of the intentions of the press freedom clause of the First Amendment was to allow for diversity of information and opinion. This diversity was to protect citizens from government control of information and ideas. Today we can add to this concern the fear many critics have of the private sector, which owns our communication system and which has profit, not pluralism, as its primary motivating force. In addition to the component of diversity of information and opinion, media pluralism also involves the existence of different ethnic and cultural subgroups in the population. A central assumption here is that no single subgroup should dominate the others.

When reduced to its fundamental features, media pluralism usually means two things: diversity of ownership and diversity of content in the communications available to the public. The two are thought to be interrelated. At one level it would seem that the question of whether media pluralism is expanding or shrinking requires only a simple empirical response. Can't we simply count the number of media organizations in society, see who owns them, and have an answer? The answer is "No, not exactly," for the problem is more complex and difficult to sort out because the number of voices is only a part of the equation. It is what's in them that counts and there is no easy, universally accepted way to measure diversity of content. The problem is even more clouded because deep-seated values, prevailing prejudices, and excessive moralizing engulf the notion of media diversity and pluralism.

For these reasons media pluralism is rarely the subject of rational debate. Critics snarl, growl, and carp. They use economic forecasts and other quantitative data as they see fit. Some of them think newspapers and other media outlets are mainly public service organizations rather than economic entities. To them chain owners and other media managers are self-serving and essentially evil individuals who would package and sell off our democratic values if they could to make a profit. Indeed, former *Dallas Times-Herald* columnist Molly Ivins once picked up on this with a bit of black humor when she told a convention of newspaper owners, "I thought you people would be a bunch of egg-sucking child molesters."

Just when the issue of media pluralism emerged is not clear, but by the 1920s critics like Oswald Garrison Villard of *The Nation* were decrying the growing economic concentration of the newspaper industry. Chain ownership, Villard and others believed, had unfortunate social consequences and would lessen chances for the Miltonian ideal wherein truth and falsehood could grapple in the marketplace of ideas. The fewer the voices, the less variety of information and opinion.

As newspaper chains became dominant and as fewer American cities had competing dailies (a trend that continues today), it was natural that critics would conclude that diversity was down and pluralism was threatened. This rather predictable reaction meshes nicely with two well-embedded American values, (1) bigness is bad and (2) localism is desirable. Media researcher Ben Compaine explains:

> Control of information, news, and ideas should be spread around as much as possible. Locally owned newspapers and broadcast stations, many book publishers, scores of independent film producers and distributors would supposedly provide greater access to diverse opinions than fewer owners controlling an identical number of media outlets (1979, 3).

No wonder that publisher Frank Munsey, known for his cold-hearted business values, raised hackles when he wrote in 1908, "There is no business that cries so loud for organization and combination as that of newspaper publishing."

Many commentators, concerned about media concentration and what they think is a decline in media pluralism, look at only one variable: the number of newspaper owners. This, coupled with the overall decline in the number of newspapers, alarms them. Less often do they consider whether group or chain ownership increases or decreases diversity of media content in a given community. Some newspaper chains like Knight-Ridder have a reputation for quality. Their papers are well-edited and have a wide range of columnists and feature material that leaves their readers with considerably more variety than some weaker independently owned newspapers. In this instance, strong ownership has real social benefits. Of course, there are also group owners like Murdoch, Thomson, and Newhouse that do not have a reputation for quality. Questions of quality are matters of opinion and taste. While there are some generally held views, there is no universal agreement about "good" and "bad" chains or about quality versus inferior papers or other media.

Not even the owners of media companies agree about the degree of pluralism, but one thing is sure: They are now quite open about criticizing each other. In the late 1980s, James Ottaway, Jr. of Ottaway-Dow Jones newspapers, owned by the media giant Dow Jones & Company, gave a speech criticizing the growing concentration of ownership and wondered if it were constraining freedom of the press. At about the same time C. K. McClatchy, another group owner, in the well-known 1987 Press-Enterprise lecture given at the University of California, Riverside, sharply criticized several newspaper groups while praising others. He named names and made clear his displeasure with some media companies and their values. It would seem that this is pluralism at its best.

In fairness, though, I concede that studies of the consequences of chain ownership and concentration paint a mixed portrait of their actual effect on quality and diversity. Generally, though, I believe that the scales tilt slightly toward the advantages that come from chain ownership, especially regarding editorial sources such as news services, columns, or comics. The record of chain newspapers with regard to editorial page offerings (as seen in endorsements for presidential candidates) is less impressive. Chain papers, studies show, are more likely to make endorsements than are independent newspapers, but are also more likely to endorse the same candidate. There are exceptions, of course, but I would rate the issue as something of a draw. While independent newspapers, according to a national study by Daniel Wackman and colleagues at the University of Minnesota, seemed to avoid controversy and thus cheat their readers out of the "diverse local voice" they might expect, the chains seemed to stamp out their presidential endorsement editorials with the same cookie cutter.

If we stopped our inquiry at the newspaper doorstep, I would be hard-pressed to make my case for increased pluralism. However, the media world includes much more than newspapers. In fact, fewer and fewer Americans subscribe to or read a daily newspaper and it is obvious that the newspapers play a less important role in our national life than they once did.

What of other media outlets? Do they contribute to diversity and pluralism? First, in broadcasting there are several thousand stations, and no one can own more than twelve AM, twelve FM, and twelve TV stations, thus preventing monopoly control. There is more broadcast news programming today as a result of the increasing cable channels.

The magazine field is a great source of diversity of ownership and content. While there is some group ownership, the magazine industry has less concentration of ownership than other American industries including newspapers, and the possibility for new magazines to develop is very great indeed. Although they were the first mass medium in America, magazines no longer court the mass audience to the extent that they once did, but rather try for a quite defined, specialized readership. They want the skier, for example, not a mythical average citizen. This means that the range and diversity of content in magazines are almost limitless, with nearly every possible special interest represented. Magazines also carry a wide variety of opinion, ranging from the far left to the far right; some are downright anarchistic. There are critics who argue that this diversity is meaningless because many magazines have relatively small circulations and are therefore not reaching enough people to make a difference. This objection is largely nonsense because a small, respected journal can have enormous impact. A specialized publication like the *New England Journal of Medicine*, which enjoys enormous respect in the medical community, can easily have more influence and impact than a network television show on the same subject by the sheer force of that publication's authoritativeness with an audience that counts.

The field of book publishing is another area where diversity of information and opinion is at a premium. While publishers have been more attuned to a marketing approach in recent years and are not likely to publish works without any profit potential, they are still offering thousands of new voices in the marketplace every year. I believe that one only need visit bookstores to see the incredible range of ideas that are put behind the covers of books. Like magazines, most individual books have a fairly narrow audience and tend to be specialized, but those with revolutionary or startling new ideas are quickly picked up and disseminated by other media.

Finally, the rapidly expanding field of cable communication and other new technologies, such as direct broadcast service, have large promise for diversity and pluralism, both because of their varied general offerings and because of those programs calibrated to specific ethnic groups, subcultures, and interests. In many cities there are at least twenty available channels, while many other cities have more than thirty and some will soon have 100 or more. Remember that each channel can be multiplied by the twenty-four hours in the day, a situation which allows a massive potential for diverse programs. Just over 55 percent of the nation is "wired," that is, hooked up to cable service, and this percentage should climb to more than 70 percent in about five years. Cable programmers offer hundreds of possibilities in special programming for women, the aged, ethnic minorities, children, and others. There are specialized sports networks, a network that covers Congress, even outlets for soft-core pornography, and much more. There are news services offered by Associated Press, Dow Jones, UPI, and Reuters. Ted Turner's Cable News Network was so successful that it has spawned other twenty-four hour cable news competition including CNBC and FNN. Most cities also have cable public access channels that will allow local citizens and groups to make their own television programs and present their viewpoints, as an alternative to the traditional media fare of commercial programmers.

All this adds up to a portrait of media diversity, both in ownership and in content, that would blow a circuit in the brains of the framers who worried about keeping newspapers free from government licensing and control. In a society where points of view range from serious commentary about foreign affairs to proposals for more nude beaches, there is clearly a good deal of diversity. Even ethnic and cultural subgroups benefit from the 1990s communication revolution in the traditional media which are developing programs tailormade for blacks, Chicanos, and Native Americans, as Felix Gutiérrez and Clint Wilson have argued.

If we once had reason to worry that national networks and conglomerate control of local newspapers and broadcast stations might lead to a nation of homogenized interests, the electronic revolution, especially as represented by cable, ought to relieve many fears. Naturally, some large firms have moved into this business (Time Warner, for example, owns Home Box Office and Cinemax), but there are still many alternative voices.

The diverse sources of information and opinion are almost mind-boggling. These are with us already in greater numbers than any of us can hope to comprehend, let alone use. In an information society with these massive offerings, the real secret of intellectual survival for the consumer lies in understanding the range of possibilities and knowing how to use them to personal advantage. There are, of course, reasons to be concerned about information-rich people versus information-poor people. Information is power and some information will no doubt be priced so high that it will be out of reach of many people. Even then, though, through the prudent use of libraries and other public sources, most of us will have such enormous choices, so rich and varied, that it will be abundantly clear that media pluralism is on the increase.

Argument Summation: Media pluralism is not shrinking.

The purpose of the First Amendment was to provide for a diversity of opinion. That pluralism of content is not shrinking today, and across the broader spectrum of all media, pluralism in ownership is growing. To look only at the number of newspaper owners ignores the effect of media chains on the diversity of message, and that is most important. Actually, higher quality and more diverse opinions survive group ownership, and the press's criticism of itself thrives through corporate competition. Newspapers are a decreasing element of the media; legal requirements preclude monopoly control of radio, TV, and cable, while magazines and books present a broad diversity of particularized information and opinions. Pluralism should continue to expand in the future, as the electronic revolution makes more avenues of communication available.

RESPONSE

Merrill: Media pluralism is shrinking.

As it is with many controversial journalistic topics, the discord connected with the issue of media pluralism is rooted in a failure to be specific as to the terms of argument. This, I think, is especially true in a discussion of media pluralism.

The topic before us is whether media pluralism is growing or shrinking. Using media as diverse as daily newspapers and books, Everette Dennis has made a reasonable case, that overall pluralism in the United States is growing instead of shrinking. When we look at all the specialized publications, tape decks, records, cable television programs, and other broadcast outlets now available to the consumer, we must agree that, in this sense at least, pluralism is expanding.

But actually when most journalists talk about the shrinkage of pluralism and the danger of increasing group ownership, they are not talking about *total* media (nonjournalistic) pluralism. Rather they are concerned about the shrinkage of *news* media.

Journalists are talking about newspapers being bought out by groups (like Gannett), about dailies (like the *Washington Star*) that are disappearing from the scene, and about one-newspaper cities, which restrict the news-commentary options of the citizenry. In effect, they are referring to a restriction of *journalistic* pluralism or diversity, not to a shrinkage of pluralism in the total communications system of the whole country.

It is true that the totality of voices in the United States is growing. I have no argument about this. We are bombarded on all sides with a constant barrage of communications pouring in on us from multiplying sources. But this is not the kind of pluralism journalists (and I) are concerned about. We are talking about newspapers, newsmagazines, and other primarily journalistic media. The names of Newhouse, Gannett, Scripps, Hearst, Knight-Ridder, and Thomson today roll off the tongue more readily than the names of individual newspapers; editors have become anonymous, as have publishers—unless they are the names of the big group owners.

I shall not argue *quality*. It is possible that a group-owned newspaper is better, as is often contended, than an independent one. But it also may be worse. Quality, I think, depends on the personnel involved at a particular time with a particular newspaper. What I am talking about is the quantity of journalistic media. There seems no doubt among people who keep up with such things that the number of newspapers is decreasing. In addition, the number of group-owned newspapers is increasing, as is the number of single-newspaper cities. All this points to quantitative shrinkage of pluralism.

By the late 1970s, for example, fewer than 4 percent of the nation's cities had competing newspapers. More than half of the nation's dailies (more than two-thirds of the daily circulation) were owned by groups. In the late 1980s almost 1,100 dailies were owned by groups (more than 70 percent of all dailies). The number of newspaper groups stood at 170, and group-owned papers accounted for nearly 80 percent of the total U.S. circulation.

While many people speak of media pluralism, meaning diverse ownerships, there is more to pluralism than this. There is also *message pluralism*—that is, diverse content even under a shrinking number of owners. It is quite clear that message pluralism is very important and that there can be a greater diversity of messages even in one newspaper than there could be in several newspapers. Therefore, there need not be a positive correlation between the number of newspapers and the number of messages. However, it is usually assumed that this is the case.

Besides the types of pluralism mentioned, there are distinct "levels" of pluralism. *System* pluralism refers to how much diversification there is in our media or press system. The total news system is what is being considered. Then there is the *community* level of pluralism. This level gets the concept of pluralism closer to home. The important question here is: How much diversity is present at the *local* level? To many persons, system pluralism is really unimportant compared with community pluralism.

Obviously there could be other types and levels of diversity or pluralism. But these are the important ones which must be considered when one is discussing or debating the topic of press or media pluralism.

It may well be that, thinking of the topic in terms of "system pluralism," my coauthor is right: Pluralism is indeed growing, not shrinking. But thinking about pluralism in terms of local or community pluralism (the really important level, in my opinion), I must maintain that pluralism or diversity is shrinking. How does it really affect me here in my locality that throughout the whole country pluralism may be expanding? The diversity that I want is here (in *my* news media), not what might be available in Oregon, Maine, Florida, Texas, or Washington, D.C.

It may well also be that my coauthor is right about "message pluralism": The number and variety of individual messages is indeed growing, not shrinking—especially on the system level. But how many people read more than one newspaper or watch more than one network newscast at a time? A good case can be made that potential pluralism is not what is important, that what matters is the actual, pragmatic pluralism—the diversity of messages that gets to the individual audience member.

In view of what I have just said about pluralism and its types and levels, I am left in the strange position of debating a "ghost topic." If we are talking about diversity of ownership media, I think I am safe in saying that pluralism is shrinking in the United States. If we are talking about diversity or pluralism as it relates to total number of units or media, I think my coauthor is correct in saying that pluralism is growing. Even if we are talking about diversity of substantive items or viewpoints, I would suspect that my coauthor is correct. Truthfully, I cannot comment on this type of pluralism because it would take detailed, thorough, and continuing content analysis to prove anything about this item-viewpoint diversity. Nobody has shown a willingness to tackle such a study, so the issue must remain unresolved, at least for now.

When my coauthor and those who agree with him say that press pluralism is growing, I cannot really disagree with them, for I do not know exactly what types and levels they are referring to. But neither can I agree with them.

This whole subject is one that demands precise definitions in the first place, and systematic research and analysis in the second place. So far neither has surfaced in American journalism. Therefore, it is my belief that the jury must remain out on this question. At present it cannot be determined whether pluralism is growing or contracting. And beyond this, there is really no way to get into the evaluative aspects of this question, given the current state of research. What I mean is this: It may well be that fewer media can (or do) provide a greater variety of information and viewpoints. This would go against the conventional wisdom, but it might well be the case. Some people contend that fewer is better; they may be right. We don't really know, and so far as I am aware, there is no real attempt to get at such questions.

For that matter, we normally assume that more information or viewpoints are better than less information and fewer viewpoints. This is nothing more than an assumption, but it is one which we use as a basis for many of our concerns about media or press pluralism. We usually assume that pluralism, in any of its forms, is good. The more information and the greater variety of information we are exposed to, the better the situation. Normally we do not take other factors into consideration—factors such as the truth or falsity of the information, differences in validity and sophistication of the viewpoints expressed, the superficiality or thoroughness of the messages presented. All these factors are vitally important, of course, and they must be tackled by any person seriously concerned with the subject of journalistic diversity or pluralism.

The reader may say that I am avoiding the debate question by falling back on the semantics problem. This is, in part, true. This whole question is packed with semantic "noise" and I am somewhat at a loss to focus the debate. Do we mean diversity of media units, or media ownerships, or media messages? I would agree with my coauthor that, all in all, the number of media units is growing. But I would have to say that media ownerships are not as diverse as in the past. As to media messages—*who knows*? Only giant and costly content analyses across the media (and over time) could answer that question.

So, in conclusion, it seems that we have a stalemate here—or a "nonarguable question." The question is really too broad and general. But before lambasting us for framing such a question in the first place, consider that when most people talk about this question they are equally vague. It is not unusual at all to hear educated and sophisticated journalists (and others) posing such a question as this: "Do you think pluralism in our media is shrinking or not?" My answer would have to be, "Well, maybe . . . and maybe not."

Argument Summation: Media pluralism is shrinking.

Media pluralism—especially in the area of journalism—is shrinking. In short, the *news* media are less pluralistic each year. Groups, networks, and multinational corporations are growing, and one-newspaper (noncompetitive) cities are commonplace. By 1990 nearly 80 percent of all dailies were owned by groups. There are different kinds of pluralism, of course, and some types may not be shrinking—but certainly news media (or unit) pluralism is. This subject is difficult to debate because of the imprecision of focus—just what kind of pluralism are we discussing: media, ownership, or message? In the above argument I am talking principally about ownership pluralism, and to a lesser degree about news media (unit) pluralism.

TOPICS FOR DISCUSSION

1. Is pluralism of the press positively related to freedom of the press?

2. Why is press (or media) pluralism theoretically good for a society? What makes it admirable in a capitalist country? Why is it not championed in an authoritarian or closed society?

3. Is group or chain ownership necessarily bad for a press system? Give at least three possible disadvantages and as many advantages for such a media situation.

4. Take television as an example and say whether pluralism (of messages—even news messages) is (a) growing, or (b) diminishing. How would this be measured?

5. Is pluralism in journalism correlated positively with *quality* of messages?

TOPICS FOR RESEARCH

1. Go to a leading political science (American government) text and see how the term "pluralism" is used. Outline its general use in government. How is the term used in terms of media pluralism? Examine the link between a pluralistic society and a pluralistic media system. How does one contribute to the other?

2. Compare and contrast a group-owned newspaper (chain) to one of similar size (and community) with independent ownership. Which one is more pluralistic in terms of content generally? Editorial policy? Columnists? Other features?

3. Defenders of the media chains say that the content of group-owned newspapers is actually richer and more diverse than that of independently-owned papers. Test this hypothesis by studying the editorial content of five group and five independent papers in similar-sized communities with regard to a major national or international issue.

4. Review the concept of pluralism in content with regard to information or news versus opinion material such as that found on editorial pages or on television commentary. How does this idea manifest itself in each of these functions—information and opinion? What are the differences? What are the similarities?

5. Most critics agree that the opinion magazines like the *Nation, National Review,* and *New Republic* contribute to diversity of ideas. Do a study of these magazines as a group or of any two of them, discussing their contribution to public discussion. How much impact do they have? How do you know?

FURTHER READING

Bagdikian, Ben H. "Newspaper Mergers in the Final Phase." *Columbia Journalism Review* 6(March–April 1977): 17–22.

———. "Conglomeration Concentration and the Media." *Journal of Communication* 30:2(Spring 1980): 59–64.

———. *The Media Monopoly*. 2d. ed. Boston, MA: Beacon Press, 1987.

Botein, Michael. *Legal Restrictions on Ownership of the Mass Media*. New York: Advanced Media Publishing Associates, 1977.

Compaine, Benjamin M. *Who Owns the Media? Concentration of Ownership in the Mass Communications Industry*. New York: Harmony Books, 1979.

Gitlin, Todd. "The New Technology: Pluralism or Banality." *Democracy* 4(October 1981): 60–76.

Gutiérrez, Felix and Clint Wilson. *Minorities and the Media*. Newbury Park, CA: Sage Publications, 1985.

Lowenstein, R. L. and J. C. Merrill. *Macromedia: Mission, Message, Morality*. White Plains, NY: Longman, 1989.

McCombs, Maxwell E. "Mass Media and the Marketplace." *Journalism Monographs* no. 24. Lexington, KY: Association for Education in Journalism, 1972.

"The New Media Barons." *Gannett Center Journal* (Spring 1989).

Owen, Bruce M. *Economics and Freedom of Expression*. Cambridge, MA: Ballinger Books, 1975.

Prichard, Peter. *The Making of McPaper: The Inside Story of USA Today*. Kansas City, KS: Andrews, McMeel and Parker, 1987.

Rucker, Bryce W. *The First Freedom*. Carbondale, IL: Southern Illinois University Press, 1966.

Sterling, Christopher H. and Timothy R. Height. *The Mass Media: Aspen Institute Guide to Communication Industry Trends*. New York: Praeger, 1978.

Whited, Charles. *Knight: A Publisher in the Tumultuous Century*. New York: E. P. Dutton, 1988.

Chapter 7

POWER OF THE MEDIA

Political candidates, television evangelists, advertising executives, and rock stars probably agree on at least one thing: that the media are powerful and do have considerable influence. There are scholars and critics, however, who doubt this, as they ask for specific evidence that it was press or media influence, not personal contact or institutional forces, that fostered a particular belief or influenced a political or consumer decision.

Whether and to what degree the mass media have power has been widely debated. For many years the concept of the "power of the press" was a given, documented by historians, propaganda researchers, and others. That the press and later other media could move minds and goad people to action was widely believed. However, in the 1940s in study after study, this popular public view was severely challenged by empirical evidence. A more modest view of the power of the press evolved, and especially in the scholarly community a theory of "minimal effects" of mass communication has been in vogue. The press and other media, this view contends, mainly have the power to reinforce what people already believe, the power not to move the public mind but to influence some opinion leaders. Other forces such as the family, social groups, religious beliefs, and political parties have greater impact on the individual than do the mass media. Texts in psychology, political science, sociology, and other fields clearly downplayed the power of the press, saying that media operate in a nexus with other factors. The jury is still out on this question of press or media power and, in one form or another, the issue continues to be debated.

CHALLENGE

Dennis: The media are quite powerful.

If at first this statement seems obvious, I can assure you it really is not. The reason is that for years new journalism and communication students have been cautioned about overestimating the impact and influence of the mass media. The conclusion was that the media were not really very powerful after all. Now something is changing.

The 1981 publication of the *Annual Review of Psychology* (Volume 32) occurred without notice in the press and with less than a resounding ripple among media scholars in the United States. Yet one chapter had a message of profound importance for media professionals and students of mass communications. In measured language, researchers Donald Roberts and Christine Bachen wrote, "The past decade . . . has witnessed a revival of the view that the mass media exert powerful influences on the way people perceive, think about, and ultimately act in their world" (307–308).

To some this may not seem such a startling statement. We are rarely without graphic examples of the alleged power of the media, whether in foreign policy (where government leaders sometimes play to the media), in national politics (where some critics claim that television has taken over the role once played by political parties), or in social behavior (where we worry whether sexually suggestive advertisements for designer jeans are corrupting the values of youth). Concern about the media clearly extends beyond the halls of academe and into everyday life, as terms like "media event," "hype," and "image" become commonplace in our language.

The media have been replete with examples like these for many years. Quite naturally this emphasis has led to the popular conception that media institutions have influence, impact, power, and, yes, effects. While it is true that these terms were never defined to everyone's satisfaction, there is an almost universal belief that mass media institutions shape our thinking, influence our attitudes and opinions, and contribute toward particular behavior such as voting and buying certain goods.

Mass communication was an invention of the nineteenth century, but did not attract much scholarly attention until after World War I. From that time until the mid-1940s, the yield of scholarly studies contributed to the conclusion that the media had enormous power. During this period, the scholarly view and the lay view were virtually congruent. Of course, there was no universal agreement about just what the media could and could not do. There were shadings of differences in interpretation and approach, depending on whether one was listening to a critic, an empirical social scientist, a media practitioner, or the uninitiated lay person. Still, at the most simple, basic level there was considerable agreement with a hypodermic needle model of media effects, wherein the media infused the minds of individuals directly with powerful messages. This was the concept of the powerful press.

This shared perspective changed under the scholarly and professional leadership of sociologist Paul Lazarsfeld (1944) and a generation of empirical researchers. By trying to isolate questions that could be probed by social researchers, Lazarsfeld and company narrowed the focus of the media effects discussion to provable impact as demonstrated by specific, short-term studies. Looking mainly at attitude and opinion change in electoral campaigns, these researchers brought us the two-step flow and a model of personal influence, wherein mass communication was not necessarily a central and dominant force, but instead one that operated in conjunction with interpersonal communication and various socializing influences. When empirical researchers were asked to explain media power, they used vague qualifying language and said they thought the earlier view of a powerful press was probably wrong. Thus came the idea of minimal effects of mass communication. This view, prominent among social scientists, had a strange and fragmenting influence on scholars' perceptions of mass communication. At the same time, the public's view of media power did not change. Even in instances when one might have doubted the power of the press to change voting behavior, for example, plausible commonsense explanations were found. When it became evident that newspaper editorial endorsements for presidential candidates did not have a direct effect on the voting public, people often chose to believe that this fact did not really challenge media power. After all, we were told, reporters are liberals and their favorable treatment of liberal candidates drowns out stuffy, conservative endorsements on the editorial page.

The notion that the media had little direct influence on people led to much confusion and outright disbelief in the research and researchers. This disbelief fostered antiintellectualism and a deep chasm between practitioners and scholars, especially in journalism education, where students received mixed messages. Students received a minimal effects indoctrination in their mass media classes and also in economics, political science, sociology, and history. Teachers, in their desire to simplify and explain, too often presented the great researchers as purist scholars who sneered at any notion of major or powerful media effects. Rarely did they suggest that thoughtful people using different assumptions and different methods might come to quite different conclusions. No wonder students found themselves in a conceptual muddle. Think, for example, of the journalism student who is told by a public opinion teacher that the media have minimal effects only to discover that the reporting teacher thinks newspaper stories can have powerful consequences. In the everyday world, then, the student watches television and perceives quite rightly that advertisers certainly act as though media can move goods by encouraging people to buy them.

While it is difficult to doubt the scholarly benefits that came with the minimal effects perspective, it did tend to fragment our understanding of mass communication and appeared to set practitioners against researchers. Contrasting the powerful effects approach with the minimal effects view does provide useful background for the continuing debate over media effects, especially now when people are arguing for a return to the concept of powerful media with some modification.

One of the main reasons we study and debate media effects is to get a handle on our own thinking, to trace our own intellectual history and chart increments and obstacles in its development.

Whether the dramatic shifts in research findings (as noted by Roberts and Bachen) truly represent what the historian of science Thomas Kuhn (1962) in *The Structure of Scientific Revolutions* calls paradigm change or complete change in our thought process is not clear, but scholars increasingly think this might be so.

The first stirrings of the apparent shift in communication research came not in a new and startling book or theory, but in the shared views of a number of scholars, some of whom were well-established, while others were just beginning their careers. The distinguished researcher Wilbur Schramm urged study of the "quiet, continuing effects" of mass communication which, he said, were largely ignored and might yield important findings. Melvin DeFleur and Sandra Ball-Rokeach (1982), authors of *Theories of Mass Communication*, said we should explore the role of mass communication in the enlargement of peoples' belief systems, which he thought might seriously challenge the narrow, limited conclusions of earlier studies. The German researcher Elisabeth Noelle-Neumann called for a return to belief in the concept of a powerful mass media. "The fact is," she wrote, "the decisive factors of mass media are not brought to bear in the traditional laboratory experiment" (Noelle-Neumann, 1973, 67). Adding to the discussion, several other scholars agreed that what people learn from communication activity is a more rewarding topic for media effects research than attitude formation or change. Offering a striking observation in his studies of media bias in electoral campaigns, John P. Robinson wrote that evidence now exists that under certain conditions, the media can have political impact. Robinson was one of the first to challenge seriously the minimal effects perspective, asking rhetorically in his 1972 *Journalism Quarterly* article, "Can the Media Affect Behavior After All?" Agenda-setting studies by Maxwell McCombs and Donald Shaw (1972) concluded that the informational-learning role of the media was its most important effect. This means that the media will tell people not *what* to think but what to *think about*. The above scholars were quite careful and understated in their new view of media power, but others were not so quiet.

Sociologist Todd Gitlin denounced the Lazarsfeld (minimal effects) tradition in an article that accused researchers of failing to "put the crucial questions" because of "intellectual, ideological and institutional commitments" (Gitlin, 1978, 205). Said Gitlin, "behind the idea of the relative unimportance of the mass media lies a skewed, faulty concept of importance, similar to the faulty concept of power" (205). To Gitlin, this had the effect of justifying the existing system of media ownership, control, and purpose:

> By its methodology, media sociology has highlighted the recalcitrance of audiences, their resistance to media-generated message, and not their dependency, their acquiescence, their gullibility. It has looked to "effects" of broadcast programming in specifically behaviorist fashion, defining "effects" so narrowly, microscopically, and directly as to make it very likely that survey studies could only show slight "effects" at most. It has enshrined short run effects as "measures" of "importance," largely because these "effects" are measurable in a strict, replicable, behavioral sense, thereby deflecting attention of larger social meanings of mass media production (203–206).

This view comes mainly from humanistic reasoning and observation. However, Roberts and Bachen (1981) reached a similar conclusion based on a review of several areas of research, including patterns of media use, probes of children, and media studies of uses and gratifications, information transmission and processing, the knowledge gap hypothesis, the cultivation of beliefs, attention and comprehension, responses to advertising, political socialization, antisocial behavior, pro-social effects, and sex role socialization. This research raises new questions and expands the arena for investigation well beyond the old targets into the largely uncharted realm of cognitive effects. It is here that many studies, with striking and distinctive findings, are encouraging researchers to consider a modification of the minimal effects doctrine. Several recent texts about media effects also make this point. It is not surprising that one of the most articulate proponents of a new view, the German researcher Noelle-Neumann, says there are clues in research that have not been considered to any great extent before:

1. *Ubiquity of the media*—the ability to be everywhere, to dominate the information environment. The media are so ubiquitous at times that it is difficult to escape a message.

2. *Cumulation of messages*—one should look beyond the individual, fragmented messages to the cumulative effect over time. There is frequent repetition of the message that tends to reinforce its impact.

3. *Consonance of journalists*—remarkable agreement and demographic similarity among journalists and other media professionals leads to a sameness in newspapers and newscasts and limits the options the public has for selective perception (Noelle-Neumann, 1974, 67–112 paraphrased).

Similarly, communication reseacher James Lemert (1981) attacks what he calls the "simple reductionist model" of the minimal effects school, which measured media influence mainly through attitude change. This, he says, is too simple an explanation because it uses only one measure—behavior—to ascertain effects. Lemert would have us discard the idea that attitude change is either necessary or sufficient for public opinion change. He believes that minimal effects researchers attempted to explain society with limited information about individuals. The mass media, he says, can have a powerful impact on the information given to decision makers. By integrating research on public opinion with the role of decision makers and journalists, Lemert proposes studies that would take effects research beyond "simple reductionism." More importantly, he recognizes that we must first understand the prevailing research patterns in order to use their strengths and avoid their limitations. Like Noelle-Neumann and others, he is concerned with the news media as collectors of attitude information and with the context of attitude information and change.

Many media people are reluctant to brag about it, but they are also aware of their power. It is the only institution that really gets no policing; it falls back on the Constitution when occasional darts begin to come close. In protecting its power, every mass medium paints its critics as uninformed cranks who would repeal the First Amendment and censor the press.

Richard Harwood, ombudsman for the *Washington Post*, pointed up media power: "Newspapers and other media enterprises . . . have acquired considerable wealth, influence and perhaps real power in this century" (1989, *World Media Report*, Washington, D.C., May–June, 3). Harwood is, of course, being modest when he says "*perhaps* real power." He and other journalists know full well that media are powerful and have far too few checks on their power. This is the very reason he thinks newspapers should have ombudsmen such as he.

When the dust is settled on the present media effects debate, I believe that a true paradigm shift, in Kuhn's (1962) term, will be evident. We have, in fact, seen an integration of all the stages of change that accompany paradigm change. There has been incremental change, as represented in the empirical scholarship wherein researchers are framing new questions that take them into cognitive areas and beyond the limitations of short-run effects studies. This change has come about by a useful collaboration between people interested in the largely externally oriented social impact and those caring more about individuals and their attitudes as well as those who care about media organizations. In the early stages of some of this research, findings that conflicted with prevailing patterns and widely held beliefs were often seen as change by exception. As these findings recurred, they eventually replaced the earlier view. Some scholars say there has been a pendulum shift and they decry the "errors of the past." If research really does tell us that we need a new view of media power, it may be due to studies that probe such issues as the social construction of reality and long-term cumulative effects. Notably, research of this kind is no longer confined to a small group of theoretical researchers in mass communication or social psychology and related fields. Persons from within mass communication with interests in history, law, institutional analysis, economics, and other topics are also working diligently on questions often central to media impact, influence, and effect. Even these terms are getting greater clarification and more precise definition as scholars raise new questions and try to make more refined calibrations.

All of these factors will help us understand the impact and influence of mass communication with greater care and sophistication than before. We will not return to the point of having uncritical awe of so-called media power, but we will understand better how mass communication works in the context of other social forces without underestimating its importance and influence. Clearly, the media are powerful.

Argument Summation: The media are quite powerful.

The general perception that the media are a powerful force in society is correct. The research of social scientists who revealed a limited impact of media on formation of opinions only fragmented our understanding of the power of the media. Today, more balanced research is leading to a growing recognition of media power. The difference is how the importance of the media is measured. Modern researchers feel that the impact of media power is in telling people what to think about, not what to think. The behavioral focus of early media sociologists led them to ignore the broader social impact of mass media by measuring its importance only in narrow, easily definable areas. It is now accepted that the power of the media comes not from single messages, but from the cumulation of messages and from the domination of the information environment by the media. Attitude change is not necessary for a change in public opinion; hence, earlier studies failed to account for the power of the media. As the terms get greater clarification and more precise definitions, the power of the media will become increasingly evident.

RESPONSE

Merrill: The media are not so powerful.

I take issue with the contention that the media are all-powerful. Still I am in good company, as even my coauthor will agree, since he points out that for years there have been researchers who have maintained that the impact and influence of the media have been overstated. Thus, this topic is, in spite of its fuzzy nature, quite controversial.

I am put in a difficult position, however, by the very wording of this proposition. I really cannot maintain that the media have *no* power and that their impact is *nonexistent*. It is all too obvious that media have some power and that their influence on society cannot be denied. Advertisers, pragmatists and realists that they are, recognize the power of the media. Sociologists have documented various trends started and maintained by media attention. Politicians have contended that their careers have been helped or ruined by attention or neglect by the media. Panics have been precipitated by the media. Riots, demonstrations, skyjackings, and acts of terrorism are thought to be stimulated by media publicity. The "contagion" aspect of events is obviously connected with public exposure.

I cannot and will not deny that the media have some power. But the question really is: Do we know for certain that the media are *in themselves* powerful? Or are they simply secondary factors, triggering mechanisms if you will, which have various impacts in society under certain circumstances?

Let us admit immediately that some media, under some conditions, with some people, have some effects or impact. Media, however, do not work in a vacuum. Certainly Paul Lazarsfeld and his colleagues (1944) were right when they concluded that the mass media operate in conjunction with many social forces to bring about certain results. The implication of much of this "effects" research is that mass communication is influential, but not central or dominant in the model of personal influence.

A candidate for office, let us say, is elected. Did the media put him in? The answer must be, "No—but they probably played their part." The candidate appeared to many persons in person—as an individual without media help. He conversed; he debated; he answered questions. He used the telephone. He and his family and friends knocked on doors and handed out cards. He spoke at the Rotary Club and at the county fair. He was an individual, as well as a media, event.

In addition, we must recognize that the candidates themselves (exclusive of the power, presumed or real, of the media) had talents, effectiveness, charisma, a friendly and trustworthy smile, and other personal attributes that made them popular and electable. The media themselves did not give them these attributes. The media may have served as channels whereby the public or portions of it were exposed to these attributes—but they were personal, not media-induced. How can researchers, seeking to perceive the impact of the media, separate personal "power" from media "power"? I do not think they can. There is no evidence, to my knowledge, that can show that all other impacting factors can be separated: So the conclusion is that the media have no more than tangential or minimal impact.

Journalists, of course, like to think that they and their media have great power and that they are movers and shakers in society. It is satisfying to them to think that they are kingmakers, agenda-setters, corruption-unearthers, society-improvers. Of course, they are not quite so sure of their power when someone points out that the negativism, violence, sensationalism and sexploitation permeating the media might be having a deleterious effect on society. They seem to see themselves as having only "positive" power and seldom, if ever, "negative" power.

While there are many communications scholars like DeFleur, Noelle-Neumann, Clarke, and Kline, alluded to by Dennis, who call for more research of media impact in the real (nonexperimental) world, hardly any research of this nature has been done. How does one perceive the impact of the media when trying to study them in a total social symbiosis? How does one separate or isolate purely media effects from other effects? These questions have been addressed, of course, but have not been satisfactorily answered. When scholars like Max McCombs and Don Shaw (1972) conclude that agenda setting by the media is an important role and has "power" in that it tells people what to think *about*, they have stated an obvious informational principle, but they have come no closer to specifying the real power of the media. Of course, I will generally think more about news events that I read much about and see prominently on the TV screen than I will about those which are ignored or minimally treated by the media. Nobody can deny that I may be aware of these events or even think about them because of their media attention, but the question still remains: What impact does such consciousness have on me?

A locked front door to a building may cause me to go around to a side door to enter. In one sense the lock has power and has caused a change in my activity; it has modified my interaction with my environment. But how has it affected me? Studying the lock will not answer the question. Neither will a study of the quantitative aspects of my new and more elongated journey to another door. Only an in-depth psychological study will cast some light on the power or impact on me of the locked front door.

What I am trying to say is that our lives are constantly affected or changed by a multitude of factors—some of which are messages reaching our brains—and these factors are so complex and intertwined as to defy clear determinations as to the impact of each. What we think obviously has some kind of effect on our lives. What we do is also important. But what we do is not always determined by what we think, so we cannot say that if we have certain information we will act in a certain way on the basis of that information—or, in fact, that we will act at all.

John P. Robinson (1972) says that evidence now exists "that under certain conditions" media can have political impact. That is almost like saying that under certain conditions an Alpine valley town can be destroyed by an avalanche of snow. Of course, media can have political impact. I can just as well say that under certain conditions media can not have political impact.

My coauthor cites James Lemert's (1981) attack on the "simple reductionist model" of minimal effects, which measures media influence mainly through attitude change. Lemert says, according to Dennis, that the mass media can have a powerful impact on the information given to decision makers. I would go even further than that: Mass media can have *total* control and impact on the *information* given to decision makers. (Impact on the *information:* Now here is a new concept!) At least this would certainly be true of the information given to the decision makers by the media. Earlier I maintained that people (including decision makers) get much information from sources other than mass media.

What we need in this debate about media power are some clear definitions. I do not think most researchers and students in this area are really sure of what they are talking about. What do they mean by "power"? What is meant by "minimal effects"? Or "maximal effects"? Just how powerful (by any definition) would the media need to be to be considered powerful or effective?

Are there not different types or forms of power? Providing information (regardless of the impact) is one kind of power. Another power is the impact or effect of such information on the *mind*. Still another power would be the impact or effect of such information on the *actions* of a person. Most often the distinctions among these kinds of power are ignored or minimized.

I would postulate that:

1. Media are most powerful in furnishing information and setting agenda for members of a public.

2. Media are next most powerful in impinging on the thoughts, opinions, and attitudes of members of a public.

3. Media are least powerful in affecting actions of members of a public.

In conclusion, I agree that media are powerful sometimes and to some extent. Just when they are and to what degree are questions crying out for more answers, more research. At present we know very little about media *power*. It may well be that media are really more powerful than media-power proponents think. But then, they may be far less powerful.

I cannot say in good conscience that media are not powerful, but I can say in good conscience that what power they have is shared with innumerable forces in society. I also say that, so far as I am able to learn, media in themselves are not nearly as powerful (in any of the aspects of power) as journalists and other media people generally contend.

Argument Summation: The media are not so powerful.

We usually assume the media are powerful, but we have very little evidence. Naturally media have some power, but it is usually overblown. Secondary factors have various social effects on audience members in certain circumstances. We do not know how *much* power media really have because we cannot isolate their impact from other influencing factors, such as conversations, peer pressure, family, school, and church. It is most likely that media have the most "power" in focusing our attention in certain directions—*attention power*, if you will—but that is quite different from power to *cause* action.

TOPICS FOR DISCUSSION

1. Assuming media have powerful effects in society, what does this suggest for (a) education of media people, and (b) ethics of media people?

2. Why do you think the issue of media power has such a fascination for communication scholars? Do you think media practitioners are "power hungry"?

3. Why do you think *what* people learn from mass media has significant effect upon them or indicates that media are, or are not, powerful?

4. When scholars say that "under certain conditions" media can have impact, are they supporting or minimizing the *powerful effects theory* of the media?

5. Explain why advertising and its large expenditures argue for powerful effects of media. Also discuss why many politicians who get more exposure than their opponents often lose the election.

TOPICS FOR RESEARCH

1. Write an essay about the academic-professional disputes over media power. Compare the perceived "power of the press" in the 1930s and 1940s with that in the 1950s and 1960s. What is the prevailing sentiment today? Do academics and media professionals agree or not? Why?

2. Compare ideas about the *power of* the media to deliver consumers through advertising as is asserted in economics textbooks versus mass communication or advertising texts. What differences in interpretation and analysis do you find?

3. Some media researchers doubt that the media can do much to change people's attitudes, opinions, and behavior in elections. Campaign managers and politicians themselves seem to doubt this, or they certainly act as

though they do. To what extent do media influence (or not influence) the outcome of elections?

4. Do a profile of a leading media consultant who works on political campaigns. What do we know about the person? How does he or she work? What evidence does he or she marshal in deciding what communications resources to deploy in a campaign? How do we know whether the strategy worked?

5. Write a "biography of an idea," that of *agenda-setting*. What does the term mean? Who originated it? How did it come to be known as "an important media effect"? What have studies of agenda-setting shown? How would you explain the agenda-setting hypothesis to a lay audience?

FURTHER READING

Altschull, J. Herbert. *Agents of Power: The Role of the News Media in Human Affairs*. White Plains, NY: Longman, 1984.

Babb, Laura L., ed. *Of the Press, by the Press, and Others, Too*. Boston: Houghton Mifflin, 1976.

Cohen, Jeremy and Timothy Gleason. *Social Research in Communication and Law*. Newbury Park, CA: Sage Publications, 1990.

Comstock, George, et al. *Television and Human Behavior*. New York: Columbia University Press, 1978.

Davis, D. K., and S. J. Baran. *Mass Communication and Everyday Life: A Perspective on Theory and Effects*. Belmont, CA: Wadsworth, 1981.

DeFleur, Melvin L., and Sandra Ball-Rokeach. *Theories of Mass Communication*. 4th ed. White Plains, NY: Longman, 1982. Also see 5th ed.

DeFleur, M. L., and Everette E. Dennis. *Understanding Mass Communication*. 3d ed. Boston: Houghton Mifflin, 1988.

Dennis, Everette E. *The Media Society*. Dubuque, IA: William C. Brown Publishers, 1978.

———. *Reshaping the Media*. Beverly Hills, CA: Sage Publications, 1989.

Gitlin, Todd. "Media Sociology: The Dominant Paradigm." *Theory's Society* 6(November 1978): 205–253.

———. *The Whole World is Watching*. Berkeley, CA: University of California Press, 1980.

Jamison, Kathleen Hall, and Karlyn Kohrs Campbell. *The Interplay of Influence*. Belmont, CA: Wadsworth, 1983.

Klapper, Joseph T. *The Effects of Mass Communication*. New York: The Free Press, 1960.

Kraus, Sydney, and Dennis Davis. *The Effects of Mass Communication on*

Political Behavior. University Park, PA: Pennsylvania State University Press, 1976.

Kuhn, Thomas. *The Structure of Scientific Revolutions*. Princeton, NJ: Princeton University Press, 1962.

Lazarsfeld, Paul, et al. *The People's Choice*. New York: Duell, Sloan & Pearce, 1944.

Lemert, James B. *Does Mass Communication Change Public Opinion After All?* Chicago: Nelson-Hall, 1981.

McCombs, Maxwell, and Donald Shaw. "The Agenda-Setting Function of Mass Media." *Public Opinion Quarterly* 36(1972): 176–187.

Mills, C. Wright. *Power, Politics, and People*. New York: Ballantine Books, 1962.

Noelle-Neumann, Elisabeth. "Return to the Concept of Powerful Mass Media." *Studies of Broadcasting* 9(1973): 67–112.

"Print Culture and Video Culture." *Daedalus*. A special issue 3, no. 4 (Fall 1982).

Reeves, Richard. "The Press's Great Threat." *Esquire* (August 1, 1978): 10–13.

Roberts, D. F., and Christine M. Bachen. "Mass Communication Effects." *Annual Review of Psychology* 32(February 1981): 307–56.

Robinson, John P. "Can the Media Affect Behavior After All?" *Journalism Quarterly* 49, no. 2 (1972): 239–46.

Rubin, Bernard. *Media, Politics, and Democracy*. New York: Oxford University Press, 1977. See especially Chapter 5, "Media and Election Trends."

Schramm, Wilbur, ed. *The Process and Effects of Mass Communication*. Urbana, IL: University of Illinois Press, 1954.

Schramm, W., and William Porter. *Men, Women, Messages, and Media*. New York: Harper and Row, 1982.

Small, William J. *To Kill a Messenger: Television News and the Real World*. New York: Hastings House, 1970.

———. *Political Power and the Press*. New York: Hastings House, 1972.

Stein, Robert. *Media Power: Who Is Shaping Your Picture of the World?* Boston: Houghton Mifflin, 1972.

Chapter **8**

QUALITY OF MEDIA CONTENT

For decades critics of mass communication have hammered away at the quality of media content. Whether one is discussing the information, opinion, or entertainment functions of the mass media, the quality of the fare offered to the public is often at issue. The standard view in communication history is that the press has become stronger, freer, and better over the course of time. We have come to think of newspaper articles, movie scripts, and television scenarios as increasing in quality. To some, media content of two decades ago or earlier not only seems dated but of somewhat primitive quality compared with what is offered today. Others disagree. Criticism of media content usually focuses on (1) the substantive information or entertainment material being present, and (2) the style or form of presentation. Especially in the first instance, there is strong support in scholarly commentary and criticism for the argument that media content is much improved. Often it is argued that audience preferences and tastes demand quality, and television programs, news content of newspapers, and magazines that do not meet this consumer quality standard simply do not survive. This argument convinces some, but not others.

CHALLENGE

Dennis: Media content is generally of poor quality and getting worse.

Evaluating media content is a difficult task. If we have low expectations, almost anything will seem better than it might have been. If we have high standards and measure what is against what *might be*, we are likely to be disappointed. Frankly, I am in the middle. I look at today's media content against a standard of what is reasonable. And on that basis I am unimpressed by what I see in almost all of the individual mass media in the United States. True, there are rare pockets of quality in some of the so-called opinion and literary magazines and on public television, but for the most part the performance of the American media can only be termed a major embarrassment.

Questions of quality almost always are equated with matters of elitism versus egalitarianism: It is assumed that quality is synonymous with a wealthy or highly educated audience, which would make an intellectual assault on what the people really want. I would argue that this is not the case. I believe that the American people have too often been subjected to low-quality media content, not because they want it, but because media professionals have an inaccurate understanding of public tastes.

The major motivating force for quality in the American media is little more than the egos of directors, producers, editors, broadcasters, and others. People who want to distinguish themselves from the commonplace have the motivation and interest to strive to do better by producing something distinctive. There is little reason beyond this to elevate accurately the media and its content. These people are often thwarted by their industry's perception of what the market will bear.

What distinguishes a quality performance by the media from one that is mediocre or poor? Contrary to the view of some egalitarian critics, appealing to rich or snobbish people is not the essential element. Instead, it is:

1. *Beauty* as expressed in design, presentation, and format.

2. *Literary style* as expressed in writing either for print or electronic media.

3. *Universal appeal* in terms of those elements that touch the heart or mind and have a lasting impact.

4. *Impact* as seen in the long-term contribution of the material that is produced.

Finally, in my mind, an elevating influence is being able to say that this is the best that can be done; it is better than that which has come before, and it can be clearly distinguished from earlier work, more primitive efforts, and less informed approaches.

While I do not believe in the full-throttle theory of Excelsior (upward, onward ever), I do think there is a difference between stagnation and forward movement in media content.

Look at the newspaper, for example. Is today's newspaper better than the one that existed a few years or decades ago? By what measure do we answer this question? First, I would look at the quality of writing. Is it more vital, more lively, more readable than that which appeared before?

Next, I would consider the substantive information conveyed. Is it accurate? Is it complete? Is it compelling? Does it have proper context? I would also look at the methods reporters use in their work. Are these tools, whether in interviewing, use of documents and records, or corroboration of sources, an improvement over those used decades ago? If so, how and why? If not, why not? I would ask whether the newspaper is in touch with its audience. Does it resonate the concerns that people have? Does it understand its readers and calibrate material to their interests and needs?

When we address these questions squarely and well, the American newspaper is a quite deficient product. Few critics assert that the writing in the American press is sterling. Good writing is the exception, not the rule. Tom Winship, the former editor of the *Boston Globe*, has excoriated the American press for its lack of attention to writing:

> Newspapers are dying, in part, because they are dull and predictable. If we are going to attempt good writing we won't be able always to play it safe; we'll have to try new forms, new subjects, new voices, stories written and reported at new distances, stories that are shorter than usual and longer than usual. Some of them won't work for good writing is always experimental (Winship, 1982, 22).

Experimental is the key word here. Most newspapers simply will not tolerate experimentation. They play it safe and what they produce results in what New Journalist Tom Wolfe calls a "paralyzing snoremonger" syndrome. Few critics think the writing in American newspapers is anything other than mediocre. The newspaper is not the home of America's best and most gifted prose. It could be. Literary giants of the past such as Hemingway, Faulkner, and others began their careers at newspapers and produced strong nonfiction prose that is memorable today. When the brilliant sports writer Red Smith died in 1982, a number of publications produced samples of his writing. This work was notable mainly because it was so much unlike the turgid copy that usually appears on the modern sports page.

Writing, of course, is only one aspect of media performance. What of the methods, tools, and techniques of the journalist? Is there evidence that today's interviewing methods are significantly better than those of yesteryear? Are reporters more systematic, more meticulous, more competent in seeking out information for a wide variety of public records and documents? In spite of the surge toward investigative reporting in the early 1970s, it can rightly be said that today's reporters are guilty of journalistic primitivism. They are ignorant of their craft's history and frankly do not care about it. Consider one example from investigative reporting. When Bob Woodward and Carl Bernstein did their Watergate investigation in the early 1970s, they were hailed as culture heroes. They were credited by some with bringing down a government and giving journalism a place at center stage again. But for journalism historians who compare this work with that of the great muckrakers at the turn of the century, the Watergate boys and other modern investigative reporters do not measure up very well. By contrast, Lincoln Steffens, Ray Stannard Baker, and Ida Tarbell, the original muckrakers, were world-class performers. Their prose was stronger; their investigative techniques about the same; the time they devoted to their projects, greater. Students will find this work in its original form, plus histories and criticism of it, in any library. After a close inspection of the performance of the 1980s investigative reporters and those of the early 1900s, I would have to give the nod to the folks at the turn of the century. This in itself is not particularly noteworthy, but it is sad that in eighty years, American journalism has progressed so little. If American medicine or science or even cooking methods had made as little progress, we would be terribly distressed, but we accept this sluggish performance by the media without much complaint. Indeed, the methods of a profession are often the best indicator of its progress.

One of the principal concerns of communicators is knowing and understanding the audience. Since the turn of the century there have been breathtaking advances in market and survey research and in other forms of audience analysis. Audiences can be examined for the intensity of readership and in other highly revealing ways. What does the average American newspaper know about its audience? The advertising department probably knows quite a bit, but little of this information filters down from the editors to reporters in the field. Reporters of the 1980s are probably more ignorant of their audience than were their counterparts in the nineteenth century. In fact, there is evidence that contemporary reporters are hopelessly out of touch with the reader because reporters tend to be part of an elite class. Researchers at Michigan State University reported that "mobility, long working hours, and an attitude that news people are different from their readers contribute to journalists feeling out of touch" (Burgoon, Burgoon, and Atkin, 1982, 5). This and other studies indicate that American journalists are not only insular, but are also quite contemptuous of their audience, referring to readers and viewers as "bozos" or "Joe Sixpack."

You might ask, why should we expect today's reporters to be more knowledgeable or better informed? The answer is simple: research, computers, and techniques for examining the audience with real precision. I recall with much disappointment the results of a study I did with science editors on daily newspapers. They were an elite group of reporters and had a better grasp of research than almost any of their counterparts had. Yet, when asked about the audience they were writing for, their responses were incredibly unscientific, as they confessed that they thought they were writing for "the Kansas City milkman." Many knowledgeable reporters genuinely thought they were writing for "everyone in the community," rather than for the highly specific and defined audience which exists today. They were not making any practical use of the research data readily available to them as a tool to stay in touch with the reader or viewer.

What of commercial television content? Few would argue that the soap operas which dominate daytime television are the best dramatic performances that we Americans are capable of producing and sustaining with advertising. Heavy-handed, melodramatic programs are the order of the day in the soaps that dominate daytime television. Evening programming is a little better, but not particularly noteworthy. Over the years some of the best quality programs have been dropped. Nearly every season, the shows that are taken off the air are often some of the best. In their place we have often seen such fare as sensational news and talk shows, sometimes called "trash" television, or the next generation of tasteless, violent fare introduced in autumn 1989, with ice skaters and gladiators competing in dangerous contests and games, appropriately called "crash television."

Television is probably the best example of the "great leveler" theory of mass communication, which posits that one must appeal to a vast, homogeneous audience in order to succeed commercially. In the early 1960s, the chairman of the Federal Communications Commission declared that television was "a vast wasteland." Since then the situation has not improved. Television programs are banal, silly, and generally poor in quality. Those of higher quality usually are destined for the trash bin.

Television news is also worth examining. In recent years the most notable thing about TV news has been the addition of the news consultants, who have had an enormous effect on program content. The addition has led, not to more serious and thoughtful coverage of the public arena in a fashion that people will find interesting, but to "happy talk" news where newscasters reflect a kind of jovial idiocy as they make jokes between reports about plane crashes and bloody coups in foreign lands. There is more emphasis on the hairstyle of the anchorperson than the substance that person presents on the evening news. There are certainly some pockets of good performance in television news as compared with radio news, which is still a headline service and an even vaster wasteland than television.

Television news has justifiably been called "chewing gum for the eyes." It emphasizes trivial events that have a visual component regardless of their importance; it is biased toward the spectacle instead of the more subtle trend; it misleads the public by following the visual cue to the exclusion of deeper meaning.

Across much of the media, the economic glue that holds things together is advertising. And what of advertising? Is it of high quality? Does it elevate the American people? Do we admire it for its ethical sensitivity? For its fairness? For its devotion to truth? Of course not. These questions cannot even be put seriously. Advertising content is better than it was in the days of patent medicine shows and quacks, but it is hardly befitting a modern society. Advertising is self-serving; it is biased and it misleads. Even comparative advertising, where one advertiser compares its wares with another, is less than desirable and hardly a serious consumer service. Without some supervision by the Federal Trade Commission and other government agencies, advertising would no doubt be worse than it is. Still, the end product of advertising agencies today can hardly be called admirable.

Many of the points made here about newspapers and television could be made for other media, but I will not develop an endless laundry list. Instead, I will return to the criteria suggested earlier as points of comparison between and among the media. If we consider them seriously, we find some intriguing, if depressing, answers. I recognize, of course, that any criticism of media content subjects the critic to charges of elitism. Fair enough. Measures of quality are necessarily subjective, although I have tried to offer some support that goes beyond personal conjecture. My views may differ markedly from those of others. However, I would note that the American people, on the one hand, vote with their pocketbooks, and in so doing they continue to support the present output of the media. Yet, when they are allowed to make qualitative judgments they are singularly unimpressed by media content. In 1981 the Public Agenda Foundation, working with the pollster Daniel Yankelovich, conducted one of the most exhaustive surveys of public attitudes toward the media. The principal finding of that survey was a general public dissatisfaction with the media. The vast majority of Americans criticized the media for lacking fairness and for the growing trend toward sex and violence on television. Other studies of public confidence in the media as an institution also gave low marks to American journalism. It is true that these studies are somewhat limited and that the respondents often have little basis for comparison except their own personal standards. Still, the public is smart enough to know what it does not like.

As for social consequences, I believe that the media have a more important and sustained role. They give us a common frame of reference, possiby because they seek the lowest common denominator audience thus giving everyone a common experience. The media, both print and broadcast, do have an influence deemed important and potentially powerful. Is this power exercised to the greatest possible good? Does the press generally serve the public interest, as opposed to its own narrow commercial interests?

The portrait of the content of the American mass media is not what it could be, even if it is better than the norm of international standards. I personally believe that the American people are intelligent, have standards, want quality, and decry the kind of brain candy that demeans and denigrates the human spirit. To date, the American media have not received this message.

Argument Summation: Media content is generally of poor quality and getting worse.

Judged by a reasonable standard, not a utopian "what might be," the American media are still of embarrassingly low quality. To measure the quality of the media it is necessary to evaluate the progress they have made over time, which in the case of newspapers is minimal. Writing is of extremely low quality. An examination of investigative reporting reveals that the methods, tools, and techniques of journalism have failed to improve since the turn of the century. Despite improved techniques for examining the audience, elitist attitudes among reporters leave them ignorant of their audience. Commercial television is no better, as quality programming is dropped in favor of talk show and tabloid news programming. Finally, advertising has improved only slightly since the days of medicine shows and quacks, but it is still biased and misleading. Mass support for the media should not be misconstrued as a vote of confidence, for, while Americans vote with their pocketbooks for current programming, when asked to make qualitative judgments they are singularly unimpressed by media content. After all, they have little real choice.

RESPONSE

Merrill: Media content is generally of good quality and getting better.

Everette Dennis has admitted that evaluating media content is a difficult task. I would certainly agree, but would add that pointing out negative aspects of the media and concluding that general quality is poor are much easier than accentuating the positive. Media critics like Eugene Methvin in a 1989 *Quill* article on "destructive journalism" normally stress the weaknesses and, by and large, ignore the strengths.

The very nature of the mass media in America opens the door to a criticism that deprecates the general media picture, points up the rather low "common denominator" quality of the media, which must appeal largely to the masses, and approaches media criticism from an arrogant and elitist perspective. *Generally*, of course, U.S. mass media are not paragons of quality; they do not exemplify consistently the highest standards; they do, indeed, reflect the basic characteristics of the very mass audiences they seek to serve. This is quite natural and it is also intelligent.

Again, as we have seen in other debatable issues in the arena of mass communication, we find ourselves squarely in the middle of a semantic thicket. Imprecise definitions and the whole concept of relativity circumscribe such "debates" as this one and cause the ensuing discussion to be devoid of the precision and lucidity that we might wish.

For example, we are talking about "media content." But we are not sure just which *medium* we are talking about, nor are we certain about what *content* we are specifically referring to. Beyond this, what do we mean by "generally poor" or "good" quality? Even though we have such questions as these about the proposition being debated and recognize that the whole issue is fuzzy, we can feel some justification for the discussion because the subject constantly thrusts itself into the public forum. The American media system is an important social force, and it is useful to ask questions about its quality and about the direction in which it seems to be going.

As I have reviewed a wealth of critical literature about the press in recent years, I have been struck by how poorly the press fares. Not uncommon at all are statements similar to this harsh one by Cecil King, publisher of London's *Daily Mirror:*

> I have to say that, in spite of all your modernization, the American newspaper is the shabbiest product in a land which has shown the world how the best designed and most elegantly finished goods can be produced for the masses (King, 1967, 19).

King's indictment of U.S. newspapers goes far beyond the above generalization about shabbiness into considerable specificity. It was a rather good summary of common criticisms of the American press. Even though Cecil King's criticism is from an earlier decade, his words reverberate today. Indictments are heard on every side: about TV programs with no substance, about design and printing quality of newspapers and magazines, about sloppy writing and deficient grammar and spelling—about almost every aspect of the modern American mass media.

My coauthor says that, when we measure American media content against what it *might be,* we are likely to be disappointed. Undoubtedly. If we measure anything against what it might be, we are likely to be disappointed. I think we should be more realistic in our expectations; we should measure American media content against media content in the mass media of other countries and against the media content of past times in American history. If we do, I think we shall see that our media are very good indeed—that they are relatively vigorous, thorough, competent, literate, appealing, and useful. Any American who travels much throughout the world and has a chance to read magazines and newspapers, listen to radio and view television will recognize that, in spite of weaknesses of American media, the overall media system is quite good. My coauthor feels the American media can only be termed "a major embarrassment." I have found that, generally, they can be termed a source of pride.

I am not thinking about what they *could* be, but am considering them in historical and worldwide contexts. Dennis extols the great muckrakers at the turn of the century and finds that modern reporters such as Woodward and Bernstein come off poorly by comparison. Dennis sees as superior to today's journalism, the "good ol' days" of American journalism, when "world-class performers" such as Ida Tarbell and Ray Stannard Baker produced prose and devoted great amounts of time to their projects.

Dennis thinks that American journalism has progressed very little, if at all, since the turn of the century. I accept this as an opinion, but I have really seen no evidence of the superiority of earlier journalism. Dennis mentions the "strong prose" of earlier journalists like Lincoln Steffens, but which modern journalists are being compared to Steffens? Scotty Reston, George Will, William Buckley, Norman Podhoretz, Nicholas von Hoffman, Tom Wicker? We are not told. We can, of course, pick certain journalists from *any* age and use them to make the case that journalism of that age was superior to another. But this is not very convincing.

There was, perhaps, a certain sophistication and low-keyed charm to the journalistic prose of yesteryear. But does this make that journalism better than today's journalism? You might find examples of good, forceful writing at the turn of the century or during the exciting Civil War period, but you will also find notable examples of sloppy interviewing, gap-filled stories, liberties taken with the facts, instances of fictionalizing, personal reportorial involvement and obvious bias, questionable ethics, and on and on. Certainly the American people were not informed as thoroughly and continuously at earlier periods as they are today. Journalistic quality cannot simply be limited to writing style or "forceful prose" attributed to a small sample of journalists. But this is what Dennis has tried to do.

From my study of elite newspapers and those aspiring to be high-quality, news-oriented newspapers, both in the United States and abroad, I am convinced that the United States has a sizable group of serious, well-edited newspapers with staffs of considerable sophistication motivated to great public service. I believe that the number of such reputable, qualitative newspapers is larger than ever before. And I know of no other country in the world with such a high proportion of reputable middle-level or "mass" newspapers. The reader of a daily newspaper in a city of 50,000 in the United States gets at least four times as much news as a counterpart would get if he were reading a paper in a similar city abroad. The United States has nothing to be ashamed of *generally* (and note that "generally" is part of the proposition for debate) when compared with media in other countries or media at other periods.

I invite the reader to take a trip abroad and look at the media situation. Do not just go to Paris, London, Tokyo, Frankfurt, or Zurich. Go to some small cities or towns of 10,000 to 20,000. Watch TV. Read the local newspapers. Note the superficiality of news treatment. Notice how few pages the publications have. Compare the information you are getting there with what you would be getting in the United States—wherever in the United States you might be.

Go to a city in an advanced European country such as Switzerland or West Germany; visit a city comparable to Louisville, St. Petersburg, Dallas, or San Jose. See what kind of journalism you are exposed to. You will come away with a more positive feeling toward the media system of the United States. We need to remember that familiarity often breeds contempt and that quaint foreign practices do, indeed, often have undue appeal. This is why foreign media do often seem more to our liking (at least in the short run) than do our own media. But it does not take long for an American foreign traveler, returning from abroad, to realize U.S. media superiority.

In his "challenge" Dennis sets up four criteria or determinants for "quality performance" by the media. Let us briefly look at these four which he has evidently used to conclude that the U.S. media system is an embarrassment:

1. *Beauty* (as expressed in design, presentation, and format): Is Dennis's determination that the American media system is of poor quality and getting worse based, in any sense, on the concept of beauty? If so, he presents no evidence of faulty design, presentation, and format.

2. *Literary style* (as expressed in writing for print or for the electronic media): Is Dennis's determination of low quality really based on evidence of poor "literary" writing? If so, he presents no evidence of poor writing generally (or even in specific cases). He gives some opinions on certain aspects of this (dealing with muckraking), but really makes no comparisons.

3. *Universal appeal* (of those elements that touch the heart or mind and have a lasting impact): Is the American media system of poor quality, in Dennis's opinion, because it has no elements which "touch the heart or mind and have a lasting impact"? Certainly some "hearts" or "minds" are touched by messages emanating from our media system. Sociologists and psychologists—not to mention pragmatic advertising specialists—would maintain that the American media have as much universal appeal as ever and certainly as much as can be found in the media systems of any other country. No evidence can be found to show that this appeal, even if it is not increasing, is diminishing. For our media system to be getting worse— qualitatively worse—as Dennis contends it is, it would have to show that, among other factors, the universal appeal is diminishing.

4. *Impact* (as seen in the long-term contribution of the material that is produced): Impact of the media, like universal appeal, has evidently been inferred by Dennis and others who hold that this is a determinant of media quality. Certainly no evidence of lack of impact or even of lessening impact, has been given in Dennis's "challenge." I think that almost anyone familiar

with the scope and potency of American mass media would be inclined to assume great impact (and even growing impact) by these media. Just what Dennis means by "the long-term contribution of the material that is produced" is unclear, but I would suggest that "long-term" implies that the contemporary American mass media cannot be faulted in this respect yet. Critics like Dennis will have to wait for the "long-term" to see what contribution today's media material *will* make to society.

Dennis puts good writing very high in his criteria of quality. And he finds the American press deficient in good writing. "Good writing," he says, "is the exception, not the rule." I would agree with this, but I would add that it is the exception *everywhere*, not just in American journalism. And only an unrealistic person would expect the best writing to be found in the *mass* media; less than the best writing is almost implied in the mass media concept. It appears to me unfair and unreasonable even to expect consistently good writing in the American press. As is true everywhere, some writing is good, some is not so good, and some is poor. Writing for the mass media is obviously not as consistently good as it could be. But I can just as well say that it is not as consistently bad as it could be, either.

Tom Winship of the *Boston Globe* is quoted by Dennis to give evidence that writing in the American press is poor. Good writing, says Winship, "is always experimental." Just what does that mean? Would not such a statement simply be based on (have meaning because of) what one means by "experimental"? How is such a statement helpful in identifying good writing? Winship says that journalists need to try new forms, new subjects, new voices, stories written and reported at new distances, and stories that are shorter than usual and longer than usual. When does a "new" form become old? How often do new forms need to come along before the old ones cease being good writing? How do new subjects and new voices determine good writing? How does the distance at which stories are written contribute to quality? Dennis does not let Winship answer such questions, nor does he attempt answers himself.

If media critics are expecting Faulkners and Hemingways to be writing the run-of-the-mill journalistic pieces for print and broadcasting today, they are, of course, living in a fool's paradise. If this is what they expect, it is easy to see why they think the American media content is generally poor.

What we need in this country are media critics who are realistic in their criticism. It does no good to insist that an impossible "literary" face be given to the American press and that outstanding literary stylists produce the general contents of the country's media. This has never been the case and it never will be the case. The modern mass media comprise a greedy giant that consumes writing at such a pace that it is logically impossible for the highest literary quality to be generally maintained. This would seem to me to be self-evident.

Argument Summation: Media content is generally of good quality and getting better.

In spite of much criticism, information about basic and important aspects of society is available in the media. And it is presented in an interesting and understandable way. Exceptions are rare. Admittedly, media messages are aimed at the masses and are not of the highest literary or intellectual quality. However, much so-called "journalism" is in time anthologized as literature. Media writers are usually well-educated and serious about their work. It is unfair to judge American media content, as Dennis does, by what it might be. We need to judge it against media content in other countries or against such content in the past. If we do, it looks very good—and it is getting better.

TOPICS FOR DISCUSSION

1. Discuss what you mean by "quality" media content. Does it refer only to message quality? What other aspects of media quality can you think of?

2. Suppose that TV programming is basically "chewing gum for the eyes." Does that refer to poor quality or does it mean that selection of messages should have been different?

3. Does the mere fact that content is part of mass media automatically make this content poor? Can "mass" audiences sustain quality media?

4. How is media *message* quality related to media quantity? As media become more prosperous, what is the tendency in the proliferation of "quality" content?

5. Are newspapers duller and more predictable today than in the American past? Compare a typical U.S. newspaper of today with one at the turn of the century—or during the pre-Civil War period.

TOPICS FOR RESEARCH

1. Write an essay defining quality in media content. Who has been involved in this debate? By what standards do they judge media quality—either in information, entertainment, or opinion? Are there different standards of quality for elites versus the mainstream of the population?

2. Discuss the idea of media quality—indicating which standards you are using—by contrasting an entertainment program on commercial (network)

television or cable with one on public television. What conclusions do you draw?

3. Discuss the quality of three major newspapers of contrasting types or approaches, such as the *Wall Street Journal, USA Today, New York Times, Washington Post, Christian Science Monitor,* or others. Evaluate the papers you choose on the basis of quality of content, design, reliability, or other criteria you wish to use. Defend and document your positions.

4. Write a paper on "quality media for the underclass," wherein you indicate how people with limited income can still get quality information, opinion, or entertainment at minimal cost. Are there communication channels from which this part of the population is "excluded?" Which ones and why?

5. People sometimes refer to the "quality" magazines, meaning publications like the *Atlantic, Harper's, Smithsonian,* the *New Yorker, Scientific American,* and others. Select a "quality" magazine and study its content over several months. What sets it apart from other publications with larger circulations and more mass appeal? Does it have a distinctive character and approach? If so, what? What do its advertisements tell you about the audience it is seeking? Do this systematically, so that you can generalize from your results. Document the work carefully.

FURTHER READING

Bagdikian, Ben. "The American Newspaper Is Neither Record, Telegram, Examiner, Observer, Monitor, Mirror, Journal, Ledger, Bulletin, Register, Chronicle, Gazette, Transcript, Nor Herald of the Day's Events . . . It's Just Bad News." *Esquire* (March 1967).

Barbato, Joseph A. "What Is a Good Newspaper?" *The Quill* (October 1965): 24–25.

Burgoon, Judee, Michael Burgoon, and Charles Atkin. *What is News? Who Decides and How?* A Report of the Newspaper Readership Project, Michigan State University (1982).

Curran, James, Michael Gurevitch, and James Woolcott, eds. *Mass Communication and Society.* Beverly Hills, CA: Sage, 1978.

Fiske, John. *Introduction to Communication Studies.* New York: Methuen, 1982.

Gans, Herbert. *Popular Culture and High Culture: An Analysis of Taste and an Evaluation of Taste.* New York: Basic Books, 1974.

Hulteng, J. L. *The News Media: What Makes Them Tick?* Englewood Cliffs, NJ: Prentice-Hall, 1979.

Kempton, Murray. "The Sound of Tinkling Brass: A Skeptical Opinion of the Press." *Harpers* (August 1974): 41–44.

King, Cecil H. "An English View of American Newspapers." *Editor & Publisher* (29 April 1967): 19, 98–99.

Lemert, James. *Criticizing the Media: Empirical Approaches.* Beverly Hills, CA: Sage Publications, 1989.

Luedtke, Kurt. "An Ex-Newsman Hands Down His Indictment of the Press." *The Bulletin of the ASNE* (May–June 1982): 16–18.

Lyons, Louis M. "A Commentary on the Press." *Neiman Reports* (June 1972).

Markel, Lester. "Why the Public Doesn't Trust the Press." *World* (15 August 1972).

Merrill, J. C. " 'Quality' Daily Journalism: An Analytical Discussion." *Gazette* 15, no. 1 (1969): 51–56.

———. *The Elite Press*, New York: Pitman, 1968.

Merrill, J. C., and Harold Fisher. *The World's Great Dailies*, New York: Hastings House, 1980.

Methvin, Eugene H. "Mephistophelean Journalism." *The Quill* 77, no. 4(April, 1989): 38–40.

Weber, Ronald. "Journalism, Writing, and American Literature." New York: Gannett Center for Media Studies. Working Paper No. 5, 1987.

Williams, Raymond. *Communications.* Harmondsworth, England: Penguin, 1976.

Winship, Thomas. "The Care and Feeding of Writers." *Nieman Reports* 36. no. 2(Summer 1982): 19–22.

Chapter **9**

JOURNALISTIC OBJECTIVITY

If there is a most important tenet of journalistic practice in the United States, it is the concept of objectivity. To some objectivity does not mean clinical or scientific precision, but instead an effort by journalists to produce news stories and newscasts that are emotionally detached and that separate fact from opinion. Objectivity in journalistic practice is often associated with the inverted pyramid news story (news organized in a descending order of importance) and with the 5Ws and H (who, what, where, why, when, and how), or other systems or sorting out the facts necessary to convey the essence of an event or issue in an orderly fashion.

Objectivity to many means factual reporting, straightforward descriptive presentation. In recent years, though, objectivity as a theory of journalism has also included analytical reporting that goes well beyond simple description. Objectivity is a distinguishing feature of American journalism, especially when compared with journalistic content in other countries and cultures. At least that is what the proponents of objectivity believe, and it has become the standard wisdom. While some of the world's newspapers engage in polemic and opinionated essays, the U.S. approach generally has been to keep the views of the journalist segregated from the story of an event and to keep factual news on the news pages and opinion on the editorial pages.

Most critics of journalistic objectivity, as well as its defenders, agree that objectivity is a high-minded value. Some see it as a helpful goal; others see it as an unrealistic and even harmful one. Many of the so-called "new" journalists and "existential" journalists scoff at this formulation of objectivity. Still, even they would argue that American journalism generally is journalism without ideology, where method goes far toward dictating factual presentation.

CHALLENGE

Merrill: Journalistic objectivity is not possible.

Many readers may think that my position—that journalistic objectivity is not possible—is like building a straw man and then proceeding to demolish it. They will say that nobody contends that journalistic objectivity is possible, and that such a "debate" simply turns into an exercise of semantic frustration.

First, let me say that I sympathize with such a position just attributed to "many readers," but I believe that we cannot ignore such an important journalistic concept. If we did, we would be doing an injustice to a legitimate concern of those who are involved with modern journalism—all of us. Secondly, many journalists and others talk and write as if they believe in journalistic objectivity. If they do not believe in it, then I propose that they stop using the term.

Perhaps the concept of journalistic objectivity is a "straw man" to those who seriously think about it, who are sophisticated, and who are realistic about the realities of journalism. But I contend that such persons are not legion and that, generally, laymen and journalists alike actually think that a news story can be "objective" or that there are objective reporters out there somewhere who can be identified as different from other reporters. Certainly we hear the term used often: "I wish he had written an objective story of that speech" or "Scotty Reston—now *there* was an objective reporter."

Let us consider "objective reporting." It would be reporting that is detached, unprejudiced, unopinionated, uninvolved, unbiased, omniscient—and infallible, I presume. Where do we find this? The objective report would, in effect, match reality; it would tell the truth, the whole truth and nothing but the truth. Where do we find this kind of reporting? No reporter knows the truth; no reporter can write a story which can match reality, for as the general semanticists like S. I. Hayakawa point out, the "map is not the territory." The story, in other words, is never what it purports to be; it is always much bigger than its verbal image.

All reporters, in addition to being limited in their objectivity by the weakness of language, are also *conditioned* by experience, by physical state, by education, and many other factors. They do not come to their stories as blank sheets of paper on which the reality of events is to be written. They may want to be unprejudiced, balanced, thorough, and completely honest in their reporting, but they simply cannot be.

Many believe that reporters are objective when they are *detached* from the event being covered. The problem here, of course, is what is meant by detachment. Detached in the sense of being "outside" the event being reported? Detached in the sense of being uncommitted to any of the positions involved in the event being reported? Detached in the sense of being uninterested (or disinterested) in the event except as something to be reported? Detached in the sense of holding one's self aloof from the event? Detached in the sense of making sure the reporter's point of view does not impregnate the story?

The obvious answer to all of the above questions is that it is really impossible to be detached, that the reporter's subjectivity—values, biases, interpretations, and news judgments—always enter into the production of the story.

Let me briefly mention short remarks by three journalists on this subject; they abjure any pretense of a nonsubjective viewpoint:

David Brinkley: "If I were objective, or if you were objective, or if anyone was, we would have to be put away somewhere in an institution because we'd be some sort of vegetable. Objectivity is impossible to a human being."

Frank Reynolds: "I think your program has to reflect what your basic feelings are. I'll plead guilty to that."

H. L. Mencken: "We talk of objective reporting. There is no such thing. I have been a reporter for many years, and I can tell you that no reporter worth a hoot ever wrote a purely objective story. You get a point of view in it."

These brief opinions are representative of some journalists, but I doubt that very many journalists really would say such things—at least for public consumption. If journalists do not really believe in objective reporting, they should stop talking and writing as if they do. They should talk more about being accurate, about being as thorough as possible, about trying to keep overt or obvious opinions or judgments *of theirs* out of their stories. In other words, they should show that they are really *aware* that "objectivity" in journalism does not exist.

Sociologist Michael Schudson has said in his *Discovering the News* (1978) that journalistic objectivity is a faith in facts and a distrust of values—and a commitment to their segregation. Bernadette Parker-Plummer, of the University of Texas believes that most working journalists operationalize objectivity by insisting on *verification* and *attribution.* But this researcher found that there is more rhetoric here than fact. In a study of the *New York Times* and the *Los Angeles Times,* Parker-Plummer noted that there had been a "dramatic increase over time of anonymous sources in the news" (1988, 62). If two of our "elite" dailies cannot even provide attribution (so as to make verification possible), then there is little meaning left for the concept of "objectivity."

So even if we apply a rather measurable and "realistic" definition to journalistic objectivity, we can see that it is really nonexistent. And when we submit the concept to more challenging epistemological standards, it tends to evaporate altogether.

As Michael Schudson notes, while valued by the media attribution sometimes is compromised because of other factors. For example, the reporter may plead ethical motivation for withholding names of sources (or even principals in the story). I understand this and will even grant that this a correct action in some cases. But it doesn't change the fact that objectivity suffers because of it. (Actually objectivity "suffering" is not right; perhaps it would be better to say that objectivity has never been born—therefore, it cannot really "suffer.")

Of course, there may really be some who actually think that objectivity is possible in journalism. How they come to such a belief baffles me, but I often get the impression that there are such believers. Somehow they seem to think that if a reporter checks the facts, verifies all statements, eliminates all first-person pronouns, makes an attempt to present "both sides" (as if there were only two sides) of the story, then the story is objective.

Listen to John Silber, president of Boston University, who wrote on press objectivity in 1988: "Today, the practice of 'personal' journalism in news reporting has persistently sacrificed objectivity for entertainment and personal gratification—and presumably the greater popularity—of the reporter.... Too often we see and read, not what happened or what was said, but the personal view of the fourth estate."

The actual state of affairs is this: Every journalist—reporter, as well as editorial writer—goes beyond descriptive facts into interpretation. Journalists cannot be objective, even if they would like to be. Every article, every sentence, every newscast, every movement before the camera, every voice inflection on radio is *subjective*. Even the so-called straight news reporter subjectivizes the story, which is always judgmental, value-loaded, incomplete, and distorted as to reality. That is the nature of journalism. In fact, that is the nature of *any kind* of communication.

News reporters, even those wanting to be as aloof and neutral as possible, are caught in the natural trap of subjectivity. They involve themselves, their ideas, their values in the story—even though they may ostensibly (verbally) keep themselves out. They are there nevertheless. They decide what aspects of the story to put in and which to leave out. They decide on the emphasis to be given various parts, which quotes to use, which parts of quotes to use, or whether to use quotes at all. When they paraphrase instead of using direct quotes, they, in essence, become *translators* and their interpretive powers come into play. Although this is not objective reporting, there is really nothing intrinsically wrong with it.

Michael Novak, writing about the journalist and objectivity, makes the following pertinent observations:

> The myth of objectivity leads to ... misunderstandings in American journalism. There are no facts "out there" apart from human observers. And human observers become not more, but less astute when they try to be neutral....

> Reporters and newscasters know that if they aim at objectivity, at presenting "the facts" without editorializing, they run the risk of giving dignity to nonsense, drivel, and outright lies. What really happened in an event is not, they know, discovered by some neutral observation machine, not even by a camera. Events are not events until they are interpreted by human beings. . . . To list statistics, or outwardly observable happenings, or quotations from witnesses, is to give a very narrow view of the human world. It is to offer interpretation and editorial comment of a very misleading sort. Reality does not come divided into "facts" and "interpretation" (1971, 40).

Novak's remarks are in the tradition of other thinkers and critics like Paul Tillich, Martin Buber, and Jean-Paul Sartre in the existentialist camp, who have great respect for subjectivity. They have attacked the "emptiness" of empirical and pragmatic objectivity beloved by Americans especially. They have said that, not only is this belief in objectivity contrary to linguistic philosophy (and they could have said also to the principles of general semantics), but it demeans and devalues the individual person and the concept of intersubjectivity.

The business of journalism is really subjective from beginning to end. And reporting is no exception. There may be an "image" of objectivity in some stories—a linguistic aura of objectivity. But behind this aura is the reporter's subjectivity; there is never any real objectivity in reporting.

Reporters are not mindless, soulless automatons who roam about without values, opinions, and preferences—simply soaking up reality and spouting it out completely. They have their prejudices, their biases, their values, their favorite topics, their heroes, and their villains. We may wish oftentimes that there were some robotized, completely unbiased and bland reporters who could report "objectively," but they do not exist.

As Donald McDonald said in a seminal article, a reporter's values are necessarily injected into the story.

> The value judgments [the journalist] must make at every critical stage in his investigation and interpretation of the facts must reflect the values he already holds. Again, these values flow from his personal history. They are products of his education, his religious experience, his childhood, family life, social and economic background, friendships and associations, national ties and culture, as well as his emotional life and experiences, and his reason (1975, 29–42).

The context in which a story happens cannot be fully reported. But the reporter's inability to explicate the total context keeps a story from being objective. In a story about a political speech, not only the words that a speaker speaks, but how the speaker says those words is part of the story of the speech. What the speaker thinks while speaking is part of the story—a part unavailable to the reporter at the time of the speech. To speculate about it would be "subjective." To leave it out is to fail to be "objective."

Audience reaction, speaker movements, gestures, smiles, and the like form part of the objective story. The *totality* of the story is the story—the truth, the whole truth, and nothing but the truth. But the reporter cannot give all this truth, so he or she strains the objective portions of the story through a mental, emotional, and psychological strainer and thereby presents the audience with a necessarily subjective account of "what happened."

Journalists are selective. They are forced by the nature of their craft to select certain facts to report, certain quotations to bring to light, certain individuals to interview, certain perspectives to give, certain aspects of an event to expose. And what happens to the other facts, individuals, perspectives, and aspects in a story? Are not they also part of the objectivity of the story? The answer to the question is that many parts of the story are ignored completely. If they are not totally ignored, they are slighted, deemphasized, or distorted in some way that keeps them from completing the objectivity of the story.

There may be something that can be called *verifiable journalism*. If as a reporter I write, "John Doe stole six cows from W. H. Arden of Winchester," and if this is indeed what happened, then that sentence is factual and verifiable. That one aspect of the story is true—in the sense that it has no overt errors in it. But when that sentence is put into a context with other sentences to make "a story," then its nonobjective nature is exposed. This sentence may be factual and as "objective" as a single sentence can be, but when it is made part of a total story, then we must begin looking at the story and not just at the sentence.

What are the gaps in the story? What is the totality of the "story" out there in reality, and what has it become in its verbal nature in the story? In essence, what happened in reality that is left out in the story? Is there a correlation between the real event and the verbal picture of the event?

Also harming the reportorial objectivity is bias. Many recent commentators (for example, Rothman and Lichter, 1986, and William Rusher, 1988) have scored the press for ideological bias in its news presentation. Woody West of the *Washington Times* offers such criticism when he contends that the press has departed from traditional sentiments and principles of the people and is substantially to the left of most Americans. He quotes a 1989 *Times Mirror* survey which says that 48 percent of the sample believed the press was "tilted" (West, 1988, 64).

Many persons will say that journalistic objectivity is not meant to be total, that partial objectivity is what is really meant by those defending objectivity. When we consider such a "partial" concept, however, we run into trouble immediately: just how partial can objectivity be? At what point will it cease being objective?

A British provincial editor, Arnold Hadwin of Bradford, has said that total objectivity might well be impossible, but that "most people recognize and welcome objectivity that is less than total" (1980, 29). People may welcome *something* that is "less than total" but it is not objectivity. Objectivity is total. And one wonders how Mr. Hadwin knows that most people recognize and welcome such partial objectivity. Why would people—especially most people—recognize objectivity that is less than total? Is it recognizable in any degree less than total? Let's say that I read a news story and say to myself: "I recognize less than total objectivity here." What have I said about objectivity or about the nature of the story? Nothing—or perhaps that I know that journalism is really always less than objective. And if it is less than objective, it is not objective.

Armand Mattelart, a French Marxist sociologist, calls objectivity the "golden rule of journalistic practice, the cornerstone of its professional deontology, and the equivalent of the Hippocratic oath" (1980, 39). But he does not believe it. He questions the concept by saying that: (1) The concept presupposes on the part of the journalist certain perceptive powers capable of penetrating reality and determining what is important and what is not; (2) the concept postulates that the description of facts (which are *what they are in themselves*, and not what the journalist *sees* them to be) goes no further than the facts themselves; and (3) facts are isolated by objectivity-oriented journalism, "cut off from their roots, deprived of the conditions which would explain their occurrence, and detached from the social system which endows them with meaning and in which they possess an intelligible place" (Mattelart, 1980, 39).

Many writers excoriate those who, like Mattelart, maintain that journalistic objectivity is a myth. For example, John DeMott, a journalism professor at Memphis State University, speaking at the Defense Information School at Fort Benjamin Harrison in 1976, called such people naive, foolish, and lacking in imagination. He even hinted that such persons might be subscribers to Communist theory. But H. L. Mencken took much the same view as Mattelart, and he was certainly no Communist.

Professor DeMott, like many of those who claim to believe in journalistic objectivity, seems to subscribe to a belief in the relativity or the incompleteness of "objectivity." He seems to be an absolutist—except when it comes to objectivity; then, he begins using all sorts of modifiers (like *greater* objectivity and *superior* objectivity), to weaken or lessen journalistic objectivity. Tell the whole truth and nothing but the truth, Professor DeMott concluded in his speech: "That's objective reporting—journalistic objectivity, pure and simple." Pure and simple? Good! When I find a journalist who gives the *whole* truth and *nothing but* the truth, I will capitulate and admit that, after all, there really is journalistic objectivity.

Argument summation: Journalistic objectivity is not possible.

Objectivity may be a worthy goal, but it is unrealizable certainly in regard to the press. In no way can a journalist be detached, unprejudiced, unopinionated, unbiased, and omniscient. The journalist must *select*, organize, and manipulate facts; that is the nature of journalism. From beginning to end, journalism is a *subjective* enterprise. No reporter knows the truth; certainly he or she cannot report it. A story of an event is no more than a partial (and poor) image of the real event out there in reality. Journalists are subjectivists, personally conditioned, and are able to provide audiences no more than superficial "maps" of the real territory.

RESPONSE

Dennis: Journalistic objectivity is possible.

There is considerable irony in this debate because the prevailing view of objectivity today—shared by journalists and critics alike and persuasively summarized by John Merrill—was heresy in the 1960s. At that time (and for a thirty- or forty-year period) objectivity was the dominant philosophy that guided most of the nation's newsrooms. Those who criticized objective journalism as a myth that was beyond human capability were hooted down by defensive editors who declared that impartial and balanced reporting could be achieved and that true objectivity was a noble goal.

With great pride, Alan Barth of the *Washington Post* wrote in 1950 that "the tradition of objectivity is one of the principal glories of American journalism." Nineteen years later, Herbert Brucker of the *Hartford Courant* agreed, writing, "We can do a good job . . . as long as we keep the flag of objectivity flying high. That will give a more honest and more accurate view of this imperfect world than trusting a latter day Trotsky, or any partisan on any side, to tell us what's what." The preceding essay reviewed some of the reasons that objectivity became an object of scorn and derision. Critics declared that "everyone is subjective and journalists have no magic powers to be otherwise." And almost everyone who had ever had a psychology course agreed.

Sometimes we forget that objectivity is merely a method and style of presenting information. Its defenders, who led the press out of a sorry period of partisan sensationalism in the 1920s, said it had three principal characteristics, namely:

1. Separating fact from opinion.

2. Presenting an emotionally detached view of the news.

3. Striving for fairness and balance, giving both sides an opportunity to reply in a way that provides full information to the audience.

What is wrong with this straightforward set of goals is that they are too simplistic and assume that complex situations can always be reduced to a balanced presentation with two alternative views. Such an approach leaves little room for ambiguity.

Beyond the underlying philosophical problems associated with objectivity was the operational difficulty in the "inverted pyramid" story, which was the mode by which objective accounts were presented to the public. In its pristine form, objective news reports contain the 5Ws and the H, and they organize information in a descending order of importance. This journalistic style was often criticized as cold and lifeless. It was also said to obscure the truth. It was what the sociologist Gaye Tuchman called a "strategic ritual," wherein journalists used four procedures to lay claim to objectivity:

1. Presentation of conflicting possibilities.
2. Presentation of supporting evidence.
3. The judicious use of quotation marks.
4. Structuring information in an appropriate sequence.

Objectivity came under attack most significantly during the 1960s and 1970s when there was a flurry of new journalistic styles and standards. Although some of them were not altogether unknown before, they constituted a journalistic movement that expressed dissatisfaction with the status quo and brought change. At the center of this movement was a vigorous assault on the concept of objectivity. Some of the developments in journalism were:

1. *The New Journalism*—with writers using such literary devices as extensive description, dialogue, interior monologue, and others previously discouraged by spare prose 5W editors.

2. *Advocacy journalism*—with its unabashed support for particular issues and causes by journalists opposing the impartial, objective tradition.

3. *Investigative reporting*—which took an adversarial stance and sometimes proposed solutions to problems as it uncovered corruption and moved well beyond the scope of disinterested, stenographic reporting.

4. *Service journalism* or the marketing approach to news—which employed a different definition of news, emphasizing that which is commonplace and of interest to the greatest number of people, rather than that which is unique and new. With this approach both the selection of material to be covered and the unity of style aim at identifying closely with the audience. Stories aim at all homeowners, not just unusual ones. This form of journalism (discussed in Chapter 10) relies heavily on market research.

5. *Precision journalism*—which is the use of social science methods, including survey research, as reportorial tools to determine what is happening in the community.

All of these approaches claimed to be more *objective* than traditional objectivity. New journalists said they provided greater tone, texture, and feeling than cold, lifeless objective reports. "What we have here," said Tom Wolfe, "is a subjective reality. It is really more objective than traditional reporting." Advocacy journalists also claimed that they came closer to the truth than their more conventional colleagues. "We all have a point of view," they said, "so why not admit it—up front." Journalists all too often presented facts, but missed the truth, wrote Raymond Mungo. Marketing approach journalists said, "We're giving people what they want. Our news is more pertinent and relevant." And precision journalists added, "We move beyond the limits of intuition. We use computers and statistics to give the most representative picture of the community that is humanly possible within the constraints of a news organization."

In the face of such criticism, support for objectivity crumbled. While much of the criticism of objectivity as it was articulated and understood in the 1950s and 1960s is warranted, I think that it went too far. As is often the case when a prevailing mode of thought is abandoned, those who push the new view feel a need to drive a stake though the heart of the old one. In this case, it does us no service. The wave of new styles and reportorial approaches has definitely enriched American journalism, but it is time once again to look carefully at objectivity before abandoning it altogether. Objectivity fell out of favor because it was seen as an impossible goal. Maybe that judgment was too hasty. Objectivity deserves another chance. What is objectivity, anyway? According to *Webster's Third New International Dictionary*, objective means:

> ... publicly or intersubjectively observable or verifiable, especially by scientific means ... independent of what is personal or private in our apprehension or feelings ... of such a nature that rational minds agree in holding it real or true or valid ... expressing or involving the use of facts without distortion by personal feelings or prejudices.

Is this so wild a dream? No one would argue that journalists can achieve perfection, but is it impossible within the context of human frailty to try to be disinterested, not meaning uninterested or indifferent, but impartial? Is it impossible to observe and report those perceptions so that others can verify them if they choose to do so? Can we not reach some consensus about what is happening in our neighborhoods or communities and still leave room for differing interpretations and speculative views? To all of these questions, I would answer with a resounding "yes."

I believe that journalistic objectivity is possible if we adopt methods that lead to systematic decisions. We can borrow from some of the admirable new styles that have emerged in recent years and use the tools of rational decision making. This need not be a complex scholarly endeavor that is well beyond the daily resources of the media, but a practical strategy that will make journalism better and more reliable. I would do this in three ways: first, through strategic planning in the reporting process; secondly, through the use of systematic tools to analyze communities and gather information; and thirdly, through the clear delineation of the presentation form used.

STRATEGIC PLANNING

For a number of years American corporations have engaged in strategic planning. They have corporate strategies that involve an agreed-upon approach, an understanding of the major decision-making points, and a well-calibrated effort to make the best possible choices. The relation of benefit to cost is always a central concern. Practical decisions are made with the expectation they will yield the best possible results. What we can learn from this approach in journalism is that news gathering and news making involve choices that can be made on a rational basis. They need not be purely subjective. Writer Ronald Buel says that news is essentially data that must be made into a product. This process involves a series of interrelated decisions. (Buel's framework is in italics below.)

1. *Data assignment: What is worth covering and why?* This will depend on the type of publication and its purpose. If the purpose of a newspaper is to cover the whole community as adequately as possible, it is not difficult to inventory various components of community life. This categorization may mean moving away from the old beat system that emphasizes what happens in public buildings (the courthouse, etc.) and to consider such issues as lifestyle, the workplace, business, fads and trends, and the environment. Within the paper's particular definition of news, it is not difficult to make rational decisions that can be defined and justified. For example, in the coverage of a political campaign, the paper should be able to explain how it covered various candidates, why some were deemed more important than others. This ought to result in a view of the race with which other observers would concur if given the paper's original assumptions about news. It would also take into account such economic factors as staff size.

2. *Data collection: When has enough information been gathered?* Again, this is a matter of definition. But there are reasonable standards by which trained reporters know when they have assembled enough information to answer the key questions that make a complete story. Again, outsiders looking in ought to be able to understand the basis for decisions. The test here is whether, within the goals of a particular story, all of the critical questions have been answered with evidence from appropriate sources. This standard of "reasonable completeness" is frequently used in defense against libel suits, and news organizations are increasingly being asked to explain their "thresholds" for finished work.

3. *Data evaluation: What is important enough to be put into a story?* Once information is gathered, only part of it can typically be included in

the story. What part? And why? Sometimes new reporters make a priority list, especially if they are asked to cut a long story to meet the space demands of an editor who cannot accommodate their first submission. This decision ought to be rational. If, for example, a reporter is covering a trial, it is not difficult to list basic facts, key sources, and interpretations. If this list must be reduced markedly, the real test is what is essential to full and accurate presentation.

4. *Data writing: What words and images will be used?* Good writing means imaginative writing, which involves interpretations that are not always verifiable. Writing adds tone and complexity of perception. Still, it is not difficult to write in such a way that the writer's impressions, legitimately expressed, are distinguished from purely factual information. This technique will provide a somewhat subjective portrait, of course, but still it ought to come close to what an average reader might have ascertained had he been on the scene. After all, journalists writing for mass media (as opposed to literary or specialized publications) should use words and images that are generally understood.

5. *Data editing: Which story should get a big headline and go on the front page or begin a broadcast, and which stories should be buried, which should be changed, and which should be cut?* Again, we return to the "corporate strategy" of the news organization. What is most vital to the audience? Once that is understood, decisions can be made about cutting material or providing emphasis. The underlying policies of media organizations are based on values. These may be that news of government is more important than that of business because it affects more people, and so forth. Nonetheless, it is important that orderly, consistent decisions be made so that readers have a clear understanding of the rules of the game. Naturally, values always play an important role. It is not possible to have universal answers to the questions raised in the Buel framework for all societies. The appropriate response in Lagos, Nigeria, will not be the same as that in Austin, Texas.

MODE OF PRESENTATION

There are at least three general types of journalistic presentation that ought to be considered. The chart on page 121 explains.

Descriptive stories can easily be verified. Certain facts are presented and can be corroborated, even if there is disagreement about details. With analytic stories we can usually inventory possible sources on a given topic. They can be listed and individual views set forth. The reporter brings an interpretive or sense-making perspective to the story, but this can be discerned by anyone who reads the story carefully. Also, if the reporter omits a possible source, the reader should be able to see this and evaluate accordingly. Consequential stories are trickier, but they too can be presented impartially as statements of conjecture and speculation.

THREE MODELS FOR NEWS REPORTING AND WRITING FEATURE STORIES*

	CHARACTERISTICS: USES	QUESTIONS ANSWERED	EXAMPLES
Descriptive story	A straightforward description of the basic facts of a situation or event—terse, to-the-point, spare writing; the minimum requirements to make sense to the reader. The nature and scope of the event or issue, major sources.	Who What Where When	Spot news stories, event coverage, singular instance coverage (e.g., natural disaster, election, parade, demonstration)
Analytical story	A story focusing on the forces at work, the competing interests, points of view, possible explanations and interpretations of how and why the situation or event occurred.	How Why	Backgrounders explaining the forces (seen and unseen) behind the event or issue; shows how multiple sources, different views influenced event (e.g., stories chronicling a political decision)
Consequential story	What the story means, both currently and in the long term. Sometimes speculative, based on authoritative sources. What consequence does it have for individuals? The community? Others?	So What	Interpretive stories that grapple with meaning of issues, events, problems. Useful in trend coverage, process stories; sometimes speculative future reports (e.g., what a tax reform will mean to citizens).

* From Everette E. Dennis and Arnold H. Ismach, *Reporting Processes and Practices, Newswriting for Today's Readers* (Belmont, CA: Wadsworth, 1981), 171.

Armand Mattelart (1980) would no doubt see this process as astoundingly presumptuous, with journalists assuming superhuman powers to penetrate reality. But then, the very act of being a journalist, of presuming to report what is happening, is by definition presumptuous. However, this process is the social function of journalism and it can be done systematically in a manner that withstands examination. The true test is whether reasonable people in the same cultural setting would have similar, if not always the same, perceptions of the event or issue if they were to have done their own reporting. Certainly a highly trained lawyer will see a trial differently from the average person, but this difference does not negate the fact that mass communication aims at the mass audience and tries to make connections with a norm. The press is the surrogate of the people in our society—it represents them as their eyes and ears—and it has an obligation to present intelligent and understandable reports that give a reasonably representative picture of society. Objectivity in journalism or science does not nean that all decisions do not have underlying values, only that within the "rules of the game" a systematic attempt is made to achieve an impartial report.

Argument Summation: Journalistic objectivity is possible.

Objectivity is merely a method or style of presenting information. During the 1960s and 1970s new styles of journalism led to an assault on objectivity, which fell out of favor as an impossible goal. However, impartiality is not beyond the capabilities of the modern journalist if procedures are followed providing for systematic decisions. This process should include strategic planning in the reporting process, the use of systematic tools to analyze communities and gather information, and clear delineation of the presentation form used. Following such guides would allow the reporters to report impartially on their communities or, at worst, properly distinguish subjective conclusion from fact. The goal should be to present the story so that individuals reading the report would have had the same perspective if they had been present themselves. That objective is not impossible in modern journalism, but it does require a systematic attempt to provide an impartial report.

——— TOPICS FOR DISCUSSION ———

1. How can a person—a *subjective* entity—write or present an *objective* story?

2. What do you think most journalists mean by "journalistic objectivity"? According to this meaning, do you think journalists are (or can be) objective?

3. Is it possible to give "the truth, the whole truth, and nothing but the truth" in a news story? How does truth relate to objectivity?

4. If a reporter refrains from naming a source of a quote in the story, or decides not to give the name of a juvenile offender, can the story be "objective"?

5. The "New Journalism" of the 1960s was said by its adherents to be more objective than Associated Press-type journalism. What do you think they meant? Do you think they were right?

TOPICS FOR RESEARCH

1. Compare and contrast objectivity in science or social science with objectivity in journalism. How do they differ in concept and practice? Indicate how a clinically objective scientific investigation might differ from a report a journalist would call objective. Use specific examples by comparing a research article in *Science Magazine* or some scientific journal with a news report in a publication like the *Wall Street Journal*. How do the "investigator's" methods differ? How much evidence is offered? What of interpretation?

2. Write an essay about the concept of "fairness." What is it? How is it defined and operationalized in the media? How would you advise laypersons about how they might judge the fairness of the media in covering a particular story or event? Assess, if you like, two or three different accounts of the same event from a standpoint of "fairness."

3. Discuss advocacy journalism. What is it? How does it differ from objective journalism?

4. Write a personal essay about how you would try to be objective (if indeed you would) in gathering information about any controversial subject you choose. Be specific and indicate how you would decide which sources to contact, which to quote, how to sum up.

5. Write an essay that takes the middle ground somewhere between Merrill and Dennis on objectivity. Assume that both are giving you their best-case advocacy position. On what points do you agree, disagree?

FURTHER READING

Cohen, Stanley, and Jock Young, eds. *The Manufacture of News.* Beverly Hills, CA: Sage, 1973.

Dennis, E. E., and A. H. Ismach. *Reporting Processes and Practices: Newswriting for Today's Readers.* Belmont, CA: Wadsworth, 1981. See especially Chapters 1–2.

DeFleur, M. L., and E. E. Dennis. *Understanding Mass Communication.* Boston: Houghton Mifflin, 1981. See especially Chapter 12, 417–45.

DeMott, John. "The News Media's Quest for Objectivity." *Vital Speeches of the Day* 42, no. 24 (1 October 1976): 744–67.

Epstein, Edward Jay. *Between Fact and Fiction: The Problem of Journalism.* New York: Vintage Books, 1975.

Gans, Herbert. *Deciding What's News.* New York: Pantheon, 1979.

Hadwin, Arnold. "Objectivity is Crucial—But Is It Possible to Be Objective?" *Journalism Studies Review* (Cardiff, U. K.: July, 1980).

Hayakawa, S. I. *Language in Thought and Action.* 5th ed. New York: Harcourt Brace Jovanovich, 1990.

Hunt, Todd. "Beyond the Journalistic Event: The Changing Concept of News." *Mass Communication Review* 1 (April 1974): 23–30.

Korzybski, Alfred. *Science and Sanity.* Lancaster, PA: Science Press Printing Co., 1933.

Lichter, S. R., S. Rothman, and L. Lichter. *The Media Elite.* Bethesda, MD: Adler & Adler, 1986.

Manoff, Robert Karl, and Michael Schudson, eds. *Reading the News.* New York: Pantheon, 1986.

Mattelart, Armand. *Mass Media, Ideologies, and the Revolutionary Movement.* Atlantic Highlands, NJ: Humanities Press, 1980. See especially discussion of objectivity, 37 ff.

McDonald, Donald. "Is Objectivity Possible?" In *Ethics and the Press,* J. C. Merrill and Ralph Barney, eds., 69–72. New York: Hastings House, 1975.

Merrill, J. C. "Objective Reporting: A Myth, However Valuable . . . " *The Quill* (July 1969): 26–27.

———. *The Imperative of Freedom.* New York: Hastings House, 1974. See especially "Quest for Objectivity," 156–61.

Novak, Michael. *The Experience of Nothingness.* New York: Harper Colophon Books, 1971. See especially discussion of objectivity, 37–40.

Roshco, Bernard. *Newsmaking.* Chicago: University of Chicago Press, 1975.

Rubin, Bernard. *Media, Politics, and Democracy.* New York: Oxford University Press, 1977. See especially Chapter 1.

Rusher, W. A. *The Coming Battle for the Media.* New York: William Morrow, 1988.

Schudson, Michael. *Discovering the News.* Cambridge, MA: Harvard University Press, 1978.

Tuchman, Gaye. "Objectivity as Strategic Ritual: An Examination of Newsmen's Notions of Objectivity." *American Journal of Sociology* 77, no. 4 (January 1972), 660–67.

West, Woody. "A Harsh Indictment of the Press." *Insight* (9 May 1988).

Chapter 10

DECIDING WHAT IS NEWS

What is sometimes called the "news-making" process is the result of a daily bargaining process between various personnel in newspapers and broadcast stations. Editors look at the world they cover with particular standards and measures. They attempt to direct reporters to cover the most interesting, newsworthy material. There are some generally accepted definitions of news and these provide the justification for what appears in the newspaper and on the newscasts. Many competing forces want space in the news columns or on newscasts. Some are self-serving, external persons who want their stories told sympathetically and well; others are reporters who want their work in the paper; still others are subtle influences ranging from values and habits to personal preferences. A standard view is that, at the bottom line, news is determined by editors and that editors' (or other gatekeepers') judgments should, in fact, decide what is news. There can be no mechanical standard, it is said, because the news of the day is dynamic and its results are uncertain. Therefore, the well-trained editor or news director makes judgments reflecting prevailing journalistic practices and the specific needs of the audience as perceived by upper management. This, it is further stated, is the essence of journalistic (and other media) leadership. It is, after all, the job of editors to edit.

CHALLENGE

Dennis: Market forces, not editors' judgments, should decide what is news.

There is a long-standing, persistent debate among media professionals and media critics about what news is and who should make decisions about it. Editors and reporters say with much assurance that they and they alone should make decisions about news, determining what will appear in the news columns and on newscasts and what will not. Some critics of the press, for example people in business, say that the sources of news, those quoted in stories or covered in some fashion, should have a role in defining and shaping the news. In actuality, news decisions are made by journalistic professionals with little guidance from anyone, no matter how much their detractors may complain. This situation is changing, though, as intuitive judgments are being challenged more and more by market forces, which we learn about most effectively through market research. In my view, this change is good, and I hope that before long many of today's smug, all-knowing editors will replace their seat-of-the-pants (or skirt) decisions with more thoughtful, better-researched, systematic decision-making. To such persons, this position is heresy, of course.

For as long as anyone can remember editors (with the help of various minions) have decided what will grace the pages of newspapers or appear on newscasts and what will not. They have engaged in a hard selection process, elevating some items to importance and public exposure while relegating others to the wastebasket. Editors are hired to make these judgments and, for the most part, they do so with the best of intentions. But how are these judgments made and are they the right ones? Against what set of criteria are news items and stories selected? On what basis are others deemed unworthy of coverage?

Most editors would tell you that they make their choices from among those news stories that they assign or that flow in from their regular channels (such as wire services), and they do so with proper regard for their audience. They would also tell you that they rely heavily on the "budgets" of the wire services (priority lists of stories deemed important or significant), as well as taking cues from such major national media as the *New York Times, Washington Post,* and the three major television networks. What will interest the audience is of paramount importance for, after all, if readers and viewers are not attentive, newspaper circulations may drop and broadcast ratings may falter. This situation would push revenues down and the editor might be fired or see the paper die.

It came as a surprise to many editors when in 1947 the Hutchins Commission on Freedom of the Press, a privately funded, blue-ribbon group that evaluated the news media, suggested that the media were failing to give readers a representative account of the day's news, let alone present a "representative picture" of the constituent groups of society. As with most media criticism, however just, editors rejected these ideas wholesale. The issue raised by the commission, however, continues to raise its head at professional meetings and in scholarly critiques of the media. The definition of news is the subject of much wrangling and for good reason. I believe that a new approach to news decision-making is needed more than ever.

1. News is a highly complex formulation that requires the best intelligence and a thoughtful strategy for professionals to fashion it properly.

2. Editors and reporters are elitists, unrepresentative of their readers and viewers and unable to act effectively on their behalf.

3. A marketing approach to news is the most effective and efficient way to select and present news that is of interest to and pertinent for the audience. In such a system, market research findings, which indicate reader and viewer preferences, are used to decide news.

Ask journalism students if they know what news is and they will tell you, "Yes, of course." Ask them to define it and confusion sets in. News is difficult to define, which explains why there is a lively continuing debate among many persons trying to sort it out. All kinds of people—journalists, sociologists, political scientists, news sources, and others—have engaged in this exercise. It is more than a theoretical discussion because knowing and understanding what news is can have real payoffs. Imagine the political candidate whose idea of news differs radically from that of the local editor. The candidate is likey soon to be a former (and defeated) candidate if that view persists. The same is true for others who want to place something in the news.

In a rather scornful view of news, Henry David Thoreau once wrote:

> I am sure that I have never read any memorable news in a newspaper. If we read of one man robbed, or murdered, or killed by accident, or one house burned, or one vessel wrecked, or one steamboat blown up, or one cow run over on the Western Railroad, or one mad dog killed, or one lot of grasshoppers in the winter—we never need read of another. If you are acquainted with the principle, what do you care for myriad instances and applications? To a philosopher all news, as it is called, is gossip, and they who read it or edit it are old women over their tea (Thoreau, 1854, 148–49).

Thoreau clearly identifies some of the negative characteristics of news. Some commentators have tried to explain the difference between facts, truth, and news with less than full success. Walter Lippmann once wrote that "news is not a mirror of social conditions, but the report of an aspect that has obtruded itself." One famous definition of news is attributed to John Bogart of the *New York Sun*, who allegedly said in 1880, "When a dog bites a man, that is not news, but if a man bites a dog, that is news!" Newscaster David Brinkley would seem to agree: "News," he said, "is the unusual, the unexpected. Placidity is not news. If an airplane departs on time, it isn't news. If it crashes, regrettably, it is."

Some of the standard criteria that are said to make up the news are

1. conflict (tension-surprise)
2. progress (triumph-achievement)

3. disaster (defeat-destruction)
4. consequences (effect upon community)
5. eminence (prominence)
6. novelty (the unusual, even the extremely unusual)
7. human interest (emotional background)
8. timeliness (freshness and newness)
9. proximity (local appeal)

Sociologist and distinguished analyst of the news Bernard Roshco says that all news has a dual origin. It is a *social* product that represents an effort to make sense out of what is happening in society, and it is an *organizational* product representing what the news organization decides to do with it.

After reading scores of articles and treatises on news, Melvin DeFleur and I came up with this definition that reflects some of the factors that go into news:

> News is a report that presents a contemporary view of reality with regard to a specific issue, event, or process. It usually monitors change that is important to individuals or society and puts that change in the context of what is common or characteristic. It is shaped by a consensus about what will interest the audience and by constraints from outside and inside the organization. It is the result of a daily bargaining game within the news organization that sorts out the observed human events of a particular time period to create a very perishable product. News is the imperfect result of hurried decisions made under pressure (DeFleur and Dennis, 1981, 422).

This is not to suggest that our definition of news changes daily. It does not. There is considerable consistency over time as to what editors deem newsworthy; the similarity (some would say sameness) of our newspapers and newscasts suggests considerable agreement about what news is under most conditions.

One aspect of what constitutes news is to be found, then, in the external events that await report. In addition, the consideration of what is news partly depends on the audience to whom it is directed. The journalist and the editor are supposedly acting as and on behalf of "everyman" in deciding what is worth reporting. It is said that they have a built-in understanding of their readers and viewers if they are any good in their jobs. After all, readers and viewers are the journalists' next door neighbors, friends, companions at sports. While this vision of the journalist may be true in very small communities, for the most part it is far from the mark. Editors and reporters are part of an elite. They simply are not like most of the citizens of the community. They are better educated, more liberal politically, less religious, more likely to be single, to live in an apartment, (as opposed to a single-family dwelling), and to have both social and cultural values quite distant from others around them. National studies have documented this condition for a number of years. They draw a portrait of journalists as relatively isolated and out of touch with their communities. As one reporter was quoted in a 1982 study:

> It is an inherent problem; inbred newspapers don't trust the people they are writing about. . . . Especially the younger reporters are getting removed from society. They come from different backgrounds than the average public. [Theirs is] a snobbish view of the world (Burgoon, Burgoon, and Atkin, 1982, 5).

That study, based on a national survey conducted for the American Society of Newspaper Editors, went on to say that journalists underestimate reader intelligence, have a poor understanding of what people will actually read, and simply do not comprehend the role of television in delivering news to people who also read newspapers. The report was a stinging indictment of the press that was not out of line with a more impressionistic speech by Kurt Luedtke, mentioned earlier in this book. Luedtke charges that his former colleagues in the media suffer from the twin perils of "arrogance and irrelevance." Arrogance keeps them unpleasantly off the track with readers; irrelevance could spell doom in an era when other information sources (data banks provided by cable systems or the telephone company) can supply much of the factual information (sports scores, weather reports) that people now gain from newspaper and television news. There are a number of steps that editors and reporters can take to get and stay in touch with their communities, but nothing will change the inevitable. Journalists will continue to be elitists, continue to be unlike their readers and viewers.

A marketing approach to news makes news decisions less of a guessing game and more of a thoughtful, systematic process that takes into account the interests and needs of the audience. The marketing approach to news is nothing new. In fact in the 1970s when newspaper circulations were sliding downward, a national Newspaper Readership Project, which has been written about in many books on newspapers and news reports such as Leo Bogart's (1989) *The Press and the Public*, collected data about reader interests, preferences, and reading habits. As a result many American newspapers changed their formats radically, offering special sections on lifestyles, neighborhoods, and entertainment. News was packaged differently, with livelier design and more vivid writing. For example, a news story on a zoning ordinance would begin by suggesting the consequences of the news story for potential homeowners, rather than simply summarizing the action of the zoning board in a procedural manner. The story would likely be presented with striking photos or line drawings and readable, attractive headlines.

The marketing approach to news depends on a regular and accurate flow of statistical data about the audience. The data are then used as one factor, a central one, in determining what will be offered to the audience and in what manner. News is matched to the interests and potential interests of the audience. Some critics have called this approach "soft and sexy in the afternoon," suggesting that a marketing approach must always emphasize soft news rather than important news of public affairs. The best papers using the marketing approach, however, have an effective blend of editorial leadership, wherein professional journalists make news selections and prepare material with strategies for reaching the reader. Those strategies depend largely on marketing research data. This process is not a mindless one where journalists succumb to hardhearted statistics while ignoring professional ethics and a desire to be complete in their coverage of a community issue or problem. Information is a calibrating tool that, when used by intelligent people, can result in a higher quality product. Market information gives news organizations a continuous source of feedback from their readers and viewers, something that is lacking in many places today.

Any discussion of the marketing approach to news naturally revives the old debate of whether the press should give readers what they want or provide leadership that gives citizens what they need. I believe that the two are not incompatible, that the public is ultimately better served if market information plays a more important role in guiding editors' decisions. If today's newspapers and television stations guided mainly by intuition are so far out of touch, it is worth making our best effort to bridge the gap. Market information, intelligently used, will do it.

Argument Summation: Market forces, not editors' judgments, should decide what is news.

Editors have too much control over selecting what news to present to the public. Selection emphasizes the editors' personal biases and fails to give a representative account of the day's news. Since news is difficult to define and numerous perspectives exist on what actually is news, it is preferable to have news selection determined by market forces, which give a broader account of events, rather than relying on an editor's preferences alone. Research shows that editors tend to be part of an isolated elite and that this lack of interaction with and understanding of the public results in poor decisions about what is news. A marketing approach focuses instead upon a regular and accurate flow of statistical data about the audience. This systematic criterion based on market forces is preferable because it relies on the interests and needs of the audience in defining "news."

RESPONSE

Merrill: Editors' judgments, not market forces, should decide what is news.

Unfortunately perhaps, my coauthor has challenged a proposition that is not contradictory to what he is advocating. What Dennis seems to be saying, though he only gets to it in the last several paragraphs of his essay, is that news should be determined by a regular and accurate study of audience desires. In this view, the audience and not the editor determines what is news. The editor, in the Dennis perspective of news, is consigned to a mechanistic role whereby he or she serves as a short-order cook preparing only what the customer orders. This is harsh pragmatism, crass capitalism carried too far, in my opinion.

The marketing approach to news relegates the press to a powerless dispenser of desired services. Editors take on a strange role; they do not make decisions, but only grant requests. They do not determine what their audiences need or should have; rather they provide the news that the audiences—the real editors in the marketing approach—say they want. In effect, if Dennis's concept of editorial leadership were taken very far, journalism would become a passive and uninspiring vocation.

Now, Dennis realizes this danger, and he tries to moderate his advocacy of the marketing approach to news by conceding that the "best papers using the marketing approach, however, have an effective blend of editorial leadership, wherein professional journalists make news selections and prepare material with strategies for reaching the reader." In other words, Dennis would have editorial leadership, while editors follow the dictates of audience research. He wants it both ways.

If this is the case, then I have very little to argue against. For I agree that market forces enter into the editor's decisions about news. Any American journalist who has ever dealt with determining what news is and how to play it has recognized the natural symbiosis between editorial decision making and audience desires. Only the most naive person would think that the editor's judgment and the audience preferences are mutually exclusive.

I am arguing that the editor (or some journalistic decision maker) should decide what is news. He or she may do this, whether taking audience desires into consideration or simply ignoring what he believes to be the will of the audience. In other words, market forces may or may not enter into the determination of news. I see news as an editorial matter, not as a public matter. This is the main business of the editor: determining what news is and how it shall be played.

No editor has ever ignored the audience. So in that sense at least, editorial determination of news has always taken market forces into consideration. But editors have generally prided themselves on their own ability to recognize and determine news. They have seen themselves as independent decision makers in journalism and not simply reactors and servants to their audiences. I feel that they have been justified in this image of themselves. Anybody who has worked for a news medium knows full well that the great majority of news decisions are made by journalists without evidence of what the audience wants. News is determined quickly, stories are selected from the many available without too much deliberation, and journalists make these determinations almost instinctively. They certainly do not have the luxury of holding various stories in abeyance until they can survey their readers to find out which of the stories might be desired. The pragmatics of journalism militates against the marketing approach to news.

This approach does not mean that the reasonable news executive does not have some general guidelines for news based on inferences drawn over time from the audience. Dennis has already presented some of the standard criteria that help determine news—and, of course, these criteria did not suddenly leap full-grown from the editor's head. Over the years, journalists came to the conclusion that *generally* these were criteria that were agreeable to news consumers. So the editors did have some overall, long-range guidelines for news; but on a daily, decision-by-decision basis, they made their own determinations as to what would be news in their news media.

As Dennis says in his "challenge," all of this brings up the old debate of whether the press should give readers what they want or what they need. I believe that the press should give readers what the editors think they want and what they need. This is, really, what the press does. What the people want can also be what they need. What they need may not, however, be what they want—that is, unless they are made somehow to realize that there are some things they need which they have not thought about needing.

A good editor is one who recognizes that it is a journalistic responsibility to provide the reader with some significant, useful news which may or may not be of great immediate interest or appeal; at the same time, editors know that, in order to get the reader exposed to such news, they must also provide types of news of a more shallow—perhaps even sensational—nature. The good editor is a pragmatist and a realist, not some one-dimensional person seeking either to entertain or to educate. The good editor wants to do both and other things as well. But in addition to being a realist, the editor is something of an idealist also, believing that readers should get certain information which they might not choose if given the chance. In this sense, the editor is much like an educator.

Editors may very well use marketing information for some of their decisions. Certainly they have access today to a considerable amount of such information. They may, however, decide not to use marketing data for their news determinations; in fact, they generally do not. They use intuition, instinct, and perceptions of news value stemming from experience and common sense. They often project their own likes and dislikes about news to their readers. This may not be scientific, but it is useful and quick—and it works very well. An editor is a kind of one-person sample, projecting to the newspaper his or her own news values. As such, the editor can retain at least the illusion of independent editorial news determination, while taking into consideration the assumed interests and desires of the audience.

Perhaps the philosophical rationale for audience-determined news is the same one that has resulted in a shift in several areas from an emphasis on the press to an emphasis on the public. Examples: increasing talk about "public access to the media" and the "public's right to know." Now we have people talking about the "public's right to determine what is news." Granted, the public (nonjournalists) can consider anything it desires to be news. As a member of the general public I have a right to determine what I want to call news; and I can pass this on to whomever I wish. But in the context of *journalism* (or of the press) such determination is up to journalists, not members of the public.

Said another way, as a private citizen I have the right to make home movies and to show them to anyone who will watch. But I do not have a right to determine for a cinema owner or a television director that my home movies will be shown in their facilities. In effect, I *can*, indeed, determine what I want to consider a "movie," but this does not, and should not, imply that I will determine what is to be shown as a movie through the mass media. This is the prerogative of the media decision makers. Market forces, of course, must be taken into consideration, for no medium of mass communication is an island. But news determination, like "movie" determination, lies with the disseminating medium.

Only a stupid or unrealistic editor would continue providing his readers with news that was not wanted or read by these readers. In fact, the newspaper would not exist very long if this were done. So it can be assumed that, in the case of viable newspapers, the editors are taking the news values of the readers seriously. However, they are not being dictated to by the readers; they can and often do go against the wishes of the readers. Admittedly, many journalistic news determiners do bow to the wishes of segments of their readership; this pandering often results in shallow, largely sensational material with negative overtones being the main news fare. Some editors do, indeed, stoop to the lowest common denominator.

But the question here is whether this *should* be the case. Should market forces determine the news? My answer is: No! An editor or any journalist responsible for news judgments should make news decisions. This is the nature of journalism. This is the responsibility and job for journalists as long as they, not nonjournalists, are in the business of news collection, definition, and dissemination.

Argument Summation: Editors' judgments, not market forces, should decide what is news.

In a free-press nation like the United States, market forces, advertisers, government, and other institutions naturally have their impact on news, but the media managers should determine what to publish or broadcast. That is the essence of press freedom in America. Obviously editors will take audience desires into consideration (when they know what they are), but these desires should not determine news decisions in a microscopic sense. The daily pragmatic nature of journalism militates against the marketing approach to news. News ebbs and flows rapidly and only journalists can make decisions as to how it is to be handled.

TOPICS FOR DISCUSSION

1. How can market research be used in the everyday newsroom decisions about news?

2. The marketing approach depends on a regular flow of statistics about the audience. Editorial staffers on a daily newspaper, therefore, would have to get this data constantly. Is this possible? If it is successful, how might this affect a publication's basic editorial policy?

3. If editors gave over their news determination right to the audience-surveyors, would they relapse into being mere functionaries with no decision-making responsibilities? How would their jobs change?

4. Would a market research approach to news constitute a new people's right—the "right to define news"—and would such a right be consistent with traditional American journalism?

5. What might be a good "compromise position" in news determination? How would it work? Is it different from what is presently done?

TOPICS FOR RESEARCH

1. Examine the proposition that editors should be quite conscious of their audience and target their work for the people who read, listen to, or view their reports. What role should the audience play in shaping the news?

2. Write a short paper on audience research in broadcasting or newspapers. What role does it play? How does it measure the relative health of a given medium?

3. What impact do ratings have on television news? Research this question by looking at the discussion in recent years involving "people meters." Does the audience data yielded by people meters tell us anything about the demographics of the audience that will likely influence the news on television?

4. Discuss news decision-making, consulting major books and studies on this subject. Can editors exercise professional standards and still please the audience?

5. Examine yourself as a "consumer" of news. If you could design your own paper tailored to your personal tastes and interests, what would it contain? What would it look like? Assume that you can create a new publication from scratch and select bits and pieces of several existing papers to create your personalized product. Discuss whether your paper would appeal to others. To whom would it appeal? Do you think there is enough of a market for it to create a niche?

FURTHER READING

Argyris, Chris, *Behind the Front Page: Organizational Self-Renewal in a Metropolitan Newspaper.* San Francisco: Jossey-Bass, 1974.

Bogart, Leo. *The Press and the Public: Who Reads What, When, Where and Why in American Newspapers.* Hillsdale, NJ: Lawrence Erlbaum Associates, 1989.

Burgoon, Judee, Michael Burgoon, and Charles Atkin. *What is News? Who Decides? And How?* A report of the American Society of Newspaper Editors. East Lansing, MI: Michigan State University, 1982.

Carey, James W. *Communication in Culture: Essays on Media and Society.* Winchester, MA: Unwin Hyman, 1988.

DeFleur, Melvin L., and Everette E. Dennis. 4th ed. *Understanding Mass Communication.* Boston: Houghton Mifflin, 1991.

Dennis, Everette E. *The Media Society: Evidence About Mass Communication in America.* Dubuque, IA: W. C. Brown, 1978. See especially Part II, "Looking Inside: The Media's Social Institutions."

Gans, Herbert. *Deciding What's News.* New York: Pantheon, 1979.

"The Business News," *Gannett Center Journal* (Spring 1987).

Gitlin, Todd. *The Whole World Is Watching: Mass Media in the Making and Unmaking of the New Left.* Berkeley, CA: University of California Press, 1980.

Sigal, Leon V. *Officials and Reporters: The Organization and Politics of Newsmaking.* Lexington, MA: D.C. Heath, 1973.

Thoreau, Henry David. *Walden, Or Life in the Woods.* Boston: Houghton Mifflin, 1854.

Chapter 11

NEWS-GATHERING TACTICS

Deeply rooted in American journalism is the notion of the *journalistic reporter*. Reporters are trained in the journalistic method, which gives them the tools and wherewithal to cover almost any situation they may confront. Essentially journalistic training means knowing how to gather the news—how to sift through documents, do background research, interview sources, and so on—and how to write a story using the usual news and feature forms employed by newspapers and broadcast outlets.

In the midst of this seemingly routine task, however, come all kinds of ethical issues (tactical decisions) including "checkbook journalism," fabrication of sources, false identification, and lying. Some of these issues, being topical, come and go. But many are recurrent.

As with news-gathering methods and writing methods, competent reporters and editors are expected to handle tactical or ethical dilemmas. But do these problems require precise and differing tactics for different situations, or responses based on *consistent and universal* standards? While such questions are regarded as worthy of debate and discussion, most reporters believe that they have somehow internalized professional values and competencies that will help them resolve any problems that may occur.

CHALLENGE

Merrill: Tactics should be situational and relative.

We come now to discuss a very real and important everyday concern of journalists: reportorial tactics, journalistic ways and means of gathering and writing stories. Should these tactics be situational and relative or should they be, as Everette Dennis will argue later, consistent and universal? I maintain that they are situational and relative; even more, I insist that they *should* be situational and relative. This position, of course, gets us into the realm of ethics.

Opposing my view, however, is a considerable theoretical tradition in this country, even if it fails to manifest itself in common practice. It is safe to say that an accepted truth in American journalism is that journalists should be consistent in their methods and their actions: They should all subscribe to universal standards and should, if they are responsible and "professional," have a profound respect for predictable and consistent practice. Consistency and predictability, we are led to believe, are foundation stones of professionalism.

Unpredictability is associated, on the other hand, with amateurism, inconsistency, and relativity, which are seen by many as deleterious to journalism, harmful to the journalist and frustrating to the audience. I would maintain just the opposite: that consistency in journalism—the journalist always using the same tactics and dealing with the elements of the story in the same way—makes for a deadly dull journalism, keeps the individual journalist from full self-realization and prevents the audience from being exposed to the multifaceted, rich, and diversified aspects of similar (but different) stories.

Perhaps it is more comfortable and satisfying for journalists to have hard-and-fast rules as to tactics of reporting. This proposition seems reasonable, but I cannot believe that it is in the best interest of the newsperson or the public to have the press tied to an absolute tactical system. Most printed codes of ethics fail because they present absolute rules or standards (or because they are so fuzzily written that they, in essence, say nothing meaningful). But perhaps their failure is, paradoxically, a good thing—for such failure assures that tactical situationalism and relativism will thrive in the absence of absolute ethical codes.

Ethics, of course, is very closely related to the subject of journalistic tactics. One cannot really separate them. Should I lie, either while getting a story or while telling the story to my readers or listeners? Should I reveal the source of certain statements or quotes which I use in my story? Should I give my readers or listeners all of the information which I have collected and verified?

These are just a sampling of questions that are both ethical and tactical:

- Should I *ever* lie as a reporter in order to get a story?
- Should I *always* reveal my sources? (Or *never* reveal them?)
- Shall I try to ascertain the *whole truth* (as much of it as I can) for my audience?

Here we have introduced the possibility of tactical consistency or absoluteness. Such consistency has a notable appeal. If I am going to reveal the source in one case, why should I not reveal all sources? If I am going to lie in one case, why not in all? If I am going to withhold part of a story in one case, what would be wrong with withholding parts from any story?

Let me give an example of each of the two tactical positions:

1. Absolute: *Always* ascertain the names of victims of all crimes.

2. Relativistic: Ascertain the names of victims in *some* crimes but not in others.

The first tactic (the absolute) does, indeed, simplify the journalist's decision making. If this tactic is accepted, all that must be done is to identify all victims—juveniles, the mentally ill, rape victims, and so on. The second tactic (the situational) is more difficult because it forces the reporter to discriminate, to think. The reporter must see distinctions and think about consequences; in short, the reporter must decide that it is not only all right but good journalism to make exceptions—to have double standards, if you will.

The reporter who is situational recognizes that there is a difference, and a very important one, between a rape victim, for example, and a murder victim. Naming a rape victim can bring mental and emotional harm to the victim; naming a murder victim cannot harm the victim at all. The thinking reporter understands that the naming of a nine-year-old boy for shooting his father is quite different (in psychological, if not in legal, terms) than the naming of a thirty-nine-year-old adult for shooting his father. The reporter believes that it is his duty to make certain editorial decisions impinging on what is and is not published. After all, he reasons, editorial decision is the nature of journalism: selection is made to some degree—among facts in *every* story that is written.

I contend that a reporter must play this tactical game rather loosely; that he must not strive for consistency in tactics; that he must consider the specific situation or circumstance. In short, the reporter (to be effective and in many cases to be ethical, too) must specifically determine not to be absolute and consistent, but rather to be situational and relative.

A reporter cannot subscribe to a tactic of always revealing his source— even if he or she does maintain that the people have a right to know. In some cases, to reveal sources would be counterproductive, as well as unethical. For example, the journalist may get information from a source who would be in great physical danger if his or her identity were known. The reporter not only wants to keep the source operative for another day, but also to avoid endangering his or her life. In similar cases, the reporter might want to keep the source from losing his or her job.

A reporter writing a rape story has the name of the person arrested on suspicion of committing the rape. The reporter also has ascertained the name of the rape victim. The reporter decides not to use the victim's name, but does not hesitate to use the suspected rapist's name. Inconsistent? Yes. This is, in effect, withholding information from the reader. At the same time the name of another person connected with the case is provided—even though this person may not have committed the rape. The reporter feels no qualms about this inconsistent procedure, reasoning that in this particular case it is tactically prudent to do as he or she has done. The reporter justifies withholding verified information from the reader on ethical grounds, on a consideration of possible consequences to the victim.

The reporter in the hypothetical rape case is inconsistent, and certainly does not subscribe to a "universal" tactic. A universal tactic in reporting would be: The reporter is obligated to report all the facts that he or she has, that are verified, that are pertinent to the story. Period.

In this rape story, certainly the name of the rape victim is *pertinent to the story,* as we will be told by our absolutist reporter. After all, the reporter has found out who the woman is; therefore, should not the name be given, especially since the name of the rape suspect has been used?

Let me reply to the above question with another question: Why *should* the reporter use the victim's name? The reporter is wise to subscribe to relativistic tactics, to play the story the way he or she wants to play it in that particular case, after consideration of possible consequences. Why should the reporter always name names? Why should the reporter subscribe to the same tactics in every story? Straightjacketing oneself does not assure better reportage by the reporter. In fact, a relativistic or situational tactical program in reporting is what is called for. Consider each story. Consider the ramifications of each story. Consider the importance of the story. Consider consequences or implications for certain persons in the story.

It may well be that when a reporter considers the importance to the public of a particular story, there will be a realization that "usual" tactics must be modified or changed. A reporter may decide that the story is important enough, for example, to steal files (or at least to make copies of papers and return the files). A reporter may even feel that in a particular case there is justification to pose as someone else. It may be that the reporter will decide to eavesdrop on certain conversations and report on them, using or perhaps not using the names of those who spoke. A reporter might decide to "bug" a room or wiretap a telephone in order to get some very important information that the public should know. A reporter might decide, in order to get some much-needed information, to tell a source that he or she knows or has heard certain things from someone else (which he or she really has not heard) in order to get a response. A reporter might decide to make up quotes and drop them into a story so as to prompt someone connected with the story, someone he or she wants to make a statement, to come forward to refute or to enlarge on the "speculated" or fabricated quotes.

We can justify these tactics by resorting to the "ends justifies the means" argument. We can say that we are thinking of the public and the public's right to know. How can the public know unless we break through the barriers of secrecy with our situational tactics? Journalists thus must resort to these tactics *from time to time* in order to do their job, to live up to their responsibilities.

We can justify relativistic or situation tactics by contending that they are more ethical; we can also justify them instrumentally or pragmatically by saying that they are needed to accomplish our ends. In any case, in a country with a free press, it is the right of a newspaper reporter to be inconsistent. If the reporter wants to reveal the source of a quote in one story and not in another, that is his or her right. In fact, if the reporter wants to reveal the source of a quotation in one part of a story and make all the other quotes in the same story anonymous, that is his or her right. Depending on the situation, there might be good reasons for:

- Using the 5W lead in one story, but not in another.
- Using only indirect quotations in one story, and using direct quotations or a mixture of indirect and direct quotes in another.
- Giving the addresses of persons in one story, and omitting addresses in another.
- Going directly to persons for information in one story, while going to someone for secondhand information in another or using old information from the files.
- Giving certain personal data (such as age, race, occupation) about some persons in some stories but not about other persons.

What is the alternative to these inconsistent tactics? Consistent and universal tactics, we are told. The intelligent and dedicated reporter can only scoff at such an alternative, seeing it as a definite voluntary placement of the reporter in a straitjacket with little chance to achieve a primary goal of journalism: obtaining the story.

Why, asks the dedicated reporter, should I *never* deviate from a kind of traditional tactical program? If the normal tactics will not work, why not use others that will work?

I may *usually* want to give sources for information in my story. But why must I always give them? I may *usually* want to avoid deceiving a person to get information, but why not deceive when I feel the issue is important enough to warrant deception? I may *usually* want to identify myself as a reporter, but there will be times when I need either to hide my identity or to pass myself off as someone else. I may *usually* want to get my interviews free as part of a news story, but why should I not pay someone for an interview if I feel my news medium wants it or that it is important to the public?

In short, I am not wise or very sophisticated if I always use the same tactics. Consistent and universal tactics are simply not instrumentally (or ethically, in many cases) conducive to effective journalism, nor are they in line with a journalist's dedication to getting the story and keeping the public informed.

As I have written elsewhere, a relativistic ethics appears to be the only rational and "situation-concerned" ethical position for the journalist to take (Merrill, 1989). I suggested there what I called "deontelic" ethics (synthesis of deontological and teleogical ethics), combining a deep respect for moral principles with a willingness to deviate on occasion from such principles after much hard moral reasoning:

> Deontelic ethics is for the journalist who is both morally concerned and rational, who respects generalized ethical principles but who is willing to depart from them. . . . Deontelic ethics is a broad moral grounding, not a set of specific rules for right action. As such, it emphasizes the journalist's own reason, not his or her ability to conform or follow orders. It is truly a socially concerned, individualist ethics that respects the journalist's own freedom and reason but is built on a respect for others, too, and for the continued moral progress of journalism (Merrill, 1989, 214).

Argument Summation: Tactics should be situational and relative.

The tactics of news-gathering should fit the particular case. In one case a reporter may have to promise a source anonymity, whereas in another there is no need. Closely related to ethics, such tactics must be flexible, and the reporter must think of *success* and *consequences*. Should a reporter *ever* lie to get his story? Yes. Should a reporter *ever* promise a source that he or she can see the story before publication? Yes. Tactics must be varied so as to reflect the importance of a particular story. Important ends do indeed justify or warrant extreme means. Good journalists know that.

RESPONSE

Dennis: News-gathering tactics should be consistent and universal.

The preceding discussion of news-gathering tactics defends the status quo in American journalism. Reporters do use relative and situational methods when gathering the news. However, there are many agreed-upon general standards and practices. These practical tactics for getting information are undergirded by ethical judgments that are self-contained, based mainly on the immediate situation rather than considered against the backdrop of long experience with similar cases. There is more than a slight temptation to reinvent the wheel with each ethical dilemma that arises.

That, in my opinion, summarizes one of the most serious problems in journalistic practice today—a thoughtless, seat-of-the-pants approach to reporting that eschews planning and thinking. It is the journalism of intuition. "Do what intuition tells you, and apply common sense to the situation"—these are accepted axioms. On the face of it this doesn't sound so bad, but consider the following:

- A reporter for NBC News is asked how he knows when he has enough information to "go" with a story. "How," he was asked, "can you be sure that your information is complete, that you are not missing major sources that would turn a story completely around, maybe with a different interpretation altogether?" The reporter replied, "You just know. There is," he added, "no answer; things just click into place and it seems right."
- An editor for a metropolitan daily newspaper is asked by a Harvard Law professor how far he would go to get a story. "Would you lie? Would you steal? Would you disguise your identity?" The editor thought for a moment, then responded, "Yes, under some conditions, I'd probably do all of those things, even though I might personally find some of them reprehensible." The professor wanted to know, "How do you make your decision; on what theory do you base your actions?" And the editor answered, "I have no theory, I just do what I think is right."

We would not accept this kind of thinking from other professional persons (say, doctors, lawyers, or architects) whom we expect to have standards, codes, and systematic bases for their decisions. We do accept it from journalists perhaps because we have no choice, or because they convince us that news is unpredictable, a matter of timing that requires on-the-spot decisions governed solely by the facts of a particular situation. "You simply can't quantify these things," goes the incantation.

There is a prevailing myth in American journalism that planning news coverage runs counter to freedom of the press. Planning is thought to be dull and routine, not spontaneous and timely. It is further said that writers are creative persons who, if left to their own devices, will produce a better kind of journalism. And God forbid that journalists should have hypotheses. A hypothesis, which is an assumption that becomes an organizing principle, is thought to encourage bias and run counter to journalistic objectivity. There is also a prevailing view among many journalists that news really defies precise definition.

This "every-day-a-new-beginning" theme in many newsrooms, the operational rule of the status quo, needs rethinking. While it certainly is not always possible to predict with scientific certainty what will happen on a given day, journalism is really much more routine than most of its practitioners *know* or will *admit*. They may not know it because American journalism is insulated and parochial. Many journalists have little work experience outside of their present assignments; few belong to national organizations where they come into contact with other journalists; few subscribe to professional publications or make any effort to keep up with the literature of their own field. Most sneer at the thought of reading "media sociology," systematic research that gives us data about patterns and practices across many journalistic organizations. Individual journalists may know their own organization intimately, but they often have little knowledge about the field generally. This situation is not unusual because many professionals are so busy doing their jobs that they have little time to think about them or to make comparisons with their colleagues in other places. For a field that is supposed to demand so much creative calibration, journalism is remarkably predictable, routine, even stodgy. Send any five reporters to cover a city council story and you can predict with considerable certainty what they will write. Why? Because the coverage of public affairs, in particular, has been standardized. Journalists agree about the form and format of stories, about what essential facts should be included, and about what most editors will accept. Reporters know what is expected of them and generally they do it.

Of course, there are stories that are more complex than routine meetings, but even with these the traditional methods of news gathering pretty much dictate what will eventually appear. And if this were not enough, we have "rewards and punishments" built into the journalistic system to guarantee conformity. At a positive level there are prizes (such as the Pulitzers) that honor imaginative work within the framework of traditional journalism. Journalism schools help out by promoting conventional approaches to news-gathering through courses and books.

Journalists believe that their work is unpredictable, situational, and relative. Communications researchers say this is not true, that reporting is not nearly as uncertain as practitioners think. Journalists say that with regard to ethics, they live in a conceptual thicket that requires instant decisions of convenience, if not conviction. They tend to justify what they do without worrying whether their choices about revealing sources or lying are consistent with what they did before. Scholars, on the other hand, because they are trained to look for patterns of organizational and individual activity, can see a method, whether haphazard or well thought out, in journalistic work, just as they do in the work of firefighters or farmers. The way the newspaper or broadcast station is organized, the selection of personnel, their training and socialization, all have a hand in shaping news practices.

The once-similar (and now quite different) practices of journalists and social scientists explain some of this discrepancy. As Philip Meyer, well-known for his work in precision journalism and now a professor at the University of North Carolina, has written:

> Social scientists used to be more like journalists. They relied on observation and interpretation, collecting the observations from public records, from interviews, from direct participation, and

then spinning out the interpretations. Like many journalists they cheerfully accepted the American folk wisdom . . . that anyone with "a little common sense and a few facts can come up at once with the correct answer on any subject" (Meyer, 1979, 216).

But something changed. First with the development of inferential statistics and later with the advent of computers, social scientists no longer worked like journalists. Instead, they used powerful quantitative tools to deal with unwieldy and massive data. Now, says Meyer, social scientists are doing "what we journalists like to think we are best at: finding fact, inferring causes, pointing to ways to correct social problems, and evaluating the effects of such correction"(216–17). He charges that journalism is being left behind because it lacks a systematic approach to news gathering.

Systematic news gathering tactics can bring a far richer yield than old fashioned, impressionistic reporting. It is now possible to determine how much information, and from what sources, will be adequate. This does not mean that journalists should be exactly like social scientists. Press people have greater time pressures and are more concerned about immediacy.

The change toward more systematic reporting is under way. In addition to the "precision journalism" advanced by Meyer and others, there was also greater use of computer-assisted reporting during the late 1980s. At first, giant mainframe computers were used by reporters to access and sift through public records to get "the goods" on public officials and others. Then with new software developments, mainly introduced by Elliott Jaspin, a former reporter at the *Providence Journal* and now at the University of Missouri, it was also possible to do some computer-assisted reporting by plugging into massive government records and documents with a personal computer and a software package.

It is one thing to develop a strategy for news coverage that lists the tactics to be employed, another to do it. No situation is ever perfect and no prearranged rules ever work in all situations. For this reason some journalists throw out the rules altogether and make expedient decisions. It is threatening to ask: Is the information complete? Have I mined all possible (and reasonable) sources? Is the evidence strong enough to warrant the conclusion, actual or implied? Are various interpretations and leaps in logic justified? If such questions could have been avoided in the past, such is no longer the case.

Systematic news-gathering tactics are not simply a theory for journalism schools to trumpet, but something being demanded by the rest of society. One of the most compelling calls comes in the courts. Frequently in libel suits news organizations must offer evidence that their story has "an absence of malice." This requirement means that the story is not marred by "knowing falsehood" or "reckless disregard" of the truth. How is this honesty of intent determined? By showing that reasonable efforts, consistent with national news-gathering standards, were employed. If they were not and the paper admits it, there is the possibility for a whopping libel judgment. Sloppy reporting is expensive. Of equal or greater importance is the fear that journalists will not have the credibility they need and deserve unless their methods are respected by the audience.

People who argue against ethical standards or moral imperatives in news-gathering tactics usually suggest that each case is so different that rules will straightjacket the reporter. They add that general guidelines are so vague that they are meaningless. I disagree. We need a theory of journalistic ethics, a fundamental framework for reporters to base their decisions on. This framework requires general understanding about ethical behavior, whether in reporting or everyday life. It means having a clear notion about how specific journalistic dilemmas ought to be handled. This general ethical understanding does not mean that rules cannot be modified or tempered to meet particular situations. We need a thoughtful policy that serves as a conscience for individual journalists and their organizations. Such a policy should spell out standards of conduct for information gathering. One minimal standard is that journalists should obey the law. In most instances this principle means they should not lie, steal, or cheat. They should not wiretap or break into places not otherwise open to them. In rare instances, a right-thinking reporter may want to be civilly disobedient, to deliberately break the law as a matter of principle because it will lead to a greater social good. In all instances where ethical questions arise, if there is not a clear answer, reporters should consider alternatives, not simply rush to judgment with the easiest solution. If the decision runs counter to conventional wisdom and standard ethical codes, there ought to be a clear and compelling rationale for making it.

For example, in most instances it is regarded as ethical to reveal one's sources in a news story. This strengthens the credibility of the story and ties information to attributed sources. If revealing names will put sources in great danger or make them reluctant to talk, a different decision may be appropriate. If it is determined that a source should not be named, the information should meet a test of public benefit, clearly agreed upon and understood by the reporter's supervising editors so that they can defend the action later. And the reporter, if subpoenaed by the courts, must be ready to go to jail if it comes to that.

The problem today is that many reporters do not have solid ethical training and do not have the kind of foundation necessary for ethical decision making.

Journalists have gotten into trouble for being inconsistent in recent years with regard to fair-trial–free-press codes. The press was a signatory to such codes, which list tactical guidelines for covering criminal proceedings from initial investigations of crimes to court judgments. Reporters generally agree to withhold some information (such as prior arrest records) in the interest of not prejudicing a jury and assuring the defendant of a fair trial. This is a social compact between the press and the legal system. When the press violates this agreement or decides not to abide by a particular provision of the code, there ought to be a good reason (beyond curiosity seeking or pandering) to justify its action. If not, reporters and editors may have to answer in court. This happened in 1981 in a notable case in the state of Washington, where a newspaper was held accountable for violation of the fair-trial–free-press code.

Naturally, it is always possible to substitute a "greater social good" argument or a "humanitarian" argument to explain why an individual journalist or publication may deviate from an accepted rule. I believe such exceptions should be justified on the basis of devotion to the public interest, rather than petty or self-serving reasons.

Similarly, it is appropriate to reconsider rules that are regarded as journalistic conventions or articles of faith. Printing the names of persons involved in litigation, for example. Withholding the rape victim's name while printing that of the person accused of rape has been mentioned. This practice would seem potentially unfair both to victim and accused. The press usually prints the name of the accused. But is it really necessary? The reasons for printing names has to do with keeping the courts open so that they do not become secret tribunals. Thus, we know who is being tried, for what, and why. But as long as the courts are open to the press and to spectators, why not defer printing this material until the trial is over? No great social good is done by heralding names of victims or accused persons in advance of trial, with some obscure exceptions.

Consistent and universal standards of reporting—with necessary escape clauses for unusual or unique situations—will do much to enhance journalistic practice in America. Such standards, if widely known (and the press can virtually guarantee this with adequate coverage), will do much to strengthen public confidence in the fairness and completeness of reporting. It will also have real advantages for individual newspapers and broadcast stations in an increasingly litigious society. Haphazard, thoughtless conduct that meets no standard, but blunders along willy-nilly is neither appreciated nor rewarded by the courts. One of the most effective ways to put the journalistic house in order is to establish coherent policies and consistent practices. This is the essence of professional performance and distinguishes competent performance from rank amateurism.

Argument Summation: News-gathering tactics should be consistent and universal.

News reporting resorts too often to situational ethics, instead of a planned approach to appropriate news-gathering tactics. Critics who argue that advanced planning or standards interfere with press freedom fail to recognize that journalism is already routine, as media sociology has revealed. There is much agreement about the form, format, and content of public affairs coverage, and the reward and punishment systems of journalism reinforce these norms. The problem is that these norms are haphazardly developed, relying on impressionistic reporting rather than finding fact and inferring causes in a systematic manner. Guidelines, based on underlying ethical and moral objectives, should be developed to give journalists a clear framework on which to base their decisions in news gathering. At a minimum, this would require the journalist to consider carefully the alternatives and to develop compelling rationales when breaking the guidelines. The public interest is served best by a press that gathers news systematically, deviating from planned procedures only when it can be justified to serve that public interest.

TOPICS FOR DISCUSSION

1. Discuss how news-gathering tactics are related to a journalist's or to a medium's editorial policy and to a sense of ethics.

2. Explain why you feel news-gathering tactics should be determined a priori instead of as the situation arises. If you do not feel this way, explain why.

3. Do you think having definite ways of practicing journalism (tactics) that are considered "proper" or "sacred" is compatible with the American idea of press pluralism, individualism, and freedom?

4. Do you think tactics in American journalism are (a) consistent or (b) inconsistent? What are the advantages for each answer above?

5. Why would a synthesis approach to tactics and ethics—called "deontelic ethics" by Merrill—be a solution to the absolute versus the situational tactical problem faced by the news reporter? If you don't believe it would be a solution, give your reasons.

TOPICS FOR RESEARCH

1. Prepare a report for your fellow students on the advantages and disadvantages of situational versus consistent news-gathering tactics. Take a position. Which approach do you subscribe to, or do you advocate some other formulation?

2. Do a study of computer-assisted investigative reporting. Where has it been done? To what effect? Does it have advantages over more qualitative approaches?

3. How does professionalism affect news-gathering tactics? Does a professionally trained reporter work differently than someone with no such training?

4. To what extent does the law of communication, especially libel and privacy law, mandate more consistent news-gathering methods? When a court is asked to decide whether a particular story under scrutiny met professional standards, what would you want the attorneys for each side to argue?

5. Write a brief for the public that is an essay explaining what responsible citizens might want in their news coverage. What information should be offered? How should it be gathered, with what technical means and with what ethical standards? How much evidence should be offered before a politician is accused of wrongdoing?

FURTHER READING

Bok, Sissela. *Lying: Moral Choice in Public and Private Life.* New York: Pantheon, 1978.

———. *Secrets: On the Ethics of Concealment and Revelation.* New York: Pantheon, 1982.

Diamond, Edwin. *The Tin Kazoo.* Cambridge, MA: MIT Press, 1975.

Hage, George S., Everette E. Dennis, Arnold H. Ismach, and Stephen Hartgen. *New Strategies for Public Affairs Reporting.* 2d ed. Englewood Cliffs, NJ: Prentice-Hall, 1976.

Hulteng, John L. *The Messenger's Motives: Ethical Problems of the News Media.* Englewood Cliffs, NJ: Prentice-Hall, 1976.

Jaspin, Elliott. "Out With the Paper Chase, In With the Data Base." New York: Gannett Center for Media Studies speech, 1989.

Klaidman, S., and T. L. Beauchamp. *The Virtuous Journalist.* New York: Oxford University Press, 1987.

Lambeth, E. B. *Committed Journalism: An Ethic for the Profession.* Bloomington, IN: Indiana University Press, 1986.

Lowenstein, R. L. and J. C. Merrill. *Macromedia: Mission, Message, and Morality.* White Plains, NY: Longman, 1990.

MacDougall, A. Kent, ed. *The Press: A Critical Look from the Inside.* Princeton, NJ: Dow Jones Books, 1972.

Merrill, John C. *The Dialectic in Journalism: Toward a Responsible Use of Press Freedom.* Baton Rouge, LA: Louisiana State University Press, 1989.

Meyer, Philip. *Precision Journalism.* Bloomington, IN: Indiana University Press, 1979.

Rubin, Bernard. *Questioning Media Ethics.* New York: Praeger, 1978.

Chapter 12

JOURNALISTIC ETHICS

Ethics is a branch of philosophy concerned with the general nature of morals and specific moral choices that people make in relationships with others. Journalistic ethics is usually taken to mean the study and application of journalistic standards of conduct and moral choices. Journalistic ethics usually links a system of values and principles with choices that must be made in day-to-day media work and assignments. These value choices most often deal with "right" and "wrong" choices or degrees of rightness and wrongness, since many journalistic choices are difficult calls. Values refer to an ideal or highly desirable situation. For example, fairness is a value which most journalists and other media people would hail. But fairness to whom? To the person being interviewed? To the public? To one's employer? To oneself? When examined closely, fairness, which seems so obvious and easy from a distance, may be difficult in a given situation. Journalistic ethics most often relates to news decision making, and ethics in journalism has for the most part been a code of conduct expected of news people, especially editorial employees of news organizations.

Until recently, the same ethical guidelines were not thought to apply to media owners, advertising and business personnel, and some special assignments personnel for whom greater license has been accepted. That is changing, however, as support for general business ethics has been advanced by educators, critics and the public. Journalistic ethics are always seen in the context of the functions and purposes of the media, which include the delivery of information, opinion, entertainment and advertising. In order to fulfill its information and news functions, media quite naturally confront conflicting rights and duties. When there is a conflict between the media's desire to publish a story that is important to the public, but which violates the right of privacy of someone, an ethical dilemma arises. The dilemma will be solved by determining what the responsible course of action is in this case. Sometimes this means balancing freedom and responsibility, in which case the freest choice to do what one pleases is not always the most responsible choice. Journalistic ethics involves making choices in specific situations that are related to general rules and principles. For journalists and other communicators this means making choices that conform with the rules and conventions of the profession, which are guided by written codes of ethics. In a practical sense ethical choices suggest freedom in decision making when there might be degrees of rightness and wrongness to consider. There might not be a single "right" ethical choice in all situations. Some ethical values and standards become codified into law, when the state requires that a person follow a particular rule or convention in making choices. Journalistic ethics is thought to be a more voluntary endeavor, however, and the American system of freedom of the press allows considerable latitude not present in other professions where ethical rules have the force of law.

Thus, in a field where there are many standard practices but few absolute rules, the journalist has many independent choices to make in sorting out ethical from unethical conduct. In such murky water, it is not surprising that there is little agreement about what, under all conditions, constitutes ethical conduct for a journalist. While seeking the truth is an ethical imperative for most civilized people, there are conditions where highly ethical journalists have lied for what they said was a greater public good. Media ethics proponents usually distinguish between general principles of ethics and the daily application of situational ethics, when ethical choices are made on the spot with little time for analysis or introspection.

CHALLENGE

Merrill: Journalists are essentially unethical.

Until the early 1960s little thought was given to the ethics of journalists. Of course, the history of American journalism had included instances of famous media "hoaxes," instances of periodic "wheelings and dealings" by media publishers, sensational news and propaganda dissemination by men like William Randolph Hearst and Joseph Pulitzer, and forays into "yellow journalism," muckraking, and questionable publishing practices. But, generally, it was assumed that journalists were trustworthy, honest, dependable, just, unbiased and concerned with uncovering and delivering the truth.

Now we are overwhelmed with publications, television roundtable discussions, "Socratic" dialogues, speeches, conferences, and workshops, all on the subject of journalistic or press ethics. Everybody has discovered that journalists have a big ethical problem. Journalists, who enjoy bashing everything and everybody in sight for ethical lapses, are beginning to get huge doses of their own medicine.

And it's about time. For too long journalists have been pushing their own ethical problems aside and enthroning their freedom, expediency, and self-interest. Pick up almost any copy of a magazine or journal, especially one dealing with the press, and you will encounter articles detailing some journalistic ethical lapse. The situation is so pervasive in the media that many critics—from Ben Bagdikian to William Rusher—have come to believe that "ethical journalism" is really oxymoronic.

Some critics, admittedly, seem too extreme in their press condemnation. Janet Malcolm, for instance, lambastes journalists with these strong words:

> Every journalist who is not too stupid or too full of himself to notice what is going on knows that what he does is morally indefensible. He is a kind of confidence man, preying on people's vanity, ignorance, or loneliness, gaining their trust and betraying them without remorse (Malcolm, 1989).

Malcolm proceeds to say that journalists "justify their treachery in various ways according to their temperaments." The "more pompous," she notes, talk about their freedom and the "public's right to know"; the "least talented" talk about art; the "seemliest" refer to earning a living (Malcolm, 1989, 38).

Naturally many journalists took Malcolm to task for her critical words, but not all. Jonathan Yardley, in a *Washington Post* column (March 27, 1989, C2), regrets the fact that Malcolm does not distinguish between the separate crafts of nonfiction and journalism, but contends that journalists should take her criticism seriously. He concludes: "People who write nonfiction, whether books or journalism, are not responsible solely to themselves, which is a lesson all of us can learn to our profit."

John L. Hess, in *The Quill* (May, 1989, 29), rebuts Malcolm's charges by saying that "the sins of journalists are more imagined than real." He dismisses Malcolm as an "apostate Freudian" who is "full of herself," as she relies on a "single case history" to make her point that journalists have little respect for the truth.

Hess represents the typical defensive reaction of journalists to criticism of their ethics. But in spite of their efforts, they are viewed (in public surveys) as arrogant, self-righteous, and power-hungry—never willing to accept responsibility for mistakes, always anxious (and able) to get the last word.

Some journalistic ethical codes (such as that of the Society of Professional Journalists) insist that journalists "take nothing of value," that they refrain from political "involvement," that they serve the truth, and that they show respect "for the dignity, privacy, rights, and well-being of people encountered in the course of gathering and presenting the news." Compare this rhetoric with the actual daily practices of journalists and you will quickly see that ethical *practice* has a long way to go.

And, what is more interesting, journalists seem to have a difficult time accepting a major code admonition: that they "be free of obligation to any interest other than the public's right to know the truth." Truth, truth, truth. The gentlemen and women of the press enshrine the word, but go about their daily business as if they were not bound by the truth. Half-truths, distortions, and outright censorship is the main game played by journalists. In fact, they even *purposely omit* or *distort* the truth when they feel it is necessary.

Many journalists will tell you that, in spite of what their ethical codes say, there are some things more important than reporting the truth. So they fill their days with bits and snippets of the truth; they hide certain truths—often, strangely, because they feel it would be *unethical* to tell them. At least these journalists have an *ethical* motivation. Others, however, because of personal biases, withhold information and names, selectively quote sources, distort their stories, and tamper with the truth.

Press people, by and large, conceive of ethics as prudential actions which will achieve some preconceived plan, whether this is to get information from a source or to keep certain bits of knowledge from the public. Journalists often obtain their ends and then rationalize the means they used. If most journalists today have any ethics it is a kind of Machiavellian ethics—the ethics of power and expediency.

Reporters have passed as mental patients in order to write exposes of mental hospitals; slanted a story in favor of a preferred candidate; fictionalized to make "life-like" points (as in the Janet Cooke case); and surreptitiously recorded a conversation or interview. In a discussion of "Machiavellian Ethics in Journalism," Ralph Lowenstein and I raise the question of American journalistic expediency-ethics, and note manifestations of Machiavellianism (1990, Chap. 17).

Machiavellianism appeals to American pragmatic journalists. It appeals to the desire for power, for success. It appeals to individualism, dedication, and pride. Machiavelli (1469–1527) said all there is to say about a sizable slice of hard-nosed American journalists and their desire to "get the story at any price." Machiavelli might well be called the father of American journalism, setting its tradition for competitive, bottom-line, winner-take-all, success-oriented media practice. The name of the game in this pragmatic media world is "using other people to achieve desired ends," as I elaborated in the British journal *Encounter* (April, 1987, 80).

Certainly I am not maintaining that *all* journalists are unethical, but that *generally* the press and its practitioners indulge in unethical practices. Even the journalists themselves must recognize their general unethical status (at least *image*) in American society, for they are extremely "uptight" and defensive about the subject. If all is well in the ethics arena, as many of them insist, then why don't they just get on with their work and stop all their ethics dialogue, conventions, workshops, and speeches?

Argument Summation: Journalists are essentially unethical.

Journalists are generally not concerned with acting rightly, doing the proper thing, informing and enlightening the people, telling the truth, and having standards that guide them. Self-interest and a kind of Machiavellianism guide their basic actions. Pragmatism, power, and success are their key motivations. Ethical journalism is oxymoronic. Ethical codes are useless and are mainly for public relations purposes. Journalists enthrone truth, but deviate from it for a multitude of reasons. They talk of the people's right to know, and impinge on it regularly. They invade privacy, tamper with quotes, select only certain stories and information that conform with their biases, and are basically arrogant, defensive, and self-righteous.

RESPONSE

Dennis: Journalists are essentially ethical.

Because journalists deal in the currency of information and news, their work is closely watched and often disputed. The reason, of course, is that they are (or ought to be) writing for their audience. While the best of them fairly represent their sources with accurate descriptions of events, situations, and quotations, there is often conflict because the source wants to be seen in the best possible light, even when his or her actions are reprehensible. This puts the journalist in an uncomfortable situation. One can serve the interests of the source, avoid conflict, and mislead the public or one can pursue the truth, cover the news, and accept the consequences.

This is essentially the dilemma described, though somewhat unkindly, by Janet Malcolm. She was not, incidentally, the first person to suggest that writers always "sell out" their sources. An eloquent statement to that effect is found in Joan Didion's *Slouching Towards Bethelehem*. When it comes to dealing with and representing the views of news sources, there are many complicated factors to consider in determining what is right. In *The Social Responsibility of the Press* (1963), J. Edward Gerald identified several factors in the ground rules that ought to govern reporters conduct. First, he asks, "What are the conventions journalists are taught to respect?" Second, "What are the rules of their trade?" To this he adds,

"What skills in communication entitle a journalist to the acclaim (of colleagues)?" And, "What errors bring loss of face?" Scores of books have been written exploring the points Professor Gerald introduced in these four questions, which travel over uncharted ground, but also over much settled territory. While recognizing the foibles of individual journalists and other communicators such as public relations personnel, I believe that there is a great body of evidence, including books describing how journalists uncovered corruption from Teapot Dome to Watergate and Iran-Contra, that suggests journalists are essentially ethical.

Journalism both suffers and benefits from its enormous freedom. Freedom of the press allows enormous latitude in communication: No law can command a journalist to be responsible or fair or just. A journalist can be a highly ethical, moral individual who makes fair-minded choices, or he or she can be a mean-spirited polemicist who is out to get people. That is what freedom of the press guarantees, and through history there have been plenty of journalists who have not been nice people. But we are not talking here about eccentric exceptions, but rather about the norm, the typical journalist who is increasingly driven toward responsibility and fair play, in other words, ethical conduct. Why do I say this is so?

The majority of American journalists today are the products of journalism schools or have at least had some course work that "indoctrinates" them to their profession. That indoctrination includes values such as freedom of the press, responsible practices in news gathering, rigorous fair-minded writing where accuracy, accuracy, accuracy is the clarion call. Journalists who do not go to journalism school have to possess writing skills and the ability to work within a media organization. Those organizations have written and unwritten rules about what is acceptable conduct for their employees. People learn these "rules" quickly and are governed by them. Otherwise they are fired. There are also many professional organizations to which one can belong, ranging from editors and reporters' groups to others for specialized journalists. Virtually all of them have codes of ethics that are widely distributed to their members. Nearly a score of new books on journalistic ethics are available, even if they are not the fastest-moving best sellers on publishers' lists. In other words, information about journalistic ethics is readily available. Journalism and journalistic practice is not exactly a hidden or inaccessible topic. There is an increasing amount of press criticism published in newspapers and magazines, as well as being included on radio and television news programs. Mention almost any topic and media coverage of it has been discussed somewhere recently. And what does that coverage and criticism typically address? You guessed it: journalistic ethics. In fact, I would guess that the typical citizen probably knows more about journalistic ethics than about medical or legal ethics. Why? Because the topic is front-row-center much of the time in our major media.

Studies of American journalists and American journalism educators by David Weaver and G. Cleveland Wilhoit suggest that ethics is a serious concern among both groups. Similarly, the several studies of media credibility done in recent years (and stretching back for a half-century) report that the public is very concerned about the ethics of journalists. While most people support the media and give journalists and others good grades, a vocal minority is dissatisfied. Media people pay attention to these "report cards" and often act upon them, especially if they feel criticism is just.

Since the 1920s, every twenty years or so has seen a burgeoning literature of media ethics. There is discussion and debate for a few years, then the topic recedes into the background only to reappear later. That was true until the 1970s, but so visible are media issues and problems these days that the rush of articles and books has not abated. Excellent studies of situational ethics have been rendered by such educators as John L. Hulteng (1985), whose *The Messenger's Motives* is in its second edition. In *Groping for Media Ethics* Eugene Goodwin (1983) similarly looks inside newsrooms and observes problems. Philip Meyer (1987) in a study called *Ethical Journalism* even suggests that editorial ethics should extend to the business side of the press. Edmund Lambeth's (1986) *Committed Journalism* is a coherent philosophy based, in part, on ethical imperatives, as well as practical conditions. These books and others that are notable join several volumes on my shelf by John Merrill, who has been writing on media ethics for at least two decades. The literature is the tip of a very large iceberg, which includes increased instruction in media ethics in journalism schools, a trend that has been traced by Clifford Christians of the University of Illinois. There are centers for media ethics at the Poynter Institute, the University of Minnesota, and Emerson College. There are training programs in ethics for journalism teachers at the University of Missouri and scores of conferences that have been well-attended for at least a decade.

Thus, it seems to me that journalistic ethics is alive and well in the United States. But are journalists ethical? Yes, they are, I believe, based on studies, personal experience, and the various incentives that encourage ethical conduct. These include: the reward and punishment system of American journalism, which rarely rewards reprehensible or unethical journalism; pressure from an increasingly sophisticated public, which is critical of the news it gets; and finally, the legal system, which, in court, takes an exceedingly unkind view of journalists who are regarded by their peers as irresponsible, reckless, or unethical. Mostly, though, journalists, like most people, are ethical because they want to do what is right. In one of the most celebrated cases of journalistic ethics in recent years, CBS News executive Burton Benjamin critiqued a "60 Minutes" story about General Westmoreland; Benjamin's report was widely applauded for its ethical stance. The CBS story, the subject of a scathing front page critique in *TV Guide*, led to an unresolved court case and to Benjamin's book called *Fair Play*. When television journalists are asked who they admire most, who would most likely be their role model, the people who did the deeply flawed "60 Minutes" documentary or Mr. Benjamin, a man of principle, honor, and integrity, Benjamin won without dispute. That says something about the present climate for media ethics.

Argument Summation: Journalists are essentially ethical.

While there are notable exceptions as in any profession, ethical behavior is the norm in American journalism. The socialization of journalists, both through school and professional exposure, indoctrinates professional values which emphasize responsible news gathering, freedom of the press, and accuracy in reporting. Journalists who do not follow these unwritten rules of their organization do not have jobs for long. Studies confirm that journalists respond to criticism of media ethics and that there is a healthy debate regarding ethics, thus keeping the profession aware of a necessity for ethical behavior.

TOPICS FOR DISCUSSION

1. What do you think "being ethical" means to a journalist? Is it possible to justify or rationalize any journalistic action?

2. Where are the main ethical allegiances in journalism—to the public, to the employer, to the audience? How would you rank such allegiances in terms of importance?

3. Where do you think journalists derive their ethical standards? If they get them from various sources, how do they know, if they do, which are more valid and reliable?

4. Do you think that codes of ethics are useful in a "free-press" society? How so? Do you think that a monolithic sense of ethics in the U.S. press would be good or bad for American journalism?

5. Give some evidence to substantiate the claim that "journalistic ethics is alive and well in the United States." How would we know if American ethics were sick or dead?

TOPICS FOR RESEARCH

1. Study the codes of ethics used by media organizations and professional societies. Compare and contrast them. How general are they? How specific? To what extent are they useful?

2. Interview one or more journalists from any medium. Ask them to articulate their "theory" of media ethics; that is, how do they define ethics in their work? How do they make ethical decisions? Ask for an example of a particularly difficult (or easy) ethical decision they recently had to make. Where does their knowledge of media ethics come from? How do they stay up to date?

3. Examine a major controversy in journalism in terms of ethics. Pick a case or controversy where the performance or behavior of a television or print journalist was under fire. What was the main issue? How was it resolved? Did this serve the public well or not?

4. Write a review essay drawing on at least two recent books on media ethics. Based on these studies, how would you develop your own code of ethics? What advice would you give to a news organization about how they might write a code?

5. Read and analyze a recent biography by a media person. Examine the person's career and decisions on the basis of ethics. Is the person a good, mediocre, or poor model for others. What of his or her ethics?

FURTHER READING

Benjamin, Burton. *Fair Play.* New York: Harper & Row, 1988.

Christians, C. G., K. B. Rotzoll, and Mark Fackler. *Media Ethics: Cases and Moral Reasoning.* 2d ed. White Plains, NY: Longman, 1987.

Dennis, Everette E. *Reshaping the Media.* Beverly Hills, CA: Sage Publications, 1989.

Dennis, Everette E., Donald M. Gillmor, and Theodore Glasser, eds. *Media Freedom and Accountability.* Westport, CT: Greenwood Press, 1989.

Fink, Conrad C. *Media Ethics in the Newsroom and Beyond.* New York: McGraw-Hill, 1988.

Goodwin, Eugene. *Groping for Media Ethics.* Ames, IA: Iowa State University Press, 1983.

Hess, John L. "Who's Conning Whom?" *The Quill* 77, no. 5 (May 1989): 29.

Hulteng, John L. *The Messenger's Motives: Ethical Problems of the News Media.* 2d. ed. Englewood Cliffs, NJ: Prentice-Hall, 1985.

Johannesen, Richard L. *Ethics in Human Communication.* 3d ed. Prospect Heights, IL: Waveland Press, 1990.

Klaidman, Stephen, and Tom Beauchamp. *The Virtuous Journalist.* New York: Oxford University Press, 1987.

Lambeth, Edmund B. *Committed Journalism: An Ethic for the Profession.* Bloomington, IN: Indiana University Press, 1986.

Lowenstein, R. L., and J. C. Merrill. *Macromedia: Mission, Message and Morality.* White Plains, NY: Longman, 1990.

Malcolm, Janet. "The Journalist and the Murder." *The New Yorker* (13 March 1989).

Merrill, John C. *The Dialectic in Journalism: Toward a Responsible Use of Press Freedom.* Baton Rouge, LA: Louisiana State University Press, 1989.

———. *The Imperative of Freedom.* 2d ed. New York: Freedom House, 1990.

Meyer, Philip. *Ethical Journalism.* White Plains, NY: Longman, 1987.

Swain, Bruce M. *Reporters' Ethics.* Ames, IA: Iowa State University Press, 1978.

Chapter 13

PRESS COUNCILS AND ETHICAL CODES

Social responsibility has been a watchword for the press for many years. In recent times, the term "accountability" has also been added to discussions of journalistic practice. It is often agreed that mandatory controls to enforce press accountability would be inappropriate, and that various methods of self-regulation would be more acceptable.

Two such methods (or instruments of criticism) are the press council and the code of ethics.

Codes of ethics have been a part of American journalism for nearly seventy-five years. Many individual publications, trade associations, professional societies, and others have promulgated codes and actively campaign for their use. Press councils are a more recent development in America, mainly since the late 1960s, although there were some important forerunners.

Press councils are private, voluntary organizations that appraise the performance of the press and other media, as well as adjudicating complaints short of actual legal sanctions. Press councils are often seen as safety valves, allowing the public to criticize press performance without formal or legal threats to the media. Ethical codes are more plentiful in America than are press councils, although both are frequently and vigorously discussed and debated. Both can be seen either as instruments for improvement of the press or as instruments for controlling the press and diminishing the potency and pluralism of the press. The debate continues.

CHALLENGE

Merrill: Press councils and ethical codes are dangerous control mechanisms.

It is not popular to take the position that press councils and journalistic ethical codes are unnecessary at best and dangerous at worst. But that is the position I must take.

Councils, codes, and their popularity in many press quarters, are evidence of a symptom of journalistic defensiveness and insecurity that has grown, with the growing sophistication of laymen in regard to the field of communication and with growing public hostility and criticism of the mass media.

One way to try to head off or diminish this flood of criticism and abuse—certainly this wave of growing skepticism about the press—is for the press to try to do a better job of policing itself. At least the press must make the public *believe* it is trying to clean up its own act. Thus there is increased emphasis on press councils and codes of ethics, two of the most obvious policing mechanisms.

Certainly there is good reason for the press to be concerned with its public image. Press performance is certainly no more commendable and ethical than the performance of other public institutions so often called to task by the press. A former Detroit newspaper editor has summarized the matter harshly:

> There are good men and women who will not stand for office, concerned that you [the press] will find their flaws or invent them. Many people who have dealt with you wish that they had not. You are capricious and unpredictable, you are fearsome and you are feared, because there is never any way to know whether this time you will be fair and accurate or whether you will not. And there is virtually nothing we can do about it (Luedtke, 1982, 16).

It is widely believed that the press itself should do something about such problems. So we put increasing faith in councils and codes. There seems to be a deep seated fear in the press that one of these days the people are going to be fed up with journalistic excesses and arrogance, and the walls of old concepts of press freedom will come tumbling down.

By using councils and codes, the press is trying to put a little mortar in the cracks that are appearing in the traditional walls. I maintain that these councils and codes can harm freedom and pluralism as much, if not more, than the criticism which might come from the public. It is not to councils and codes that the press must trust for ethical practice and more public responsibility: Individual journalists must be more ethical and more truly concerned with the excesses and shady actions of their daily work.

The idea of news councils is not new, although the rhetoric surrounding them has escalated greatly in the past few years. The first press council was established in Sweden more than a half-century ago. Today there are some thirty press councils in the world. Some are government-connected and some are run exclusively by the press itself. Some have press and lay members. Typical of this last type is the British Press Council (created in 1953 and revised in 1963). The basic purpose of such bodies is to investigate and rule on public complaints against the press, so as to make the press more responsible and to avoid restrictive government regulation.

In the United States, the National News Council was formed in 1972 and lasted until 1984. Various state councils—as those in Minnesota and Hawaii—and local councils—such as those in Redwood City and Santa Rosa, California—were also founded. All news councils in America have been controversial. Many editors and journalists oppose the concept of news councils, since it is seen as a possible first step toward government regulation.

There are nations that, through their press councils, exercise control over the press, issue (and revoke) journalistic licenses, and impose jail sentences on reporters, as well as levy fines on newspapers.

Proponents of news councils feel that the press needs to be criticized, to have its work observed and commented upon regularly. This, they say, is the purpose of a news council; it is not designed to coerce, and its pressure is only the pressure of publicity. This, they contend, poses no real danger to press freedom.

Nevertheless, the NNC's short existence did not improve American journalism in any notable way. It, like the press itself, had credibility problems.

When groups like the News Council presume to define for the press what "good practice" and proper ethical behavior are, there is the danger of pushing the press in the direction of a monolithic conformity which is traditionally anathema to a libertarian journalistic system.

In 1973 Clayton Kirkpatrick, editor of the *Chicago Tribune*, stated that the price for press councils was simply too high and the evidence that they were needed was "too subjective." He believed, as I do, that press councils inevitably must set up universal standards and that these will lead to conformity. "Out go the rebels, the undergrounders, the angry, daring, and uncouth," he wrote. "America," he said, "would be poorer for that. Maybe the press would be more respectable, but not so exciting or effective."

In concluding these remarks about press councils, I thus would say that all this talk of "press responsibility" subordinates press freedom and journalistic diversity and gives an ominous clue to the priorities of any press council.

And, now, to codes of ethics.

The dangers I see implicit in news councils can be projected to ethical codes also. There is an implicit "conformity desire" in codes as in news councils. Somebody or some group is setting itself up as an arbiter of media conduct—and this in a system which is theoretically pluralistic and self-determining. Although codes of journalistic ethics have considerable support among media people, many journalists insist that a code is useless because it cannot cover all the problems which a journalist will encounter. Actually, they say, each journalist must make ethical decisions for himself and cannot—and should not—be hemmed in and directed by some code devised by someone else. "Most codes are just a bunch of platitudes," says William Thomas, a former editor of the *Los Angeles Times*. In blunt language he continues, "I've never seen a written code of ethics that wasn't so damned obvious that it was clear that you were doing it more for its outside PR [public relations] value than for any inward impact."

Many media groups and organizations, however, do have codes of ethics, CBS and NBC, the American Society of Newspaper Editors, and the Society of Professional Journalists, for example. Some newspapers have their own ethical codes; others do not.

Let us look for a moment at the Code of Ethics of the Society of Professional Journalists. It is a good example of what is wrong with ethical codes. In 1973 the code, an updated version of an older 1926 version, was adopted to make it stronger.

The Code of Ethics, written by a committee chaired by Casey Bukro of the *Chicago Tribune*, is a loosely and vaguely written document filled with generalizations and semantically foggy clichés. Such phrases stating that SPJ'ers believe in "public enlightenment as the forerunner of justice," "obligations that require journalists to perform with intelligence, objectivity, accuracy, and fairness," and "serving the general welfare" are sprinkled throughout the code. We are told that journalists uphold the right to speak unpopular opinions and that journalists must have no obligation to any interest except the public's right to know the truth.

We are given the usual litany of don'ts—not taking gifts, free trips, special treatment, and secondary employment. And on and on goes the code, setting up guidelines for members of the society—and for all journalists. Numerous meaningless pronouncements and directions are given. For more specific criticism of the SPJ Code of Ethics, the reader is referred to *Existential Journalism* (130–32) and to my chapter "Rhetoric" in *Philosophy and Journalism* (1983).

The careful reader of the code (and all journalistic codes) will recognize the uselessness of such codes, while at the same time understanding the potential danger they could inflict on freedom and diversity if taken seriously. Fortunately, such codes are not taken seriously; this is their redeeming feature, in my opinion.

In conclusion, let me reiterate: Press councils and journalistic codes of ethics are dangerous control mechanisms that stand alluringly at the door of American journalism, waiting to be let in and welcomed. Seductive though they may be to a journalistic world often looking for redemption from a multitude of actual and assumed transgressions, they should be banished lest they get into the Journalistic House of Freedom and contaminate it in the name of journalistic responsibility.

Argument Summation: Press councils and ethical codes are dangerous control mechanisms.

Not only are councils and codes likely to bring about conformist media activity, but they have not succeeded in bettering the American media system. The National News Council died and state councils are nearly nonexistent. In a competitive, open society like the United States, there is no need for editorial direction other than that provided by each media unit. It is not to councils and codes that the media must turn for ethical and ideological direction; individual media managers and journalists must determine their own pathways. In codes of ethics there is an implicit "conformity desire," as there is in news councils. Somebody or some group is setting itself up as the arbiter of media conduct. This is dangerous in a system which is theoretically self-determining and pluralistic.

RESPONSE

Dennis: Press councils and ethical codes are useful instruments of criticism that can improve the media.

Professor Merrill argues quite convincingly that press councils and ethical codes are superfluous, self-serving, and even dangerous. This purist position almost instantly conjures up an image of crazed Naderesque crusaders who would shackle the press and emasculate freedom through a system of constraining rules. But a look at the real world gives us quite a different view.

Those who promulgated codes and organized press councils were not activists with Draconian values, but sensitive media professionals and public-spirited citizens who want a strong, free press that is ethical and competent in its performance. This is not a lofty ideal, but a belief that the press can be improved if there are formal channels for public comment and criticism, and if professionals have standards against which they can make individual decisions. And notably, no one is imposing anything, since both press councils and codes of ethics are *voluntary*. They have only an advisory function; they make suggestions; they are not the rule of law; if they have any power it is only the "power of embarrassment." They can point to poor practices or praise good ones. In fact, they are preventive mechanisms that can head off legal sanctions and heavy penalties. For example, most press councils require those bringing grievances to waive their right to sue later on. "Ethics," as Professor Merrill has pointed out in *The Imperative of Freedom*, "is that branch of philosophy that helps journalists determine what is right to do in their journalism; it is very much a normative science of conduct, with conduct considered primarily as self-determined voluntary conduct" (Merrill, 1974, 165). Later in the same book he asks whether ethics should be "individualistic" or "group-approved." Not surprisingly, he prefers the individual choice to that of group norms. I do not think the two need to be mutually exclusive. One can have codes of ethics and press council proceedings that become a kind of "common law" of media ethics, against which individuals can exercise their minds and good judgment with regard to individual cases. That is as it should be.

In fact, Professor Louis Hodges of Washington and Lee University makes this point when he says the real value of ethical codes may not be so much in the finished product—the code itself—as in the *process* that professionals go through in writing codes. "I'd have everyone write a code; then throw it away," says Hodges. Those who participated would learn from the experience. In Hodges's ideal situation all media professionals would engage in the code-making process. In reality, of course, this is not likely to occur. Therefore, codes of ethics fashioned by journalists for journalists are the next best thing. Codes set standards and help distinguish virtuous practices that serve the public interest from those that do not. They would enhance the position of the press in society by seeing that it is truly independent, free, and responsible.

Codes of ethics developed by professional societies or editors' associations are general philosophical statements that promote impartiality, fair play, and decency. Codes formulated by individual news organizations are usually much more specific. They have rules on such matters as gifts, outside employment, conflicts of interest, advocacy, accuracy, and plagiarism, among other topics. In some instances, these guidelines become conditions of employment, but exceptions and waivers are always possible. Who is to say that it is not all right for a newspaper or television station to tell its employees that they do not want them accepting "freebies" such as trips, tickets, or other gifts? Or that they should not misrepresent themselves or plagiarize material from other sources? Such standards spelled out in codes enhance the credibility of journalism and give the audience more confidence in the news. Of course, ethical codes are mostly insiders' rules and not widely publicized.

By contrast, press councils are more public. To begin with, they are private, voluntary organizations which are usually (in America, at least) made up of a mix of media people and public members. The public members represent such interests as education, business, labor, minorities, and religion. A press council is a channel where public complaints about the media can be aired. Thus, the citizen has a neutral forum in which to raise questions about media performance. Press councils have no power of enforcement; they issue opinions and no one is obliged to accept them. In fact, far from being dangerous, press councils are most often criticized for being ineffective. I personally do not think this is necessarily the case, as I will point out later. What press councils do is encourage healthy, public discussion to the mutual benefit of media and public.

While the discussion of press councils and ethics codes is nothing new, this debate had added urgency in the 1980s because of strong public dissatisfaction with the press. This is important because the media exist in society with many competing forces and organizations. Media need not be popular, but they must inspire enough public confidence to carry out their necessary information and opinion functions.

Thus, it is disturbing when pollsters report that the media face deepening public distrust. It is as though the individual citizen, like Paddy Chayefsky's deranged anchorman in Network, is saying, "I'm mad as hell and I'm not going to take it anymore!" In a 1982 survey ABC News reported that six of every ten Americans favored a law that would prevent TV reporters from questioning people who do not want to be interviewed. Personal privacy, the respondents said, is more important than freedom of the press. A poll conducted by the Los Angeles Times found that only one person in three believes that news reporters are fair. A Gallup study revealed that the public ranks the honesty and ethics of reporters considerably below those of police officers and just above those of business tycoons. Elsewhere in this book we mention studies by the Public Agenda Foundation indicating that the public believes that the media constrain individual freedom of expression by noncoverage or denial of access to divergent views. Similarly, a study by the American Society of Newspaper Editors shows that media professionals have a contemptuous view of their audience. These are not good signs. Personally, I believe that most of these assessments are patently unfair. Most journalists are scrupulously honest and their organizations take precautions to ensure fairness. The degree of professionalism in the media is stronger than ever. Yet few people know this and the media do little to let the public in on the secret.

The rights of a free press ultimately depend on the consent of citizens. Television and other media, says George Watson of ABC News, "cannot protect that freedom simply by invoking the First Amendment. It needs to debate its rights and responsibilities and that demands a great effort to provide an attentive ear and open mind to the public's concern and criticism" (Watson, 1982, A23).

One reason we have this deplorable situation, in which the public gives the media such low marks, is that we have so few channels for feedback, so little opportunity for criticism. There are very few press councils, and codes of ethics exist mostly in professional organizations and media industry groups. A relatively small number of individual news organizations have their own. Both codes and councils are the exception in America, not the rule. Ethics codes are not particularly controversial, but press councils are. I believe this is because they are poorly understood.

Press councils are not ancient Star Chamber tribunals. They are settings for rationale debate and their findings are usually publicized in the press. For more than ten years, I was able to observe at close range the Minnesota News Council. More than anything else, the Minnesota Council was the conscience of journalism in that state. I saw complaints that questioned fairness in news coverage, the presentation of poll data, reporter interference with pending criminal investigations, and many more. One notable grievance from a defeated candidate for governor led to a lively discussion of how campaign issues are determined. In several instances, news organizations drafted new rules and policies for their staffs as a result of council findings. In other cases (about half, I believe) the council tilted toward the press and pointed up misunderstandings in the complaint. In short, the process was healthy. Charles W. Bailey, former editor of the *Minneapolis Tribune*, himself a somewhat reluctant convert to the press council idea, stated publicly that the council had a strong, positive influence on his paper and on journalism in the state generally. As Bailey put it:

> In a society where the government cannot regulate the press—and that prohibition, though periodically dented by the courts, has so far fortunately been preserved—it is healthy to have some noncoercive device to monitor the performance of so powerful a societal institution (Bailey, Minnesota News Council brochure, undated).

A. H. Raskin of the *New York Times*, who worked closely with the National News Council, agrees: "Of all the institutions of an increasingly complicated society, none is so addicted to self-righteousness, self-satisfaction and self-congratulation as the press" (Raskin, Minnesota News Council brochure). Press councils, he adds, provide an important check for the public.

The knowledgeable observer Cameron Blodgett, former director of the Minnesota News Council, argued vehemently in favor of councils because, he says, they can:

- validate news media coverage;
- reduce the number and costs of libel suits and complaints to the Federal Communications Commission;
- provide audience feedback ... and point up public perceptions and misperceptions;

- enhance credibility;
- educate the public about how the media work;
- preserve media freedom through a fair and effective press;
- improve media performance and set standards of competence.

Adds Blodgett, "Press councils will not censor, fine, or regulate, nor will they result in government control."

Have press councils and ethical codes brought any notable improvement to the press in America? Perhaps they have not had a profound impact, but I would argue that is because there are relatively few councils. Several local communities experimented with press councils in the 1960s. Professor William L. Rivers and several colleagues in a notable study, *Backtalk: Press Councils in America* (1973), reported that local community councils were generally effective. The Minnesota press council is documented in detail by Robert Schafer in a master's thesis (1982). The National News Council had a modest impact, but its mandate was large and its resources limited. It would seem that press councils work best at the state and local levels.

The impact of ethical codes is difficult to measure. Most historians of the press, though, would agree that the performance of the press has improved markedly since the wide acceptance of social responsibility theory, which is linked to the development of ethical codes. Certainly the press is considerably more professional and more responsible today than it was in the 1920s. I suspect that ethical codes have played some small part in this transformation, in concert with journalism education, media criticism, growing professionalism, and other forces. They are interrelated and difficult to separate. Certainly, there are notable examples at particular American newspapers—the *Louisville Courier Journal* and *Milwaukee Journal* are among them—where strong ethics codes are proudly mentioned by staff members as a rationale for particular processes.

Critics of press councils and codes fear that they will become stalking horses for those who would limit press freedom or push for government controls, but this is not the case. In fact, there are instances where newspapers, locked in litigation with angry defendants, cite codes of ethics to justify what they have done as standard journalistic practice.

While codes and councils may not have had a profound and powerful influence to date, they are positive forces that benefit both the press and the public, and they should be encouraged in every way possible. The maturation of a profession is measured by its ability to encourage and cope with criticism. Journalism is on its way thanks to councils and codes.

While I would be the first to admit that press councils and ethical codes really have had a rather modest impact—most members of the public have never heard of them—they have been a stimulus for other kinds of feedback between the media and the public. Robert Chandler, an Oregon editor, for example, has championed a community accountability council that can adjudicate disputes. In 1989, more than thirty U.S. newspapers, ranging from some that are quite small and others that are large, signed up for the Chandler experiment. There are television programs that allow the public to talk back to the media, as well as those that critique and evaluate performance. Additionally, in the late 1980s and early 1990s, there was a growing tendency of newspapers and magazines to "cover the media" as a beat, thus giving the public more insight and understanding about what the media do.

Argument Summation: Press councils and ethical codes are useful instruments of criticism that can improve the media.

Theoretical criticisms of ethical codes have some merit, but an examination of the realistic implications of councils and codes confirms their importance. Since the codes are voluntary they do not restrict freedom of the press, and by heading off legal sanctions they can in fact enhance press freedoms. Codes and councils serve journalism by pointing out poor practices, while preserving the journalist's right to exercise individual judgments. Codes developed by each news organization reinforce behaviors necessary for audience credibility, and councils provide public access to a neutral forum for voicing complaints about the media. These functions are crucial for redressing the rising public distrust of the press, which threatens to undermine support for free press ideals. Currently there are too few councils, but the few experiments indicate potential for success. Journalism must look to more press councils and increased reliance on codes in order to achieve these objectives and restore public confidence in the media.

TOPICS FOR DISCUSSION

1. Why do you think press councils and ethical codes are not taken seriously in the United States?

2. Are press councils and codes contradictory to the American ideal of a pluralistic and self-determined media system?

3. Are general terms like fair play, impartiality, and decency, found in many ethical codes, helpful guides to the practicing journalist? If so, how? If not, why not?

4. If codes and press councils are to be useful in "cleaning up" the American press, should they be more powerful—have "teeth" in them? In other words, should there be sanctions against offenders?

5. Are codes and councils simply "PR" instruments, mainly designed to reassure the public of media seriousness and concern for social responsibility?

TOPICS FOR RESEARCH

1. Assume that you have been assigned to create a press council on your campus, one that would be a channel for grievances against the student newspaper. How would you go about the task? What would the council's charter be? How would it operate? Who would serve on it? How could it serve students and still not interfere with freedom of expression?

2. Compare and contrast a major electronic media or broadcast code of ethics or set of standards with one from the print media. How do they differ? How are they similar? Do they have any influence or effect?

3. Should fields like advertising and public relations have codes of ethics? If so, should they differ from those of news organizations? Do codes vary depending on the purposes of the communication activity—for example, advertising versus news?

4. Codes of ethics and press councils always move back and forth between freedom and accountability. To what extent are press councils threats to freedom of expression? To what extent do they enhance it? Examine both arguments, then offer your own view.

5. What is the obligation of media to children? Should television programming be governed by a voluntary code that takes into account the special case of children, whether in exposing them to objectionable sexual content or making them shills for advertising? How can this be done without impairing the media's First Amendment rights? Discuss.

FURTHER READING

Balk, Alfred. *A Free and Responsive Press.* New York: Twentieth Century Fund, 1973.

Brogan, Patrick. *Spiked: The Short Life and Death of the National News Council.* Winchester, MA: Unwin Hyman, 1985.

Chandler, Robert. "Controlling Conflict." Working paper. New York: Gannett Center for Media Studies, 1990.

Cooper, Thomas, et al., eds. *Communication Ethics and Global Change.* White Plains: Longman, 1989.

Hulteng, John L. *The Messenger's Motives*. Englewood Cliffs, NJ: Prentice-Hall, 1976.

Lowenstein, R. L., and J. C. Merrill. *Macromedia: Mission, Message, and Morality*. White Plains, NY: Longman, 1990.

"Media Freedom and Accountability." A Conference Report. New York: Gannett Center for Media Studies, 1986.

Merrill, J. C. *The Imperative of Freedom*. New York: Hastings House, 1974.

———. *Existential Journalism*. New York: Hastings House, 1977.

Merrill, J. C., and Ralph D. Barney, eds. *Ethics and the Press*. New York: Hastings House, 1975.

Meyer, Philip. "An Ethical Audit." Occasional paper no. 3. New York: Gannett Center for Media Studies, 1986.

Murray, George. *The Press and the Public*. Carbondale, IL: Southern Illinois University Press, 1972.

National News Council. *In the Public Interest, 1973–75*. New York, 1975.

Rivers, William L. *Back Talk: Press Councils in America*. San Francisco: Canfield Press, 1973.

Schafer, Robert. "The Minnesota News Council, a Ten Year Study." M.A. Thesis, University of Minnesota, 1982.

Watson, George. "TV Hears Viewers." *New York Times*, 25 August 1982: A23.

Chapter 14

PROPAGANDA AND THE MEDIA

In its most basic formulation propaganda is a neutral term for the spread of ideas. In *A Dictionary of the Social Sciences* propaganda denotes: "The techniques and methods of influencing or controlling the attitudes, and behavior . . . by the use of words and other symbols," as well as "the statements and impressions issuing from the use of such techniques or methods." Propaganda is a communication process that makes use of certain techniques and methods to accomplish its ends. Although the term originated with the Roman Catholic Church and had to do with the "propagation of the faith," it made its way into political communication by the early twentieth century. World War I was said to have involved a propaganda battle between the British and Germans, and the U.S. public was the target of messages delivered in pamphlets, tracts, posters, cartoons, and other forms of communication. During World War II, the Nazis developed an elaborate system of progaganda to build support for the regime, both within Germany and outside.

During that period the Institute of Propaganda Analysis promoted a serious study of propaganda, defining the term as "an expression of opinion or action by individuals or groups deliberately designed to influence opinions or actions of other individuals to predetermined ends." Propaganda usually involves the state (or government) promoting a point of view to gain influence or even control. George Orwell's *1984*, is the story of a state where propaganda is used to control thought and action. Social scientists studying propaganda and the press identified various propaganda techniques, ranging from name-calling to glittering generalities, testimonials, and the band-wagon devices.

The interest in propaganda presupposed powerful media effects, but as this view of media lost ground in the 1940s, so did propaganda analysis. In time, the term was all but shelved among media scholars and used only occasionally in media and communication studies. Except for references to Soviet or Chinese propaganda, where the government and press were comingled, the term had an antiquated ring in America. This changed by the 1980s as students of the media abandoned the minimal effects model. While media in the United States are not official instruments of state propaganda as they are in the Soviet Union or some Eastern bloc countries, they are sometimes accused of being instruments of propaganda for various interests.

The term propaganda now has a clearly pejorative connotation to the general public. Among media scholars, the prevailing view is that the press is independent and acts as a shield against propaganda. But some critics argue that media are manipulated by propaganda, whether from our own government or that of other nations. They charge that the U.S. press is subject to influence from various interests, often through propaganda and public relations. Conservative critics accuse the media of having a liberal bias.

CHALLENGE

Dennis: Media are defenses against propaganda.

Those who readily use the once-discarded term "propaganda" to examine and assess the U.S. media have to accept one of two views: Either the media are being manipulated by external influences and are thus unreliable, or they are staffed by people who willingly participate in the deception. In such a system the media are either willing or unwitting soldiers in the propaganda war. In the Soviet Union and a few other countries, the media are, in effect, part of the government and have a propaganda function. Even there, however, under the *glasnost* policies of Mikhail Gorbachev, even the seemingly monolithic Soviet media began to loosen up, even to the point of being openly critical of the government. Still, they are far closer to being propaganda organs of the government than our media ever have been. An example of a media system under strict government control is that of the People's Republic of China. Although Chinese newspapers, wire services, and television were liberalized to the point of engaging in something closer to western style reporting, this quickly ceased after the student revolt of 1989 when key editors were replaced by government functionaries. In both the Soviet and Chinese examples the media are typically, though not always, instruments of propaganda.

Is there any fundamental difference between what the media do and what propaganda agencies, do? I would argue in the affirmative. Propaganda agencies typically are government agencies, and their main function is to support and nurture their backers. They do this by persuading, sometimes overtly with great passion, sometimes through a complex web of subtle messages. They are simply a channel between government and people, and they almost always promote the status quo or change that will give the government greater authority and power.

Media typically exist to communicate with audiences, either on their own behalf or on behalf of their owners and managers. They are guided by international standards of journalism or media entertainment fare. If they are an uncritical mouthpiece for a government, business, church, or other entity, they are still instruments of mass communication, but they are hardly independent media operating in concert with media elsewhere in the world. A newspaper revealed to be funded by the CIA or the KGB will be regarded by journalists the world over, not as an independent newspaper, but as a suspect and captive voice. Of course, governments can publish newspapers or magazines or engage in state broadcasting. The products they produce will be perceived for what they are. The BBC, for example, is one of the most respected broadcasting systems in the world. It has always had great independence and operates with high professional standards. Its main product is unbiased information and news, as well as first-rate entertainment and cultural programming. Its relative independence of the partisanship of particular British governments is well known, and when Mrs. Thatcher complained during the Falklands War that the BBC was not enthusiastically pro-government, there was a firestorm of criticism mainly defending the BBC. Some media outlets in other countries are known to be sympathetic to the government, but few are slavishly so and survive long. Of course, some government-run news organizations in Third World countries are more propaganda organ than news organ. That is the reality of the situation, but for the most part, the world over, one can distinguish between the broad purposes of public media and the narrower concerns of government propaganda.

This brings us to the media of the United States and many western countries. They are hardly mouthpieces for propaganda, government or otherwise. True, for most of their history they generally followed the government lead on foreign policy, but even that tradition seemed to end during the Vietnam War.

Are the component parts of the U.S. media system either willing or unwitting instruments of propaganda? Of course not. Whatever its faults— and they are many—the U.S. press is independent and vigorous. Ask any recent American president whether the press was a cheerleader for his administration and the answer will come back a resounding "No." Similarly, the Congress is often under fire in the press and it was, in part, critical media coverage that for the first time brought the downfall of a Speaker of the House in 1989, when Congressman Jim Wright was forced to resign. Similarly, the Supreme Court hardly gets a free ride. Its decisions are watched and are dissected and analyzed. Outside government, whether at the national, state, or local level, even the private sector gets fairly tough and independent reporting. Ask business leaders whether they like the way they are portrayed in the press generally or even in such publications as the *Wall Street Journal, Forbes,* and *Business Week.*

Conservative critics claim that the media are too liberal and that journalists are biased. Some scholars who call themselves critical theorists and who generally oppose many of the capitalist values of the media say that the U.S. media do have an ideology, and that this ideology generally supports business and the status quo. I agree with one commentator, who said, "Yes, the media are ideological, and for American media the ideology is objectivity." Objectivity, for all of its faults, is a defense against propaganda. The tendency of the American media is to ignore the commonplace and to highlight differences. Hundreds of honest politicians are virtually ignored while a corrupt one is pilloried.

The American press and public are particularly sensitive to the blandishments of propaganda. The South African government, for example, has tried to propagandize the U.S. press with little success. Other foreign governments and interests have had active campaigns to change their image in America. Typically, the American press views such efforts with caution and even with criticism. The *New York Times* has, for example, carried paid advertising supplements from the South Korean government, while vigorously investigating influence peddling by the Koreans in Washington. On occasion media critics have feared that the press has been getting too cozy with a particular government official. No doubt this happens, but so does criticism of the kind that uncovers it.

No, the American media may have many faults, but being fall guys for propaganda is the exception. Perhaps this is why the term "propaganda," which only recently came back into use by scholars who had for years abandoned it as meaningless and pejorative, still seems a bit passé.

Argument Summation: Media are defenses against propaganda.

Media cease to be news organs and become tools of propaganda when they are captive voices. For example, the press in China and the Soviet Union could be characterized as propaganda organs due to their institutional ties to the government. In the United States, the press is independent and vigorous—hardly a mouthpiece for propaganda, government or otherwise. The media's criticism of the president, Congress, and courts bears out its adversarial relationship to government, while the private sector is covered critically, disproving any claim that the U.S. press is a propaganda organ. By encouraging detached commentary on events and even criticism of fellow media members when they become too supportive of a single viewpoint, the objective style of American journalism assures that it is a defense against propaganda.

RESPONSE

Merrill: Media are instruments of propaganda.

We have just been treated to the case of media as protectors of the public against propagandistic assault. It is somewhat surprising to hear that media are basically innocent of propagandizing and seldom turn themselves into vehicles of the propaganda of others.

Of course, one big initial problem in such a controversial issue as "propaganda in the media" is how we define the term propaganda. If we limit it to overt and large-scale lying or purposeful misleading, then perhaps we can say that the media are not major participants. But if we take a more realistic view of propaganda as intentional persuasion to some belief or action, then the media are filled with propaganda.

In a basic media-and-society textbook my coauthors and I suggested a "PASID" formula, identifying propaganda as Persuasive, Action-oriented, Selfish, Intentional, and Devious—or Deceptive (Merrill, Lee, and Friedlander, 1989). Such a formula is necessarily superficial, but it is handy in summarizing propaganda's key characteristics.

Many persons will insist, as Dennis does earlier, that media seldom try to practice deception in order to persuade. My study of and familiarity with a wide assortment of journalists convinces me, however, that purposeful persuasion—along with techniques of bias and deception—is far more common than Dennis and others believe.

Biases exist in journalism. And they manifest themselves in stories and filmed reports through purposeful selection of acts, sources to be interviewed, the types of questions asked, emphases and deemphases. These and other techniques are used by skilled journalists to distort, bias, and persuade in subtle ways.

One reporter will use direct quotes (to depict a person either positively or negatively), while another will use indirect quotes. A journalist will quote one person in a story to provide a "typical" viewpoint. A faculty member at a university will be quoted to let the public know what the faculty is thinking. The "one-person cross section" device of propaganda is commonly used in journalism. And reporters often quote out of context, giving one impression when another could be given by providing proper context. And who has not seen the common sentence, often at the end of a controversial story, that "Mr. X was unavailable for comment"?

A journalist who is covering a debate between political candidates will be prone to "push" his favorite. He will play up parts of what "his" candidate says that show him in a good light and will minimize (or omit entirely) those comments which are illogical, crude, ungrammatical, or otherwise easily open to criticism. It may be that what he or she does choose to report is true, true in the sense of being accurate as to those parts reported. And, of course, they will be sure that their favorite's opponent receives neutral or negative treatment. If the journalist is a photographer, he or she can do the same thing with a camera—looking for certain angles, awaiting the proper smile or frown or scowl or what have you. In one sense, a picture may not "lie," but there is no doubt but that a picture can propagandize by giving impressions that are false to reality.

A reporter provides a source in Case A but not in Case B. News management, propaganda, forthright reporting? The reporter uses such generalizing devices as "Americans believe that the South African government is immoral and must change . . ." or "China experts are predicting that the hard-liners in Beijing will be toppled in the next few weeks." Which Americans? Which China experts? How did the reporter come to these conclusions?

Another reporter digs out of the library old quotes of a person currently in the news and weaves these quotes into the story to substantiate a dominant position being taken—often not even making it clear that they are "old" quotes. The reporter often gives "the other side" a chance to have a say (thereby feigning "objectivity"), thus telling the audience, in effect, that complex issues have only two sides.

Journalists, of course, never speak of themselves as "propagandists." The term has a negative connotation and usually is applied to persuasive efforts during wartime—or perhaps to efforts made by politicians, evangelists, and advertisers. But after all, are not *journalists* above such things? Are they not solely concerned with "truth" and evenhanded information-presentation? Are they not persons with no "axes to grind"? Such questions as these only reveal the sophistication of the "antipropaganda" propaganda of institutionalized journalism.

What journalist can say that he or she is guiltless of intentionally persuasive techniques? Who does not in journalism indulge in reportorial half-truths, distortions, news "management," exaggeration, false analogies, *ad hominem* tactics, hidden evidence, emotional appeals, Machiavellian strategies, and other purposeful techniques to achieve their special objectives?

Hiding propaganda in what purports to be "impartial news" is, of course, extremely effective because of the faith most people must have in such reports. In *The Information Machines* Ben Bagdikian wrote: "There are growing numbers of men who understand how news is generated, organized, and transmitted, and it would be unintelligent of them if they did not use it to their own advantage" (1971, 293).

I am maintaining that journalists are propagandists in the sense that they "propagate" or spread their own biases and opinions as they attempt intentionally to affect attitudes and actions of their audiences. Large numbers of journalists, among them the so-called straight news reporters, spread propaganda every day—if not their own, then somebody else's.

Leading propaganda scholar Terence H. Qualter says:

> Any doubts that even the news columns have propaganda significance can be settled by comparing the way in which several papers react to the one story. Each paper will make its own decision on the importance of the story—a decision which will be reflected in the page on which the story appears, its position on that page, and the size and style of type used in the headlines (1965, 91).

Qualter continues:

> At one time it was customary to distinguish the expression of opinion on the editorial pages of a paper from the straightforward presentation of facts on the news pages. With the growing appreciation of the extent to which opinion governs the selection and manner of presentation of news, it has been concluded that this division is unrealistic and it is now generally admitted that the news columns can also contain propaganda (91).

Many people, especially journalists, will disregard contentions like those made by Qualter and will say that the readers already have such-and-such opinion or ideological position and are simply seeking newspapers which reflect them. Jacques Ellul, an acclaimed French writer on propaganda, considers such a reaction "simplistic, removed from reality, and based on liberal idealism." He also says:

> In reality, propaganda is at work here, for what is involved is a progression from vague, diffuse on the part of the reader to rigorous, exciting, active expression of that opinion. A feeling or an impression is transformed into a motive for action.... The reader is subject to propaganda, even though it be propaganda of his choice. Why always fall into the error of seeing in propaganda nothing but a device to *change* opinions? Propaganda is also a means of reinforcing opinions, of transforming them into action. The reader himself offers his throat to the knife of the propaganda he chooses (1965, 104).

Some propagandistic journalism is rather overt and crude. Sophisticated and skilled journalists, of course, make every effort to avoid this kind. They propagandize in far more subtle, effective ways. Instead of injecting their own values and judgments into their journalism in readily recognizable ways, they resort to subterfuge by resorting to tactical selectivity and emphasis to accomplish their purposes. And instead of expressing a point of view, a position, or an opinion *themselves*, they let others speak for them. They selectively quote, using the device that *U.S. News and World*

Report pioneered and best exemplified. It is a common practice among journalists, and most honest ones will admit that they are guilty of it.

Propagandistic inclinations of journalists make it difficult for the audience to know when they are getting the truth. Nobody, of course, receives the full truth in journalism. Truth put into the journalism grinder comes out in bits and pieces, incomplete and sifted through the subjective value system of the journalist. So the truth is something that is tarnished when journalists finish it. One should remember Jefferson's famous quote in his later years when he wrote to a friend that, "Truth itself becomes suspicious by being put into that polluted vehicle [the press]."

Media play their parts in spreading the propaganda of others. In so doing they inadvertently (or purposely) propagandize. Take the case of CBS's Dan Rather (March 30, 1987, "Evening News") when he cooperated with the Soviet Union in its propagandistic attempt to make the United States appear guilty for the spread of AIDS. He reported: "A Soviet military publication claims the virus that causes AIDS leaked from a U.S. Army laboratory conducting experiments in biological warfare." Rather reported this even though he admitted that CBS has no evidence, and the Defense Department had earlier put the rumor to rest—or so the Pentagon thought.

I am not maintaining that journalists alone participate in propaganda. We all do. Even academic persons who, like journalists, uphold the ideal of neutrality and dispassionate search for truth. Scholars push their pet theories and emphasize their favorite political figures; they quote most often their ideological "allies," and they make sure their students get nothing or very little of the ideas of their ideological "foes." It has been said that you can tell the politics and values of teachers by noting whom they quote, and by looking at the footnotes and bibliographic entries of their publications.

Here are people—academics and journalists—who claim that they are not "grinding axes." Here are practitioners who pay allegiance to fairness, balance, an unbiased perspective, and a desire to get at the truth. Their audiences do not expect to get propaganda. In the case of advertisers, public relations people, politicians, and evangelists, on the other hand, there is a normal expectation of propaganda; nobody contends that these people are not advocating something, trying to "sell" something. There is no hypocrisy here.

No hypocrisy adheres, of course, to some journalists, editorial writers and columnists, for example. Propaganda in their products does not surprise us. But with reporters it is different. But perhaps it should not be. Perhaps we should expect propaganda from *all* journalists. I certainly do.

Argument Summation: Media are instruments of propaganda.

Practitioners both transmit the propaganda of others and initiate their own. Probably three-fourths of all media content (maybe more, considering advertising) contains propaganda for some cause, policy, idea, institution, party, or person. Journalists especially are people of strong beliefs and their biases come through in their journalism. Innumerable ways exist for journalists to propagandize—selection of information for stories and use of quotes, for example—and the journalists make use of them. Advertising, of course, is almost all propagandistic, and without a doubt, it accounts for the bulk of media content. Media are in the "ax-grinding" business, as well as the information and entertainment business. Fortunately, a pluralism of propagandas keeps the activity from doing great social damage. The people can select their favorite propaganda from the variety furnished by the media.

TOPICS FOR DISCUSSION

1. Discuss the value of the acronymic formula P-A-S-I-D as a useful definition of propaganda.

2. Explain how many persons would see the media as "shields against propaganda." Do you think this is a valid view?

3. Why is propaganda so often identified with *government* communication efforts rather than with other groups, or individuals, such as the press or the television anchor?

4. Discuss why propaganda in the U.S. media would not be as effective as it would be in the media of Iran or the U.S.S.R.

5. Is there a natural inclination for people in control of mass messages to propagandize? Give some examples of journalism which you feel *do not* indulge in propaganda.

TOPICS FOR RESEARCH

1. Write an essay on how propaganda got a bad name. After all, it was once a neutral term.

2. Prepare a report on governments and propaganda. How do governments develop propaganda machines? How do they work? To what effect? Mention both democratic and authoritarian societies.

3. Read two or three books about propaganda and write a review essay, asking whether propaganda is still a useful modern concept.

4. Considering changes in the Soviet Union, Eastern Europe, or China, examine the changing role of propaganda. Does a more pluralistic press challenge propaganda?

5. Examine the claim that public relations and propaganda are one and the same. True? False? How do we know?

FURTHER READING

Altschull, J. Herbert. *Agents of Power: The Role of News Media in Human Affairs.* White Plains, NY: Longman, 1984.

Bagdikian, Ben. *The Information Machines.* New York: Harper & Row, 1971.

Christians, Clifford G. "Jacques Ellul and Democracy's 'Vital Information' Premise." *Journalism Monographs,* August 1976.

Ellul, Jacques. *Propaganda: The Formation of Men's Attitudes.* New York: Alfred A. Knopf, 1965.

Ewen, Stuart. *All-Consuming Images: The Politics of Style in Contemporary Culture.* New York: Basic Books, 1988.

———. *Channels of Desire: Mass Images and the Shaping of the American Consciousness.* New York: McGraw-Hill, 1982.

Gitlin, Todd. *The Whole World is Watching.* Berkeley, CA: University of California Press, 1980.

Jowett, Garth S., and Victoria O'Donnell. *Propaganda and Persuasion.* Beverly Hills, CA: Sage Publications, 1986.

Lemert, James B. *Criticizing the Media: Empirical Approaches.* Beverly Hills, CA: Sage Publications, 1989.

Merrill, John C. *Existential Journalism.* New York: Hastings House, 1977.

Merrill, John C., and Jack Odell. *Philosophy and Journalism.* White Plains, NY: Longman, 1983.

Merrill, John C., John Lee, and Jay Friedlander. *Modern Mass Media.* New York: Harper & Row, 1990.

Qualter, Terence H. *Propaganda and Psychological Warfare.* New York: Random House, 1965.

Schiller, Herbert I. *The Mind Managers.* Boston: Beacon Press, 1973.

———. *Mass Communications and American Empire.* Boston: Beacon Press, 1971.

Sproule, J. Michael. "Propaganda Studies in American Social Science: The Rise and Fall of the Critical Paradigm," *Quarterly Journal of Speech* 73(1987): 60–78.

Chapter **15**

ADVERTISING

Advertising is both a communication process and an industry that is inextricably linked to mass media in America and in some other societies. It is defined in dictionaries as the action that attracts public attention to a product or business, as well as the business of preparing and distributing advertisements. According to the American Marketing Association, advertising is "any paid form of nonpersonal presentation and promotion of ideas, goods, and services by an identified sponsor." Advertising has also been called "controlled, identifiable information and persuasion." Advertising becomes a matter of controversy for several reasons. Its role in society and in the economy has often been debated.

Advertising has a well-established place in American life. The component parts of the advertising industry—ad agencies, media service organizations, media advertising departments—employ nearly 200,000 people and generate about $100 million in gross revenue annually. Advertising is generally accepted by most Americans who recognize that it funds most of the media they enjoy, provides consumer advice, and promotes a capitalist economy. It has been said that American society is a commercial culture and advertising is an essential ingredient in that formulation.

While advertising is a historical reality and one that provides "fuel" for most commercial media in the United States, there are those who would prefer a communication system without advertising. Questions are frequently raised about whether advertising unnecessarily stimulates needs and wants of people, whether it encourages class-consciousness, materialism, and other values that are not universally applauded. Such discussion is related to advertising's impact and influence in society, assessed by historians, philosophers, social scientists, and media researchers. The social criticism of advertising often centers on whether advertising is truthful. While few critics today advocate the abolition of advertising, there is an active movement to control this form of controlled communication, presumably to serve the public interest. Special attention has been given to the impact of advertising on children, the portrayal of women and minorities in advertising, and other topics that have generated controversy.

CHALLENGE

Merrill: Advertising is a negative social force.

A principal deity of a capitalist society and of a competitive marketplace media system is the Great God Advertising. GGA is everywhere, raising its gaudy face across the land, beaming its insistent messages into our offices, cars, and homes. It fills billboards along our highways, drops in the form of coupons from our magazines and mailboxes, blares at us in all of its resplendent redundancy from our TV screens, and fills our newspapers.

The power and crassness of the advertiser is a negative social force. It contaminates our country from one end to the other. This advertiser power has been called by George F. Kennan "the greatest evil of our national life." How can we, asked Kennan, have a healthy intellectual climate, successful education, a sound press, or "a proper vitality of artistic and recreational life" until advertisements "are removed from every printed page containing material that has claim to intellectual or artistic integrity and from every television or radio program that has these same pretensions?" (1968, 201).

These are strong words from one of twentieth-century America's foremost diplomats. But that's not all that Kennan had to say about advertising. Listen:

> Is it a revolution I am demanding? Yes—a revolution in the financing and control of the process of communication generally. And if this revolution brings in the government as a replacement for the advertiser in many of these processes, I still wish for it. The government's commitment and conscience as an educator its commitment to truthfulness and integrity in communication— may not be all that we could want. But it has at least *some* responsibility here to the public weal, and *some* obligation to keep in mind the public needs. This is more than one can say about the advertiser (1968, 201–202).

Another luminary of the twentieth century, Aldous Huxley, with his exceptionally keen eye for blemishes in social institutions, devoted the whole of Chapter 6 of his well-known *Brave New World Revisited* (1965) to the "arts of selling," with special emphasis on advertising. He speaks of propaganda in the West as having two faces—one (Dr. Jekyll) the democratic editorialist, the other (Dr. Hyde) the antidemocratic person in charge of advertising.

This propagandist—the advertising expert—is a Ph.D. in psychology and has a master's degree in the social sciences. Here is part of Huxley's depiction of this advertising "Dr. Hyde":

> This Dr. Hyde would be very unhappy indeed if everybody lived up to John Dewey's faith in human nature. Truth and reason are Jekyll's affair, not his. Hyde is a motivational analyst, and his business is to study human weaknesses and failings, to investigate those unconscious desires and fears by which so much of man's conscious thinking and overt doing is determined. And he does this, not in the spirit of the moralist who would like to make people better, or of the physician who would like to improve their health, but simply in order to find out the best way to take advantage of their ignorance and to exploit their irrationality for the pecuniary benefit of his employers (1965).

Irrational, exploitive, seeking pecuniary profit, manipulating the audience's desires and fears: This is the picture painted of advertisers. These two men have capsulized neatly the major characteristics and concerns of advertising in America. Obviously such advertising is not a positive force in our society.

Mention "Madison Avenue" and what comes to mind? The thoughtful, perceptive citizen does not have to read a book critical of the advertising business (like Samm S. Baker's classic *The Permissible Lie*) to feel antipathy toward the omnipresent commercialism that surrounds us all. Coke and Pepsi battle it out everywhere, each claiming superiority, with their slogans couched in abstract vagaries.

Brand X is best by taste test. Four out of five doctors recommend this mouthwash. Discerning people choose this brand. All one has to do is "squeeze" the toilet paper to know it's superior. My aspirin is stronger than yours. My automobile is like a bird; just watch it here on TV—it actually takes off and zooms into the night sky. Here come all the ads that hawk their products as "new" and "improved." And there is that advertising that insults one's intelligence; for instance, a commercial on television tells us that its product (a cereal) "might reduce the risk of certain types of cancer." It *might reduce the risk of certain* types. I am not reassured.

I sit before my TV set and, lo and behold, the alleged "positive force" of the commercials strikes me constantly. I learn useful and important things. I learn that "a double pleasure" is waiting for me if I buy a certain kind of chewing gum. I am urged to "come into Kirshmann's Furniture Store and feel the excitement." And, if "coffee tastes your way," it's X-Brand. And if I drink this kind of beer, "the best comes shining through." And I'll get "taste free in every bite" if I'll eat a certain breakfast cereal.

Important stuff. A positive social force. Just knowing that there are double pleasures, the chance to feel the excitement, things tasting my way, having the best shine through, and getting a "free" taste with every bite. Now, that's a positive (useful, socially significant) social force!

But all is well, for the "Creative Code" of the American Association of Advertising Agencies (representing at least 15 national communications groups) has determined to keep this "positive social force" intact and progressing. The public, we are told, has the right to expect advertising to be reliable in content and honest in presentation. And the code assures us that advertisers will "extend and broaden the application of high ethical standards."

Advertising, says the code, will not: deal in misleading statements or exaggerations; present testimonials which do not reflect the real choice of the testimonial-giver; make misleading price claims; make insufficiently supported claims; or present statements or pictures offensive to public decency. I would say that advertising consistently does *all of these things.* If you don't believe it, just take a few moments and analyze the ads that flood from the media upon you.

Advertising—a positive social force? I think not. Advertising causes people to buy what they don't need, causes people to discard perfectly good merchandise, causes poor people to want things they can't afford, causes the spread of vulgar culture, and creates exorbitant and unfillable expectations, thus promoting a "materialistic" society.

Here is what Michael Schudson has to say about advertising:

> Whatever advertising's direct effect in stimulating and making people buy more goods, it fully merits its reputation as the emblem of fraudulence. . . . A great many [ads] are positively informational. But there is a persistent, underlying bad faith in nonprice advertising. I take as emblematic the old McDonald's slogan, "We do it all for you." That, of course, is a lie (1984, 13).

As Samm S. Baker tells us, Madison Avenue condones and encourages half-truths and exaggeration. He adds:

> The overwhelming aim of advertising is to make a profit; to serve the public becomes a secondary consideration. A lie that helps build profits is considered a permissible lie (1968).

Former magazine editor Richard L. Tobin quotes Baker from *Printer's Ink:* "In a single half hour of browsing through magazines I found more than a dozen ads claiming that their products were smoother; longer-lasting; cheaper; better; washed whiter; stayed fresh longer. . . . Are we really suckers that we swallow these pointless hooks?" Perhaps we are not so foolish as to swallow them, but even if they are relatively harmless from that perspective, it still seems rather obvious that such advertising does not serve as a positive social force.

Now, my coauthor Dennis will surely maintain that much advertising is not of that type, that much of it is straightforward and factual, and that it provides a much-needed public service. I must admit that this is true. There is *some* honest, information advertising, just as there are some "helpful" morphine and cocaine. But what about the generality? Advertising, *generally*, is not a positive social force; it does more harm to the society than good, and certainly it should be deemphasized.

Advertising is to a newspaper as intercollegiate athletics is to a university. Both advertising and athletics deemphasize the real purpose of their "carrier." Neither is perhaps bad per se, but, to quote two old clichés, each has "gotten out of hand" and we have a case of "the tail wagging the dog." A newspaper (a misnomer these days when only about 10 percent of the total "newspaper" space contains *news*) reader must increasingly search diligently for tiny oases of editorial material, surrounded as they are by vast deserts of advertising.

In conclusion, I must contend that advertising is not a positive social force. It is simply the economic foundation for the money-making proclivities of media owners and the machine that stimulates exorbitant profits by manufacturers, wholesalers, and retailers. And what about *political advertising?* I won't even get into that. It's too sleazy. But I suppose that three out of four of the nation's politicians highly recommend it. Undoubtedly, 100 percent of media owners give it the "go" sign. This, of course, must mean that it is a positive social force. But that's Dennis's position. I don't buy it.

Argument Summation: Advertising is a negative social force.

Advertising clutters our media, overpowers serious news and discussion, encourages unnecessary buying, worsens class envy, and leads to wasteful consumption. Advertisements may largely finance American media, but that would be the only way it could be called a "positive force." Advertising exaggerates, misleads, appeals to sex and frivolity, gives irrational testimonials, creates exorbitant expectations, and generally promotes a materialistic society. At best, advertising in America is a necessary evil. It could hardly be called a positive social force.

RESPONSE

Dennis: Advertising is a positive social force.

If the reader were seated in front of a VCR, I would insert a selection of advertisements that urge safe sex practices to avoid AIDS, promote literacy, encourage racial tolerance and environmental improvement. Then I would ask the reader to find equally powerful advertisements reaching mass audiences that promote the opposite of these causes and values or any other advertising that truly does damage to our way of life, fosters racism, or promotes pollution. I would guess that the reader would have difficulty with that assignment. I might then ask what in the world Professor Merrill is talking about, but perhaps that would be too easy. So, I will respond to several of his protestations about the evils of advertising.

First, a touch of reality. Advertising is a reality. It has been with us since ancient times and has played a particular role in American culture since before the revolution. It is so well-integrated into our commercial media—and that is most media sans public television and radio—that they probably could not survive without it. No one I know of, not even Professor Merrill, is seriously suggesting that advertising be abolished or even curtailed by legislation. In fact, I doubt that this is possible because it is well to remember that advertising is protected speech. It is commercial rather than political speech, but it is a form of free expression and it has some constitutional protection. With some irony, advertising executive John O'Toole writes:

> *The Pennsylvania Evening Post* of July 6, 1776 contained the text of the Declaration of Independence and ten advertisements, thereby exhibiting a certain insensitivity to a distinction between news and commercial speech that has taken on enormous importance over the ensuing centuries (*Gannett Center Journal*, vol. 1, no. 1, Spring, 1987: 97).

While once accorded less freedom than political speech, commercial speech has gained important ground over the last ten years, a trend that is likely to continue. So it seems that my colleague, who sees no problem with the free distribution of all kinds of political and social messages and generally abhors censorship, somehow is uncomfortable with the impact and influence of what he calls "the great god advertising." I refuse to capitalize this rather hackneyed expression.

Of course, I am not so silly as to argue that all advertising is elevating and socially responsible, any more than I would make the case for all printed and electronic communication. Some advertising is misleading, unsavory, and generally reprehensible, but the vast majority of it is not, and if one really believes in freedom of expression, we take the good, the bad, and the ugly as part of the package, while hoping, of course, that positive social forces will reward responsible communicators and shun those who are not. In the case of advertising, ads that make fraudulent claims are subject to legal penalties, just as writers who libel others can be sued and thus punished. But that really isn't the point.

To argue that advertising has a positive social impact, I believe that its value is principally in providing consumer information to the public. Advertising is the means by which we learn about new products, services, and causes. Discerning people look at advertising with a somewhat skeptical eye because advertising is advocacy for a product and there are simply too many products for any of us to know, understand, use, or for that matter, afford. We know that there are many brands of cereal, all competing for our attention. Some will make nutritional claims, others emphasize taste. Probably no one—not even young children—accepts literally everything in an advertisement, even though it may be true, because there is something called "consumer choice," and we make our choices based on our own needs, interests, income, and other factors. Advertising thus provides an educational service.

Advertising stimulates the economy. One only need visit a socialist country to see how few products are available. And while it sometimes seems that our materialistic society has generated more products than we need or can possibly consume, if the choice is between the empty shelves of Moscow and the crowded displays in Los Angeles, I know where I would prefer to shop. Of course, our economy does have a wasteful aspect—we have more firms and more products in the market than can possibly survive. Some do. Some do not. And advertising plays a role in showcasing both to the American public. On the positive side, advertising expands consumer choice and promotes diversity. It if were otherwise, someone would have to make arbitrary choices about which products would be manufactured and which ones would not be allowed to develop. In socialist economies this is done by the government. In our system, ultimately the consumers choose and they are aided by advertising.

There is considerable controversy over whether advertising has any real impact on consumer behavior. Some economists and social scientists say it has little or none. Others argue that it is all powerful. Sociologist Michael Schudson, whom Professor Merrill quotes, has some real doubts about the influence of advertising, arguing that, "Advertising is much less powerful than advertisers and critics of advertising claim, and advertising agencies are stabbing in the dark much more than they are practicing precision microsurgery on the public consciousness." Still, in his book on advertising Schudson also concedes that "advertising serves a useful informational function that will not and should not be abandoned"(1984, 239).

Schudson is among those who doubt that advertising affects consumer choice all that much, but he does suggest that it may affect the goods available to consumers. Consumers are not the only factors to consider. The entrepreneurs want to create and sell products. They can do this efficiently and try their wares on the public—sometimes successfully, sometimes not—because of advertising.

Modern advertising is not the carnival barker of old, nor is it indiscriminate shotgun messages sent out over mass media. It is carefully calibrated and controlled communication. It is aimed at a particular segment of the market or audience. A particular ad, for example, may target only black Americans or only persons in a particular income bracket or with a given educational background. This also encourages diversity and even stimulates the number and range of media organizations in the marketplace. The magazine industry, for example, exists mainly because of advertising aimed at specialized audiences. There are women's magazines, for example, mainly because there are products and services that are for women only. They advertise in *Ladies Home Journal* or *Ms.* to reach a selected, target audience. As some critics have said, this is not delicate brain surgery, but it is an efficient way to see that appropriate people know about certain products and issues that will influence them. Advertising ranges from national to local, from display to classified. It is hard to imagine that anyone, even Professor Merrill, would argue against the utility and efficiency of classified advertising unless, of course, it was the personals, which sometimes transgress good taste.

My colleague saves his final stab for political advertising, which he quite superficially denounces, and then with the dagger in his shawl retreats from the stage. In light of the many attacks on political advertising in recent presidential campaigns, the subject is worth addressing here. Many will remember the Willie Horton ad run by the Bush-for-President campaign in 1988. It was said to be racist and misleading and I believe it was. At the same time, it was widely debated and I don't think, in the end, it unduly influenced anyone who wasn't already going to vote for George Bush for other reasons. Certainly there is no evidence to the contrary. True enough, there were misleading, low-grade political ads in the 1988 campaign, but they generally reflected an issueless campaign and the messages of the two candidates, both of whom were mean-spirited. At the same time there were thousands of positive, elevating political ads used by candidates at the local, state, and national levels. And, if past elections are any indicator, the general trend in political advertising has been quite positive, pointing up the virtues of a given candidate rather than tearing down that person's opponent.

The fact that there is so much discussion about the content of advertising suggests that people are paying attention to it. When ads have been sexist, there has often been an outcry against them. Fairly often, these ads are dropped and new ones come on in their place. Is the net result here negative? No, not at all. The sexist ad which probably was prepared to appeal to people's predispositions was challenged and brought to public attention, thus unwittingly doing a service to the feminist cause. And it is through this kind of criticism and response that attitudes and public images do change over time. Once minorities and women were portrayed in a denigrating fashion in the ads or not at all. Now that is changing, reflecting changing social attitudes. That is for the better.

There will always be some offensive and potentially damaging advertisements, but in our system they can be challenged, criticized, and protested. That is not a bad process and probably reflects the advance of civilization generally. After all, our culture wasn't created in a day and it will continue to mature with the help of advertising, which is, of course, a positive social force.

Argument Summation: Advertising is a positive social force.

There is no realistic justification for the restriction of advertising: It is a form of protected speech and is crucial to the financial survival of media industries. While some advertising is generally reprehensible, the vast majority is not, and there is virtually no advertising that promotes causes or values which truly do damage to American society. Instead, by providing consumer information to the public, advertising plays a positive social role. The public knows that advertisements are advocating specific views and accepts them with skepticism. Advertising also is a positive force for economic stimulation. Targeted advertising is valuable to increase the diversity and range of media organizations like specialized magazines in the marketplace. Political advertising, even when misleading, reflects the nature of the candidates and rarely goes unchallenged by the opposition or a critical news media.

TOPICS FOR DISCUSSION

1. What are some of the ways the American media system could be financially supported if we were to eliminate advertising?
2. Can advertising be considered a positive social force because it is "a reality" that has been with us from ancient times?
3. Does advertising in the United States keep the press free? If so, how? Could the press be just as free if there were no advertising? What does press financing have to do with First Amendment press provisions?
4. Make a case for political advertising. Do you know of anyone who voted for a certain candidate because of advertising? Have you or any of your family? Do you think political advertising is issue-oriented?
5. Does most TV and newspaper display advertising appeal to a person's reason or to one's prejudices and emotions? Explain and give examples.

TOPICS FOR RESEARCH

1. Look at public service advertisements that promote an important social cause or issue. Be specific and examine them in terms of their appeals and likely success (or failure).

2. Write an essay after researching the topic of political advertising on "Political Advertising: The Good, the Bad, and the Ugly." Give examples of positive and negative political advertising. What kind works best? Why?

3. Is advertising a positive social force on the movement of goods and services? Compare and contrast the advertisements of two competitors. Do they distinguish their products? Do they make compelling cases? If this were your only source of information about the products, which would you choose based on the advertisements?

4. In recent years comparative advertising, wherein one product promotes itself by attacking a competitor either overtly or with subtlety, has been in vogue. Compare two advertisers who use this approach. Do you think it works?

5. Set up your own criteria and standards for advertising that is a positive social force. Then grade several ads or ad campaigns using your own criteria. Be a tough grader.

FURTHER READING

Baker, Samm S. *The Permissible Lie: The Truth About Advertising*. Cleveland: World Publishing Co., 1968.

Huxley, Aldous. *Brave New World Revisited*. New York: Harper & Row, Perennial Library, 1965.

Jamieson, Kathleen Hall. *Packaging the Presidency*. New York: Oxford University Press, 1984.

Kennan, George. *Democracy and the Student Left*. New York: Bantam Books, 1968.

Packard, Vance. *The Hidden Persuaders*. Paperback ed. New York: Washington Square Press, 1980.

Pope, Daniel. *The Making of Modern Advertising*. New York: Basic Books, 1983.

Potter, David M. *People of Plenty*. 2d ed. Chicago: University of Chicago Press, 1969.

Rotzoll, Kim B., James E. Haefner, and Charles H. Sandage. *Advertising in Contemporary Society*. Cincinnati, OH: South-Western Publishing Co., 1986.

Sandage, C. H., Vernon Fryburger, and Kim Rotzoll. *Advertising Theory and Practice*. 11th ed. Homewood, IL: Richard D. Irwin, 1983.

Schudson, Michael. *Advertising: The Uneasy Persuasion*. New York: Basic Books, 1984.

Chapter 16

PUBLIC RELATIONS

Public relations (PR), like advertising, is variously a communication system, a subset of the media system, a series of practices, a profession, and the object of derision and scorn. The leading text by Scott Cutlip and colleagues says: "The term public relations is used in at least three senses: the *relationships* with those who constitute an organization's public or constituents, the *ways and means used* to achieve favorable relationships, and the *quality or status* to the relationships. Thus the one term is used to label both *means and ends,* to name a *condition* and to express the *conduct or actions related to that condition*" (Cutlip, Center, and Broom, 1985, 120).

The field of public relations, like advertising, is part and parcel of the communication system in the United States. There are independent public relations firms, public relations offices in businesses and government, and communications consulting firms that do everything from training executives for television appearances to designing an information campaign and strategy for a political candidate or a foreign government. Hundreds of thousands of persons work in the public relations field and it would be hard to estimate the amount of money spent on this activity. While public relations certainly has its detractors, it also has a national professional association—the Public Relations Society of America—an accreditation procedure for professionals, a code of ethics, and a growing scholarly and professional literature. Some critics—especially some journalists—would abolish public relations altogether. That, however, is an unlikely scenario because public relations is nothing more than controlled and organized communication. And in a communication society, public relations has grown since there is simply more demand for communication services. As information increasingly becomes a renewable resource through the recycling of messages, public relations strategies and services are needed to promote and market the product. Public relations differs in an essential way from advertising because it is not generally identified with a sponsor or product. When one sees a guest on the "Today Show," chances are that person has been "placed" there by a highly paid public relations practitioner or firm, yet the viewer is never told this. Thus public relations can be more subtle and less visible than advertising.

CHALLENGE

Dennis: Public relations manipulates the news.

Pause for a moment and consider the general image that public relations has in American society. Public relations in the minds of many is equated with deception. A "public relations solution," for example, implies an emphasis on appearances and stage-managing rather than a blunt recitation of facts. Remembering that public relations is an arm of top management, whether in the public or private sector, it can be noted that public relations is a process meant to benefit those creating PR messages. A company's public relations department is not charged with reporting bad news, should there be any in the firm. Instead, the mandate is to put the best face on the situation, to explain and rationalize it. This can be done positively in a fashion beneficial to the public but often is not, since it is the client, not the public, paying the bill. Some argue that this is simply the right to communicate and that all persons are entitled to put forth their views, with or without the help of a public relations firm. That is an important factor in the debate over the utility of public relations, since some critics argue that it not only tends to be deceptive, but also gives undue advantage to those who can afford to have their own public relations counsel. In general, even after years of high quality professional attainment, the field of public relations still has a somewhat unsavory reputation in American society and the term itself is much disputed. Whether this is fair and accurate or not is not the issue here. It is the prevailing image.

Of course, even the origins of public relations in the United States are unsavory. Public relations historians are fond of recounting the history of this questionable enterprise, which they say was established by Ivy Lee, an ex-newspaperman who created a publicity agency. One of his clients was John D. Rockefeller, the oil tycoon who had a deservedly bad reputation for his unfair business practices and his cruelty to the people who worked for him. The great muckraker Ida M. Tarbell documented Rockefeller's practices in her brilliant work "The History of the Standard Oil Company," which appeared in *McClure's Magazine* in 1902. Those articles and other social criticism brought pressure on the Congress to clip Rockefeller's wings and those of other robber barons. The result was antitrust legislation and penalties for unfair and illegal competition. Rockefeller hired Ivy Lee to convince the public that he was a kind and loving family man (which he was) and generous as well (which he was not). Lee, for all his genius and his role in modern business communication, helped change Rockefeller's image and, in effect, manipulated the news media and public attitudes. Today, Rockefeller is remembered more favorably than those who campaigned against his excesses. Ivy Lee and public relations must share much of the blame.

Although there have been noble people associated with the public relations field and some of them, like the pioneering Edward L. Bernays, have campaigned for professionalism and ethical practice, it still must be said that public relations is a force that packages news and information on behalf of its clients. A vigilant press ought to be able to see through deceptive and dishonest communication—and it does—but still there is an advantage for those who are well-represented by public relations counsel versus those who are not. Think of the homeless, for example, coming face to face with a giant developer who would remove them from a particular district of a large city. The developer will have a much greater capacity to argue his case in the press with the help of public relations people. There is nothing inherently wrong with this on a case by case basis, but, considered as a whole, there is no doubt that public relations strategies do influence press coverage and portrayals in the media. It isn't always a matter of money, but usually that is the case. Some social movements, from civil rights to the women's movement, have successfully marshaled public support with limited resources, while their opponents have sometimes failed to curry support even with superior budgets. These, however, are exceptions to the rule.

The political campaign consultant Roger Ailes, who assisted President Bush in his successful run for the presidency in 1988, is a master of public relations manipulation. By his own admission, he planted doubts in reporters' minds about his client's opponent, even when he knew the imputation he was making was false. In many instances, I believe, a lazy press corps failed to check out charges and the Ailes view prevailed.

The excesses of public relations—and there are some—are less important than follies and foibles of a sometimes overworked, sometimes understaffed, often lazy and poorly trained corps of journalists in this country. There is simply too much information for most media organizations to cope effectively with it. Instead of hiring legions of specialists to help—they have hired a few—the media make heavy use of handouts (press releases) and other information provided free by public relations people. Clearly, this is not fair and does not serve the American people very well.

I know scores of talented public relations people and even more talented journalists. The PR people I know are, for the most part, responsible professionals. They have every right to do what they do, but they are paid promoters for vested interests, and those interests want publicity and public support. The PR people use many ploys to get their way with the news media and to influence the public through other means. To a large part they succeed and in the process are major information providers for the American people.

Argument Summation: Public relations manipulates the news.

Public relations, by its very nature, is intended to benefit those creating the message, whether the source is public or private. In the information marketplace, public relations manipulates the news by packaging information for the media with a specific client's interests in mind. While there have been laudable uses of public relations, on the whole the practice serves to flood the media with biased news. When the press is unable to verify the reports, due to the sheer quantity of information available or because of laziness, distorted public relations reports appear in the media as objective facts, and the news has been distorted to favor the public relations position.

RESPONSE

Merrill: Public relations provides an essential news service.

It has been said that public relations is a manipulative force in news presentation. Perhaps it is, to some extent. So what? There are many manipulative forces impinging on the news: editors' fears, reporters' biases, advertising pressures, government secrecy. Public relations, in spite of normal manipulative aspects, is a valuable—even essential—adjunct to the news dissemination activities of journalism.

It has been estimated, even by journalists, that nearly 50 percent of the news stories found in the media show some signs of PR influence. Journalists themselves must think PR sources are important to news gathering, for they certainly make use of PR releases and background material which is offered them by the PR establishment. It would be hard to deny that PR sources are helpful in supplying background material and even some "hard" news to news media.

Of course, much PR material is ignored or discarded, but it is used more often than many journalists might like to admit. I myself have spent five years in college public relations and, on the basis of keeping careful clipping books and records, I can say that in this small PR sample my *public relations-generated news was used up to 80 percent on a weekly basis.* Use of releases by radio and TV was much less dramatic, but there is no doubt but that newspapers rely heavily on news releases coming to them.

Seymour Topping, former managing editor of the *New York Times*, has said bluntly that PR people contribute to the news in a functional way: "Quite a lot of our business stories originate from press releases. Often the first hint of a newsworthy event is first heard of by us from a press release." Topping has gone so far as to say that PR is becoming a news network behind the legitimate news media, "a second network that feeds the real news media more and more of its news" (Blyskal and Blyskal, 1985, 46–47).

The Blyskals also quote Charles Staebler, assistant managing editor of the *Wall Street Journal,* who acknowledges the help provided by PR people. "We look at press releases positively as a source of tips. They can alert us to things that are going on." Staebler estimates that perhaps 50 percent of the average *Journal* stories are spurred by press releases, and adds, "In every case we *try* [emphasis added] to go beyond the press release" (Blyskal and Blyskal, 47).

According to Scott Cutlip, longtime professor of PR, the 150,000 public relations practitioners play an important role in setting the public agenda and have a far more important role in opinion-making "than the public perceives, or than journalists (who themselves are only about 130,000 strong) are usually willing to admit." And Cutlip estimates that 40 percent of all "news" content today comes from the desks of PR people (*Gannett Center Journal,* Spring 1989, 105).

There is no doubt but that PR does provide a news service. And in the common or loose sense of providing "essential" news, meaning a *very important* service, I would contend that public relations fills the bill. No one is saying that PR is journalistically relevant in all of its aspects, but in providing basic news, commentary on certain news events, tips on news stories, and access to news sources, the practitioner in public relations is extremely valuable to the news media.

In a strict sense of "essential" (meaning "absolutely necessary"), perhaps PR is not essential. True, a newspaper, for example, could provide news without any help from PR. But how thorough would it be? How many additional gaps would such news presentation have? One might as well say that the news media could "present news" without interviewing politicians. Certainly it could be done; there would simply be far less political news. So we might say that politicians are "essential" for *the best possible* political news, and that public relations practitioners are "essential" for *the best possible news* related to the PR person's area of knowledge.

It may be true, as Dennis contends, that public relations manipulates the news. *All* factors impinging upon the collection and writing of news are manipulative to some degree. I could say, just as well, that *reporters* and *editors* manipulate the news. So? But since "manipulates" is a word with a negative connotation, it is not used to describe a journalistic function. But with public relations it is different: from the point of view of the journalist any "news" function connected with PR automatically seems to imply skulduggery and self-serving bias, with an accompanying intent to mislead the reader.

This may be true in some cases. But in others this is simply not the case. Truthful and conscientious reporting is not the sole province of the journalist. Such reporting can also be found among historians, sociologists, lawyers, and even farmers talking alongside a country road. Why not among PR people?

Because of its financial support by groups, organizations, and persons with vested interests, public relations is a field that is understandably suspect by news media people who pride themselves on being "detached" and "unbiased" in their news presentation. Perhaps PR people *are* prone to accentuate the positive when it comes to news about their special interests. But don't journalists generally accentuate the negative? Is negative bias any better than positive bias? Undoubtedly PR people do feel considerable loyalty to those who pay their salaries. But does employer-loyalty necessarily imply dishonesty?

But let us assume PR people are biased. Are they *more* biased in their normal newswriting activities than are the general run of media reporters who usually have their own strongly held values and biases, political and otherwise? This, of course, is a question that cannot really be answered. But it is worth asking.

In spite of biased news from PR sources which undoubtedly appears from time to time, there is no reason to believe that most PR people are not honest, at least no more so than others. Surely they *intend* to be honest, forthright, and truthful; for one thing, the Code of Professional Standards of the Public Relations Society of America (PRSA) says they must be.

For instance, the Code stresses (in Standard Seven) that a member "shall not intentionally communicate false or misleading information and is obligated to use care to avoid communication of false or misleading information." That is strange wording, to be sure, but it points up PR people's concern for providing the truth. Earlier in the same code, the PRSA members are urged to "adhere to truth and accuracy" and to refrain from engaging "in any practice which tends to corrupt the integrity of channels of communication" (quoted in Lovell, 1982, 41–42). Not much different from language in a journalist's code, is it?

William Ramsey, president of the PR firm of Bill Ramsey Associates, Inc., insists that public relations people "must communicate better . . . to the public" and that "we must tell the good news of our firm's accomplishments—and level with the public about our firm's or our institution's shortcomings." In fact, he says, "credibility is the key" (Haberman and Dolphin, 1988, viii).

In spite of PR people's attempt to professionalize, to write ethical codes, to use the status initials APR (Accredited in Public Relations) after their names, and to pay allegiance to truth and credibility, they still have a problem with the press. Journalists are suspicious of their forthrightness in news matters. Robert T. Reilly, APR member and professor at the University of Nebraska (Omaha), notes that, "Even reporters who have never experienced a problem with a PR person harbor the concept of the practitioner as a self-serving person who will try to interfere with truthful encounter" (1987, 9). He adds this backhanded slap at news reporters: "As reportorial success is measured more and more by exposé, and as media rely increasingly on the profession they criticize, you're apt to see this nagging hostility expand."

But he's right. Journalists will undoubtedly continue to snipe at public relations people—while using considerable portions of their news releases. In retaliation, PR people will take their verbal slaps at what they often see as the unrealistic and arrogant journalists who make no real attempt to understand and appreciate public relations.

All right. There's a kind of continuing cold war going on between the two "professions." Is that bad? I see it as a good thing because this kind of mild adversarial relationship may help to keep both groups honest. Perhaps here we have another "check" mechanism in our society. But in spite of this "unease" that exists between the two groups, I still maintain that PR expands the public discourse, helps provide a wide assortment of news, and is essential in expanding the pluralism of our total communication system.

The image of PR is beside the point. The fact that ethical lapses occur in PR is beside the point. The fact that journalists are naturally suspicious of any other person or group in the "news" business is beside the point. The fact that PR people do have a loyalty to their clients is beside the point. What is not beside the point is that PR people do indeed provide news to various publics (including the general public through the mass media) and, in doing so, provide an essential public service.

Argument Summation: Public relations provides an essential news service.

Public relations generates information for use by the media; it fills gaps in the news and provides similar services to those offered by advertising agencies. PR helps set the public agenda. It may not be "essential" in the ultimate sense, but neither is a newspaper or a TV station. Public relations may have an ax to grind, but so do advertising agencies. It is true that not all PR is ethical; is that not true of *any* institutionalized communications endeavor? Public relations serves as a supplement and aid to news media, a gap-filler and, in general, does a valuable job of expanding message pluralism in society. A PR person may do many things other than news gathering and dissemination; but is this not also true of newspaper staff members?

TOPICS FOR DISCUSSION

1. Is truth related to a PR news release in the same way that truth is related to a news story on TV or in a newspaper?

2. Is it any safer to believe an advertiser than to believe a PR person? In what ways are the two types of practitioners similar? Different?

3. Why would a person who loves independence and truth want to be a part of a PR organization? How can there be so many PR people today who were news media reporters at one time?

4. The assumption is generally made that newspaper reporters are neutral, unbiased, and objective—and that PR people are not. Is the assumption valid? Why, or why not?

5. PR people work for and are paid by their clients. Media news people work for and are paid by their media. What is the difference? How does their employment status affect their loyalties? How do their loyalties affect their work?

TOPICS FOR RESEARCH

1. Study a local firm or nonprofit organization in terms of its public relations program, assuming it has one. What publics do they try to reach? With what methods or tools? How do they measure their effectiveness? How do you assess their efforts and success (or failure)?

2. Assume that you have been asked to document the public relations of your college or university. What is its prevailing public image? Does it differ with different publics, say students, faculty, and alumni? In your paper indicate how public relations is carried out at the institution, by whom, with what channels or tools, and to what effect. Does the effort work or not? Why?

3. Is there any "right" to public relations in what is increasingly an information or communication society? Argue the case that all people and

organizations involved in public life need and deserve a public relations program. How can the public be protected in such a scheme?

4. Document the ethics movement in public relations. What does professional public relations do to assure ethical practice? Interview a public relations practitioner on this issue. How would you assess that person's approach to ethical public relations? How are decisions made? With what help or sources?

5. Interview a news person about contacts between his or her news organization and public relations personnel. Is public relations a help or a hindrance? Be specific about the impact and influence of public relations, if any, based on this interview.

6. What does the public need to know about public relations? Outline a speech you would give to a civic group about public relations and what citizens should know about it.

FURTHER READING

Bernays, Edward L. *Crystalizing Public Opinion*. New York: Boni and Liveright, 1923.

Blyskal, Jeff, and Mary Blyskal. *PR: How the Public Relations Industry Writes the News*. New York: William Morrow and Co., 1985.

Cutlip, Scott, Alan Center, and Glen M. Broom. *Effective Public Relations*, 6th ed. Englewood Cliffs, NJ: Prentice Hall, 1985.

Grunig, J. E., and Todd Hunt. *Managing Public Relations*. New York: Holt, Rinehart and Winston, 1984.

Haberman, David A., and H. A. Dolphin. *Public Relations: The Necessary Art*. Ames, IA: Iowa State University Press, 1988.

Lovell, Ronald P. *Inside Public Relations*. Boston: Allyn & Bacon, 1982.

Pavlik, John V. *Public Relations: What Research Tells Us*. Beverly Hills, CA: Sage, 1987.

"Public Relations: The Manufacture of Opinion," *Gannett Center Journal* (Spring 1989).

Reilly, Robert T. *Public Relations in Action*. Englewood Cliffs, NJ: Prentice Hall, 1987.

Wilcox, Dennis L., Phillip H. Ault, and Warren K. Agee. *Public Relations Strategies and Tactics*. New York: Harper & Row, 1986.

Chapter **17**

JOURNALISM AS A PROFESSION

Although scholars and practitioners debate over what constitutes a profession, most journalists believe that journalism is a profession. There is a Society of Professional Journalists. Journalism is included in various standard listings of professions in America.

Even the most rigorous critics and scholars studying professional ethics include journalists in their discussions. Efforts to enhance the professionalization of journalists abound in seminars, workshops, codes of ethics, and other activities. Although it is said that freedom of the press, as guaranteed by the First Amendment, prohibits the control or licensing of journalists, newspapers still strive toward professionalism.

Clearly, journalists like to be associated with professionalism and they see no particular advantage in being members of a trade or a simple vocation. Professionalism is associated with competence, with training, with a body of knowledge, with standards of evaluation and improvement.

Is journalism a profession? If it is not, *should* it be? The debate goes on.

CHALLENGE

Merrill: Journalism is not a profession.

Contrary to conventional journalistic wisdom, journalism is not a profession. There really is not much tradition behind the idea of journalism being a profession. It is of recent vintage. For most of America's journalistic history, professionalism was no issue; if anybody thought of what journalism might be called at all, it was usually simply referred to as a trade, craft, or vocation.

Today the term and concept of *profession* has proliferated in journalistic rhetoric—in publications, speeches, and conversations. Journalists generally like to think of themselves as "professionals" and journalism as a "profession." I recently had a journalism student so emotionally tied to the idea that journalism is a profession that the very idea that it might not be distressed her greatly. "That's the reason I wanted to go into journalism—because it was a profession," she stated with apparent consternation.

Journalists seem to be impressed with the general esteem, respectability, and even awe that surrounds any organized activity carrying the name "profession." They have also observed that law and medicine, for instance, in being accepted as professions, have taken on an elite image and that their practitioners are generally paid better than are most nonprofessionals.

It is understandable that journalists, often intellectuals or pseudointellectuals, find the lure of professionalism very strong. It would give them the aura of respectability, of public acceptance, of dignity, of exclusivity, and, at least, the collective psychological comfort denied them if they simply functioned as "journalists."

The notion that journalism is a profession is undoubtedly growing in America, but individual journalists do not really know what journalistic professionalism entails, what being a "professional" really means. Even two journalists with similar backgrounds may act in ways which each would consider "unprofessional." Even members of the Society of Professional Journalists do not agree in many basic and important respects about journalism and its practices.

Professor Jay Black of the University of Alabama, editor of *The Journal of Mass Media Ethics,* writing on "Professionalism in Journalism," maintains that journalism is not a profession. Summarizing, six characteristics of a profession (as provided by Abraham Flexner in 1915) that have served through the years as a standard definition, Black shows that journalism does not have these characteristics.

Here is a brief summary of the six characteristics: (1) an extensive and complex body of knowledge; (2) knowledge not only of the *what* and the *how* but also a theoretical grasp of the *why*; (3) a definite and practical goal; (4) agreement with other professionals about the ends to be served and about education necessary for practice; (5) common criteria or standards for practice—agreed upon entrance requirements; and (6) a motivation that is altruistic, not self-enhancing or based on a profit motive.

Dr. Black concludes that "clearly journalism falls short of being a full-fledged profession on several counts" (World Media Report, Spring 1987, 13–15). Admittedly, some of Flexner's criteria for a profession are rather vague, but they are helpful.

The observer looking at American journalism today can see very easily that journalists really do not have a single identity, nor do they share the same values, nor do they have a common definition of their role.

Originally *profession* meant simply the act of professing; it has developed from that fundamental concept to mean, according to the *Oxford Shorter English Dictionary,* the "occupation which one professes to be skilled in and to follow ... a vocation in which professed knowledge of some branch of learning is used in its application to the affairs of others, or in the practice of an art based upon it."

Even now, professionals profess; they profess to know better than others the nature of certain matters, and to know better than their nonprofessional clients what they need to know and in what proportion they need to know it. Professionals claim the exclusive right to practice, as a vocation, the arts that they profess to know.

William J. Goode, one of America's foremost sociologists, has insisted that professionals constitute a homogeneous community whose members share values, identity, and definition of role and interests. He has said that members of a profession "are bound by a sense of identity" and "share values in common."

The Bureau of Labor Statistics lists these requirements for a profession: (1) prescribed educational standards; (2) licensing; (3) enforcement of performance standards by the profession itself.

Here are some other characteristics of a profession which are given in the influential *The Professions in America:*

- A member of a profession is expected to think objectively and inquiringly about matters that may be, for the outsider, subject to "orthodoxy and sentiment which limit intellectual exploration." (Is this true for the journalist?)
- A member of a profession assumes that he can be trusted since he professes to have certain expertise that the layman does not have. (Can a journalist say this with justification?)
- A member of a profession believes in close solidarity with other members and thinks that it is a good thing to present a solid front to those outside the profession. (Is this true of a journalist?)
- A member of a profession is able to meet various minimum entrance standards for the profession—such as a degree in the professional area, a special license identifying him as a professional member in good standing, and so on. (Is this true of a journalist?)
- A member of a profession is not only certified or licensed but can expect to be put out of the profession (in the case of a journalist—"depressed") if he does not live up to professional standards. (Is this true of a journalist?)
- A member of a profession has a code of ethics governing his or her activities in concert with other professionals and submits to a high degree of group control. (Is this true of a journalist?)

- A member of a profession participates in a system of rewards (monetary and honorary) for those who conduct themselves most notably within their code of ethics. (Is this true of the journalist?)
- A member of a profession shares in a discrete and substantive body of knowledge available to those in the profession. (Is this true of a journalist?)

After looking the above characteristics of a profession, we should ask: Is journalism a profession? Obviously it is not, although it has some of a profession's characteristics, or it approaches in some respects a profession. (A donkey, we might say, has many of the characteristics of a horse; it "approaches" a horse. But we must say quite definitely that it is not a horse.)

There is no direct relationship between journalists and their clients. A journalist is not a self-employed person; he works for an employer. In journalism there are no formal minimum entrance requirements; anyone can be a journalist who can get himself hired—experience or no experience, degree or no degree. No journalist is expected (or required) to abide by any code of ethics. No journalist is certified or licensed, at least in the United States. No professional standards are commonly agreed upon and followed by journalists. A person working for the *National Enquirer* is just as much a journalist as a person working for the *New York Times*. A person writing news for the *Podunk Weekly Bugle* is just as much a journalist as a newsperson working for the *Wall Street Journal*.

Journalists do not share in common a "high degree of generalized and systematic knowledge." They do not claim the exclusive right to practice the arts (all borrowed from other disciplines) of their vocation. Finally, American journalists do not comprise "a homogeneous community."

Listen to contemporary commentator Irving Kristol: "Even to speak of the 'profession' of journalism today is to indulge in flattering exaggeration. Journalism has not, as yet, acquired the simplest external signs of a profession" (1975, 26).

Even though journalism is not a profession, it *can*—through increased stress on ethical codes, press councils, peer pressure, licensing of some kind, entrance requirements, and more rigorous standards for journalism education—grow into a true profession. I don't contend that it is impossible for journalism to become a profession, just that it has not yet happened. But I think that it is *undesirable* that it evolve into a profession.

Philosopher William Barrett, writing about professions, states my feeling very well:

> The price one pays for having a profession is *deformation professionelle*, as the French put it—a professional deformation. Doctors and engineers tend to see things from the viewpoint of their own specialty, and usually show a very marked blind spot to whatever

falls outside this particular province. The more specialized a vision the sharper its focus; but also the more nearly total the blind spot toward all things that lie on the periphery of this focus (1958, 4–5).

There appears to be a deep-rooted desire among press people to belong to a select group (a "hierarchical longing within the press," as Lewis Lapham has called it in *Harper's*). It seems clear to me that this tendency, if carried very far, would stamp out unusual or eccentric concepts and, ultimately, also the journalists who embrace them. Lapham wrote that the more the press becomes a profession, the more it will "discourage the membership of rowdy amateurs" and, as it is with other professions, encourage the promotion of people who are "second-rate."

No doubt, professionalism will certainly restrict the ranks of journalism, eliminate the "nonprofessional" from practice, and make the press appear more respectable, at least from the perspective of the elitists making up the profession.

In addition to a loss of diversity, another reason why journalism should not be a profession has been put forward on numerous occasions by James W. Carey, dean of the College of Communications at the University of Illinois: If journalism were a profession its practitioners would increasingly turn inward on themselves, thinking more and more about their own vested interests and mechanisms for self-protection, and less about their responsibilities to their audiences. Professions, believes Carey, become ingrown and selfish, with a complacent and arrogant spirit contagious among their members.

I totally agree with Carey; it would be a pity if journalism, one of the most open, diversified institutions in the country—one that is largely dedicated to public service—were to change into a narrow, monolithic, self-centered professionalized fellowship devoid of an outward-looking service orientation.

So, I maintain that journalism is not a profession and that it should not be.

Argument Summation: Journalism is not a profession.

Journalism is a vocation, an occupation, a craft, or something—but not a profession. It is a calling that is open to all, regardless of education. There are no entrance requirements, no discrete body of knowledge, no elite inner group to "depress" wayward members, no code of ethics, and no licensing system for journalists. Naturally, journalism resembles a profession in some ways, but it is not yet there. Lewis Lapham was right to view the trend toward professionalization with alarm. He said that the more the press becomes a profession, the more it will discourage eccentricity and innovation, and the more it would encourage the promotion of second-rate people. Certainly, journalism as a profession would shrink pluralism and cause journalists to think less of the public interest and more of their own interest.

RESPONSE

Dennis: Journalism is a profession.

Whether journalism is a profession is one of the oldest, continuing controversies in journalism. It used to be easier to take sides when the debate was simply whether journalism was a profession or a business. Liberals lined up on the side of professionalism, while conservatives liked to see journalism as a profit-making enterprise. But those were simpler times. Today we can look back on a half century of striving by journalists and journalistic organizations to achieve professional status.

Journalism is commonly regarded as a profession made up of professional communicators, dedicated to professional standards. Journalists themselves believe this, and even some of the most elite of American institutions engaged in the study of the professions consider journalists—warts and all—to be professionals. The Harvard-Hastings Program on Ethics in the Professions, for example, has no problem calling journalism a profession. Neither do such distinguished sociologists as Morris Janowitz or Herbert Gans, who have contributed mightily to the literature of professionalism generally, as well as journalism specifically.

Admittedly some scholars quibble with this designation, preferring instead to call journalism a "subprofession." They would, no doubt, say that the terms *profession* and *professional* are too widely and indiscriminately used in America. The commonly understood definitions of *profession*, *professional*, and *professionalism* vary widely from those who say that a *profession* is simply a "principal calling, vocation, or employment" versus a more rigid view that insists a profession is "a calling requiring specialized knowledge and long, intensive preparation." (Both definitions are found in *Webster's Third New International Dictionary*.)

Most students of the sociology of work, concerned with professionalism, acknowledge that professions *evolve*. They are not created with all the finishing touches on Day One, with their standards and practices intact. Medicine, for example, had little in the way of universal standards or educational requirements in this country until after 1915. Some commentators say that the law did not truly become a profession until the establishment of law schools.

Journalism has most, if not all, of the distinctive marks of a profession and deserves to be so classified. This assertion reflects not a caving in to popular parlance (as with "professional" actors or "professional" athletes), but the fact that most of the major criteria that distinguish a profession from a trade or calling are integral to journalistic practice in America. What's more, dedication to professionalism is growing in journalism.

Like other professions, journalism shows most of the characteristics of professionalism, with different degrees of intensity. One of the primary marks of any profession (and not mentioned in the "Challenge") is "the kind of work that has for its prime purpose the rendering of a public service." Journalism is, in fact, engaged in a public service— the free flow of information and ideas is at the core of First Amendment freedom in the United States. The press has special protection under the Constitution, not simply to allow newspaper and broadcast owners to make a profit, but because, as a matter of law and social policy, we believe that a free press is essential to a functioning democracy. Of course, the press must make a profit if it is to survive, and reporters and editors have salaries and get various ego rewards for their work. Yet, most of them would contend (and with justification) that they render a public service. Certainly law, medicine, architecture, education, and the other professions engage in public service activity and still provide a living for their practitioners. That does not exclude them from the august company of professionals. Under the most rigid definition probably only the clergy, and then only the highly trained clergy—could qualify as professionals.

For purposes of this discussion, I accept the standards set out in *The Professions in America*, even though they present a rather dated and stodgy view of professionalism. Does journalism qualify under this definition? I believe it does. Can a journalist "think objectively and inquiringly about matters" which by "sentiment and orthodoxy" limit outsiders? Certainly one of the purposes of journalism is to provide an impartial, disinterested synthesis of information. It identifies and explains conflicting viewpoints. This process helps the uninitiated understand what is happening in society without being subject to deliberate bias, or distortion. Journalism tells us that a "supply side" economist says one thing while a Keynesian says another.

Does a journalist have expertise that a layman does not? Yes, of course. Journalists are experts at news gathering—searching out, assessing, and presenting information; standard definitions of mass communication specify that "professional communicators," not amateurs, are required.

Does a journalist have "close solidarity" and "a solid front?" Not in the sense that medicine might, but that is because journalism is so diverse, involving many different kinds of media enterprises and professionals. Certainly journalists are organized through professional societies, guilds, unions, and other more specialized subgroups. I can think of few professionals with more solidarity than journalism when a fellow journalist is jailed or when a lively First Amendment issue emerges. Powerful publishers join with lowly reporters to right a common battle. One of the clichés of the media when a story is attacked or seriously questioned is, "We stand behind our reporter."

What of minimum entrance requirements? While there is no formal licensing, most media organizations do have minimum standards of education or experience before hiring anyone. They can deviate from these requirements if they wish, but rarely do. Increasingly journalists are graduates of professional schools of journalism accredited by a national body that is sanctioned by the government through the U.S. Office of Education. This procedure is not the same as licensing, but there are many other types of "conformity" and "sanctioning" within journalism. There is considerable agreement among journalists on a whole range of values and craft attitudes, as studies by communications researchers have shown. It is by no means an "every man an island" profession.

Can someone be "put out" of the profession? Not by the government, but certainly by the informal hiring practices of media organizations. Someone who consistently violates professional norms and standards or who is regarded as "sleazy" by his colleagues may have difficulty getting a job at a reputable publication. There may always be an outlet for that person's work, say in the *National Enquirer*, but not likely on the *Washington Post* or *New York Times*. After the celebrated Janet Cooke episode at the *Washington Post* in 1981, many media executives tightened up their hiring policies and developed clear standards. Increasingly, press councils, which make public pronouncements and have the power of embarrassment, provide a voluntary, policing function in journalism. Their work is advisory, but it does help guide performance.

Journalism has codes of ethics. They help define professionalism and assist journalists with ethical dilemmas. On some papers a reporter who violates the code can be fired. In that instance, adherence to the code is a condition of employment. *The Editor & Publisher International Yearbook* lists several pages of awards, both financial and honorary, available to journalists. Some of the most prestigious, such as the Pulitzer Prizes and Nieman Fellowships, can have a marked impact on their recipients' careers. These awards are given for exemplary performance.

The criterion of a "discrete and substantive body of knowledge" is more difficult. Because journalism is part of a system of freedom of expression, it is not possible or desirable to prescribe just what every journalist must know. However, there is a standard curriculum in the journalism schools that includes courses in communication theory, media history, law, and ethics, as well as other substantive topics. It is also generally agreed that journalists should be broadly educated in the liberal arts and sciences. In addition, professional schools have professional practice and skills courses in reporting, editing, photojournalism, and other topics. There is also a substantial literature of journalism, which includes both scholarly studies and such anecdotal materials as memoirs and media criticism. There are even subfields—journalism history, law, economics, theory and methodology, international communications, media sociology, and others. Each of these subfields has enough of a "corpus" of scholarship worthy of considerable attention by scholars. Journalism studies are also part of a larger literature of mass communication that has strong links to psychology, sociology, anthropology, and political science. Students of journalism have a rich lode to consider if they which to master the field. Of course, there is no formal requirement that anyone do this.

More than half of all journalists in America are graduates of journalism schools, and virtually all have at least a liberal arts education. Increasingly, some journalists have specialized education or training in such areas as science, law, politics, or the arts. The diversity of journalism in America makes the implementation of one single model of education or training impossible. Some professional communicators in broadcasting must hold federally-issued broadcast licenses attesting to certain technical competencies.

Fundamentally, journalists must know enough—gained either in formal education or on the job—to function in their work. If they do not, they are fired or otherwise excluded from the profession.

Just because all journalists do not march to the beat of a single drummer does not mean they are not professional. As Morris Janowitz has written:

> Practitioners in any particular profession hold differing conceptions of their tasks and priorities. The differences between the "public health" doctor and the clinician is a long-standing distinction that has had a strong impact on the practice of medicine. Since World War I, journalists have come more and more to consider themselves as professionals and to search for an appropriate professional model. The initial efforts were to fashion journalism into a field, similar to medicine, where the journalist would develop his technical expertise and also a sense of professional responsibility (1975, 618).

That was the "gatekeeper" tradition, which emphasized the search for objectivity. Other journalists disagree with this view and instead say journalists should be advocates for causes and participate in public affairs. This conflict, according to sociologists John Johnstone, Edward Slawski, and William Dowman, "would reappear to pit proponents of a professionalized objective, restrained, and technically efficient journalism against those advocating a socially responsible journalism inspired by some of the same journalistic norms which were the objects of earlier reforms" (Johnstone, Slawski, and Bowman, 1976, 523).

Is journalism a profession? The evidence is resounding. Sociological quibblers can find flaws in all of the professions that might put them outside of purist definitions, but this is not reality. Journalism is a profession not because its practitioners say they are professionals, but because it more than meets most of the criteria that, taken together, constitute a profession.

Argument Summation: Journalism is a profession.

A profession is defined most narrowly as requiring "specialized knowledge and long, intensive preparation" and involving "rendering a public service." Whether journalism was a profession when it began, it has evolved (as medicine or law did) into one and deserves recognition as such. Journalism renders a public service by preserving the free flow of information. Even by the dated criteria suggested by Merrill, journalism possesses the objectivity, expertise and organizational characteristics of a profession. A discrete substantive body of knowledge is required, in the sense that there is an expectation that journalists be broadly educated and there is a standard curriculum in the journalism schools. A uniform perspective of practitioners is not necessary for a field to be considered a profession; many doctors and lawyers possess differing conceptions of their tasks. Sociological quibblers might find distinctions which could put any profession outside a purist definition, but for all practical purposes journalism is a profession.

TOPICS FOR DISCUSSION

1. Why do you think many journalism students and journalists want journalism to be a profession?
2. Do you see any real dangers to journalism being a profession? If you do, what are they?
3. Can journalism be as diversified (pluralistic) as a profession as it can as a nonprofession?
4. More than half the journalists in the United States are journalism school graduates. What would the proportion be if journalism were a profession like medicine or law? Is common education really important for members of a profession?
5. Is a single code of ethics necessary for a profession? Why not have many codes, all similar, but differing somewhat? Should a professional code of ethics have "teeth" in it? Who should decide?

TOPICS FOR RESEARCH

1. Discuss the proposition that the public deserves professionalism in journalism. Indicate why and document your case carefully.
2. Study codes of ethics in terms of their promotion of professionalism. Do they promote professionalism or not? Be specific and give examples.

3. How do schools of journalism and communication promote professionalism? Does professionalism apply to all areas of communications? Does professionalism apply to all media functions—information, opinion, and entertainment? Discuss and analyze.

4. Compare and contrast journalism as a profession with any other profession you choose. How do they differ? How are they similar? Be sure you consider the role of education, codes of ethics, licensing, and other issues.

5. Some critics say that professionalism is simply a control mechanism whereby owners of the media control their employees. Is this true or not? Is it a good or a bad thing? How do we know?

FURTHER READING

American Society of Newspaper Editors. *What Is News? Who Decides? And How?* Preliminary Report on the World of the Working Journalist, Washington, D.C. 1982. Also cited in earlier chapters as Burgoon, Burgoon, and Atkin, 1982.

Barrett, William. *Irrational Man: A Study in Existential Philosophy.* Garden City, NY: Doubleday Anchor Books, 1958.

Carey, James. "The Communications Revolution and the Professional Communicator." *Sociological Review* (University of Keele) 13(1969).

Gerald, J. Edward. *The Social Responsibility of the Press.* Minneapolis, MN: University of Minnesota Press, 1963.

Janowitz, Morris. "Professional Models in Journalism: The Gatekeeper and the Advocate." *Journalism Quarterly* 52, no.4 (Winter 1975): 618–26, 662.

Johnstone, John W. C., Edward J. Slawski, and William Bowman. *The Newspeople: A Sociological Portrait of American Journalists and Their Work.* Urbana, IL: University of Illinois Press, 1976.

———. "The Professional Values of American Newsmen," *Public Opinion Quarterly* 36 no. 4 (1976): 522–40.

Kristol, Irving. "Is the Press Misusing Its Growing Power?" *More* (January 1975): 26–28.

Lynn, Kenneth S., ed. *The Professions in America.* Boston: Houghton Mifflin, 1965.

Public Agenda Foundation. *The Speaker and the Listener.* New York: Public Agenda Foundation, 1980.

Southern Newspaper Publishers Association. *Education for Newspaper Journalists in the 1970s and Beyond.* Reston, VA: SNPA, 1973. See especially "Professionalism of the Press" by William E. Porter.

Chapter 18

GLOBAL COMMUNICATION DOMINANCE

The inequitable distribution of resources of all kinds—economic, human, military, and others—has been a central thread in the history of civilization. It has also been a vital topic in communication, with a longstanding debate surrounding information-rich and information-poor societies, the haves and have-nots of the information age. Discussions of global communication dominance has several dimensions. There is the issue of dominance in ownership and control of media, with large industrialized countries, especially the United States, having a disproportionate share of the world's communication resources. This is connected to the world flow of news and the portrayal of various societies. Most news flows from large, wealthy countries to smaller, less affluent countries and societies.

It is said that the United States as the information superpower has a disproportionately large role in defining and shaping the news, and thus determines what the rest of the world will know (and presumably think) about other less affluent nations, especially the Third World nations of Africa, Asia, and Latin America. This debate erupted in the 1970s into a United Nations debate over the New World Information Order, which pitted Western news agencies against Third World leaders and communicators. The issue was always imbalance and control of information. The Third World demanded self-determination in their information policies and decried their portrayal in the Western media. The Western media including the United States thought this was an intrusion on their freedom of the press, especially when criticism came from countries where journalists were licensed and regarded as a part of the government structure.

When all is said and done, the main issue here is how much influence and control should the United States have in the world of communication? How much is too much and what can be done about it?

CHALLENGE

Merrill: The U.S. media have an unhealthy dominance.

Most of the scholarly publication (research reports and academic critical essays) since 1970 concerning international communication and transnational news flow has highlighted the inequity in global information. This publication emphasis has been reinforced by myriad conferences (many sponsored by UNESCO) at which the dominance of U.S. media has been repeatedly assailed by participants from the Second and Third Worlds.

Out of all the research and empirically based perceptions have come four major conclusions, well summarized in 1986 by Dr. Hamid Mowlana of the American University in Washington, D.C. (*Global Information and World Communication*, 37–38). These conclusions follow:

1. Most international news flows from the developed (the West/the North) to the developing nations (the Third World/South).
2. Proximity—physical, psychological, and political—is a major factor in news coverage throughout the world.
3. The United States and Western Europe receive the largest amount of coverage, followed by the socialist countries and the Third World.
4. Vertical flow of information (North to South) is the dominant flow pattern of the world (1986, 37-38).

I doubt if these research conclusions will surprise anyone; they are rather commonsensical and obvious. But they do bear out the charge leveled at the United States that it is among the dominating nations so far as information is concerned. The first, third, and fourth of Mowlana's conclusions indicate U.S. dominance; the second one is irrelevant (and truistic).

Professor Mowlana goes on to highlight what clusters of researchers "infer" from their data. "A good number of writers and researchers" see Northern-dominated news as neglecting progress in the developing countries (in culture, economics, and politics). Others, say Mowlana, conclude that it has resulted in a "massive consumer culture" that erodes national identity in many parts of the world. Still others, he points out, note that such imbalances have led to dysfunctional consequences—such as international instability, global conflict, and national discontent (40).

Many of the harshest critics of American communications policies see in them a desire and attempt to impose U.S. values on other nations and to foster world domination through a kind of "media imperialism." For example, Professor Herbert I. Schiller of the University of California at San Diego refers to the free flow of information in the world as "a myth." According to him, there are "selectors and controllers" (mainly in the United States and "the West") who shape the messages they disseminate throughout the world. From this sad state of communication affairs where huge Western multinational groups control the bulk of information, therefore, it is only natural that the fears and frustrations of the Third World are increasing (1981, 20.).

Many foreign scholars, such as Armand Mattelart, Kaarle Nordenstreng, Cees Hamelink, D. R. Mankekar, and Jeremy Tunstall, have insisted that American media are dominating the world and that this dominance is unhealthy. Magazines such as *Time* and *Newsweek*, for example, participate in journalism of "concealment and omission," try to protect the status quo, and are "militaristic." Even U.S. magazines such as *National Geographic* are pictured by such critical scholars as not giving a true understanding of the Third World and appealing mainly to "Middle America and illusion" (Schiller, 1973, 86-94).

C. B. Pratt, writing about U.S. newsmagazines and their news coverage of Africa, in the Dutch journal *Gazette*, found that they gave very little attention to that continent (less than 4 percent of editorial space) and that they pictured Africa as "politically gullible, naive, and immature." Pratt's study also showed that the newsmagazines consistently highlighted negative and conflict news—coups, political problems, economic woes, and public executions—while giving little or no attention to national progress (1:26, 1980, 35).

Little doubt exists that American media (and media content) dominate world communication. The reasons for this dominance are obvious. We produce more programming and make it available more economically than any other nation in the world. Naturally, we are the primary supplier. Some people say that in time all countries will create their own software and programs. But the impact in the intervening years may be profound. Unfortunately, there is little research on questions of impact, effects, and influence, so we are left with much speculation. But what research there has been seems to show that American media dominance is significant *and harmful* to a balanced and fair picture of the world.

The continued dominance of Western communications enterprises and technology in the Third World is linked both to economic and political interests that have great benefits for countries like the United States. If much of the direct daily impact of this activity is not caused by malevolent planning, the planning is at least insensitive. The United States, of course, sees itself as a leading nation of the world, and possessing much status. News media help continue and reinforce this self-image. A Swedish communications scholar, Einer Ostgaard, has stressed that "news media tend to reinforce or at least to uphold the divisions of the world between high-status nations and low-status nations" (*Journal of Peace Research*, 2, 1965, 55).

A few years ago Ethiopian Radio imported dramatic programs from the United States. Around Christmastime, these programs promoted the European and American tradition of Christmas trees and gift-giving. Then a Coptic Christian nation, Ethiopia considered Christmas a strictly religious holiday; therefore, the programming was considered insensitive. But, beyond this, the American programming led to a demand for Christmas trees and gifts. Was this not an unfortunate intrusion on local culture and customs? Such American activities have been dubbed by many critics as media-induced cultural imperialism that has a direct impact on people's behavior.

As American professor Dr. William Hachten has pointed out, a basic issue has to do with senders' rights versus receivers' rights, with the right to inform put over against the right to be informed (1988). Is it right that the prevailing image in the world of most Third World nations is controlled by Western news agencies and consists of bits and pieces of negative and sensational information?

Third World nations contend that they are misrepresented through the U.S.-dominated global communications network. They say they get no continued and conscientious coverage: that they get only periodic short-term visits from Western newspeople who superficially paint hasty pictures of atypical events and persons. There is no meaning, no continuity, no perspective, no attempt to reveal the progress and the cultural dignity of the Third World countries. It is, indeed, an unhealthy dominance of communication.

Of course, U.S. journalists are defensive when such situations are pointed out. After all, they say, Third Worlders are naive if they think American journalists can take much interest in the mundane, day-to-day activities of the developing countries. U.S. media are operating out of a competitive, free-market philosophy where their audience members exert great influence on what kind of news is collected and presented. American media (and journalists), therefore, must work within this context. Besides the fact that U.S. media enterprises cannot possibly keep full contingents of journalists in all these countries, the nature of news is such that only big, atypical, world-important stories can be gathered and disseminated. A bridge being built across a river in the Ivory Coast may be important there, but not in the West—or, for that matter, even in nearby Nigeria.

American apologists to the contrary, I am maintaining that American media have an unhealthy dominance in the world. Something should be done about it. But what? A wide assortment of serious, concerned people have wrestled with this question as part of the debates on the New World Information and Communication Order (NWICO). As yet the answer has not come. Suggestions, of course, have been forthcoming—for example, that Third World nations develop their own news agencies, that they concentrate on serious news themselves, that they cover better their own countries, that they try to develop their own "kind" of media system, that they improve their own journalism education, and even that they boycott American media messages if they think them damaging to their cultures.

In many—maybe most—cases these suggestions are Western-based and are not reasonable for the Third World countries. The economic and educational infrastructure is just not adequate to institute many of these suggestions. But it is possible for the Third World nations to do more than they have been doing. And it is possible for them to screen out American programming (at least to some extent) if it demeans their cultures. And if these countries do not agree with the basic American concept of "news" and journalistic values generally, they can actively excise them from their countries. They can develop their own journalistic and communication values; they can push them in their schools and in their media, and they can be more reluctant to send their students to American universities to be indoctrinated with alien communications values.

American journalistic and communications values, I'm afraid, will continue into the twenty-first century to dominate the world. Affluence is the engine that runs the mega-communications machines of the United States. Economic power, not intellectual insight, is what makes American media dominant in the world. The coming of global satellite communication will probably only strengthen American (and Western) dominance. Discrete cultures around the world that have not already suffered badly before the American onslaught will surely face the threat of extinction in the coming decades.

This is unhealthy. It is immoral. It is devastating to a great nation that was built on a foundation of reason, justice, and democracy. World domination of cultures through massive media infiltration is as morally reprehensible as world domination through military force. America must somehow lay aside here global economic ambitions and determine to make the world safe for diversity, for autonomous nations and cultures, and for differing forms of development.

Competition may be a good thing within a single nation where the playing field is more or less level. But competition as an ideal in the world as a whole—where competing nations are far from equal—is bound to result in the demeaning and diminishing (maybe even the elimination) of cultures and in the personal and national loss of identity and respect. It has been said about military weapons that when a country has them, it will eventually use them. The same holds with communications weapons: if we have them, we will use them.

The United States has the communications "know-how," the gigantic conglomerates of communication, the escalating potency of technology, the far-flung network of news gatherers and news disseminators, and the challenge and will for informational domination. All the ingredients are in place for the new century which I see as the Century of American Domination of World Cultures. It is an unhealthy prospect, and it can only be hoped that the developing nations of the world will renew their determination to thwart it. The prospect is for more American dominance of global communication, and how can anyone doubt but that such dominance is unhealthy?

Argument Summation: The U.S. media have an unhealthy dominance.

Research shows that there is a great inequity in international communication and transnational news flow. Information about the advanced Western countries— the United States in particular—dominates the global transmission networks while news of Third World nations hardly exists. American media and communications conglomerates largely determine what national images the world receives; American journalistic values, through their pervasiveness, increasingly crowd out values of other nations. This is unhealthy for a multicultured, pluralistic world communications network, in that it deemphasizes the smaller and poorer countries and tends to impose on the world the communications values of dominant Western powers, especially the United States.

RESPONSE

Dennis: The U.S. media contribute fairly to communication equity.

It is an empirical fact that there is an imbalance of resources in the world. Some people, some countries, some societies have more (or less) than others. An ideal state where there is universal economic and political equity may be an admirable goal in some people's minds, but it is certainly at odds with reality. In communication, which is essentially an economic entity in a larger society, those who invented early, invested well, and managed their resources with vision are better off than those who did not. The United States has an extraordinary advantage over other countries of the world in this regard. We developed a complex communication system early and it became a model for the rest of the world. This does not mean that things are static, however. Look at the Japanese. Here is a country with limitations in land area, natural resources, and location, yet after their devastation in World War II they came back to be an economic superpower and a great information society power.

John Merrill has joined various angry Third World and Eastern bloc voices, the same ones who unsuccessfully tried to implement the McBride Commission Report in the 1970s and 1980s and establish a New World Information Order. That failed plan, which had admirable goals, would have virtually dismantled aspects of Western communications industries, not to mention challenging freedom of the press. Who should control communications enterprises such as wire services, the movie industry, television entertainment programming, and data moving from one country to another? Should it be strictly the entrepreneurs who developed the long distance phone lines and fiber optics or the movie industry or should there be some sharing of information power? Should the United Nations and the World Bank provide incentives to strengthen the communication systems of smaller and poorer countries that are disadvantaged in the modern world? Should those with the ingenuity to create global communication systems be punished for their resourcefulness?

These and other questions can be debated forever, and people will find themselves taking different positions depending on their ideology or the stake they have in the argument. One would expect a giant communication firm that controls entertainment programming to want to make maximum profits, not necessarily to do economic charity work in the Third World, however noble that might be. One also expects the head of a military government in West Africa to want to control the media of his country without Western or other interference.

While there might have been a time when colonialism meant that a foreign state like Britain or France could run the newspapers (and later broadcast stations) in one of their colonial possessions, now it ought to be pointed out that much of the so-called communication dominance of the United States is "by invitation"; that is, political and economic leaders of a given country have invited U.S. and other Western information companies and interests behind their borders. Thus, if the Saudi television system has a large percentage of dubbed U.S. programs, it is because someone in Saudi Arabia bought the programs and put them on the air. This example can be multiplied a thousand times.

Speaking with alarm about the way that information flows around the world is like complaining because more ships or airplanes travel to New York than they do to Bali or some distant port. Information, including news and data, travels where it is called, where it has an interest. Ironically, the very Third World countries where the most criticism is heard are typically places that have benefited from Western communication development, whether the setting up of newspapers and broadcast stations or the training of journalists. Whether this was motivated by positive or negative goals, there has nevertheless been a strong link between the development of communication enterprises and economic development. Even scholars like Robert C. Hornik, who worries about the slow pace of change in the Third World in linking information to agricultural production and better nutrition, believe that better strategies and new commitments to change could transform some problems of undeveloped countries. In *Development Communication*, Hornik explains that failed efforts in developing nations usually can be explained as follows:

1. Information is no solution for a lack of resources.

2. Audiences for information programs are unresponsive even when such information might help.

3. Information programs have not worked because they have not been done appropriately (Hornik, 1988,155).

Without going into all the details of the arguments, it is clear that issues like general economic resources and institutional motivation are factors in creating effective information programs and systems in countries where they are lacking.

Elie Abel, professor of communication at Stanford and a distinguished former journalist, says that "few decisions taken in the name of any people more accurately reflect their underlying political philosophy than those having to do with the ownership and control of their information networks." Abel and many Western observers are in favor of a diverse system of communication around the world, with some help for the Third World, but with the United States and other nations having a right to exploit their advantages in the economic marketplace (Graff,1983, 238).

Over the years, the United States has fostered technology transfer, helping various nations and peoples communicate better. We have also set up training programs for journalists, broadcasters, agricultural communicators and others. We have welcomed thousands of foreign students who have taken knowledge about communication back to their home countries. And we increasingly have had joint economic ventures in various countries, leading eventually to their self-determination.

The fruits of the information age—computers, satellites, printing technology and everything else that blurs the old distinctions among media as quickly as it creates new media— will spill over into the Third World in the 1990s, despite anyone's efforts to prevent it or to promote it. It is unlikely that this spillover will speed economic and political development in the way that architects of the old paradigm hoped, or that it will help shape the vision of Third World cultural independence that advocates of the new order proposed.

But this is often forgotten by critics who believe that "balanced news" means that a given country or political system should determine what news flows out of that country to the rest of the world. The danger and fallacy of such a proposition was seen in 1989 during the turmoil in Tiananmen Square in Beijing, when Western news crews brought that tragic scene to people everywhere. The Chinese government later would block coverage, arguing that their official version was more accurate than was the portrayal in the Western press. The boundaries that used to keep communication within national borders are breaking down, as the situation in China indicated. In fact, new technologies are allowing the transmission and receipt of messages almost anywhere. With jamming stopped in the Soviet Union, people in that country are able to listen to the BBC, Voice of America, and even get Western European television signals from the satellite.

The United States does make the largest imprint on the world's communication system, but it is not the only one. European communication companies and governments are gearing up for a fully operative common market in 1992 and will be important communication competitors. U.S. media firms, especially book publishers, often have British owners, and many foreign interests are investing in media companies in the United States. The global village that Marshall McLuhan predicted is with us, and it is difficult to tell which national interests are represented in communication media without looking at the ownership papers.

True, the United States is the greatest communication power today, but the Japanese, French, Italians, West Germans, Canadians, and others are right behind, competing vigorously for everything from high definition television to videotex and data transmission. The information war is on and there is no assurance that the United States will win. After all, it is part of economic competition and we have seen the role that Middle East oil producers or Japanese electronics firms can play.

The arguments about U.S. dominance of communication and news in the world are passé. There is much more diversity and pluralism today than ever before, as was indicated by developments in Eastern Europe and the Soviet Union in 1989. I would argue that almost any nation can develop communication power in some realm if they have incentive, will, and a competent business plan. Little Barbados is a telecommunication competitor; Italy competes in publication design and high technology; the British are consuming the book trade in the United States, and people like Rupert Murdoch, the Australian media baron who owns communication media on three continents, are proving that communication is a global phenomenon.

Argument Summation: The U.S. media contribute fairly to communication equity.

The imbalance in global information systems in favor of U.S. media is a natural result of entrepreneurial spirit and American media's maturity, but it does not follow that U.S. media unfairly dominate global communication. The prevalence of U.S. communications in global information occurs because information goes where it is requested and the Third World nations have invited American media to their countries, not because of colonial dominance. Quite often it is the very Third World nations criticizing U.S. dominance that benefit from improved education and social services due to communications development. The United States has also fostered native information systems through the transfer of technology and communications systems. True, the United States does have a large impact on global communications, but the Japanese, French, Italians, West Germans, Canadians, and British are right behind and challenging U.S. media on all technological and informational fronts.

TOPICS FOR DISCUSSION

1. Is it necessarily the case, as Merrill maintains, that American dominance of world communication is "unhealthy"? Might it not be that this provides the world with a higher type of communication, more credible messages, and more professional examples for other countries?

2. How do you feel about the term "communication imperialism" used by many Third World spokespersons to indict the U.S. media system? Is it a proper term? Why or why not?

3. What do you think a "balanced news flow" among countries means? If such a state of news flow ever comes about, what ramifications would this mean for world economics and politics—and for national development generally?

4. When Dennis says that arguments indicting the United States for dominating world communication are passé, what is the basis of his belief?

5. Think of the kinds of changes that would have to come about in *all countries of the world* if one or two of them did not dominate information flow. Do such changes seem probable in the near future—or even possible?

TOPICS FOR RESEARCH

1. Study the impact of U.S. television programming on other countries. Read what critics and commentators say about this. Why should anyone care? Is there a possibility that our programming will have a negative effect on other countries and systems, debasing their culture? What evidence is there for this?

2. Report on the current status of the New World Information and Communication Order (NWICO) debate.

3. Study U.S. news coverage discussed in the McBride Commission Report, as it was portrayed in magazines, newspapers, and other outlets retrieved through libraries or data bases. Was the portrayal of the report

clearly and easily understood? Was coverage positive, negative, or neutral? Did most people have access to the information?

4. Link the discussion of information-rich and information-poor societies and countries with arguments over U.S. communications dominance. What is the state of this debate? Should anyone care? How can we measure access to information in different countries and societies?

5. Do a case study of news coverage of a given international event by reading or viewing television, news magazines, and newspapers. What were the sources of the news? To what extent were American and international information and points of view included? Was there, in your opinion, a proper balance? If so empowered, how would you change it?

FURTHER READING

Graff, Robert D. *Communications for National Development*. Cambridge, MA: Oelgeschalager, Gunn & Hain Publishers, 1983.

Hachten, William. *World News Prism*. Ames, IA: Iowa State University Press, 1988.

Hamelink, Cees J. *Cultural Autonomy in Global Communications*. White Plains, NY: Longman, 1982.

Mankekar, D. R. *One-Way Flow: Neo-Colonialism Via News Media*. New Delhi, India: Clarion Books, 1978.

Mattelart, Armand. *Multinational Corporation and the Control of Culture*. Atlantic Highlands, NJ: Humanities Press, 1979.

Merrill, John C., ed. *Global Journalism*. White Plains, NY: Longman, 1990.

Mowlana, Hamid. *Global Information and World Communication*. White Plains, NY: Longman, 1986.

Nordenstreng, Kaarle, and H. I. Schiller. *National Sovereignty and International Communication*. Norwood, NJ: Ablex, 1979.

Pratt, C. B. "U.S. Newsmagazines' Coverage of Africa." *Gazette* 1, no. 26 (1980):31–45.

Schiller, H. I. *The Mind Managers*. Boston: Beacon Press, 1973.

———. *Who Knows: Information in the Age of Fortune 500*. Norwood, NJ: Ablex, 1981.

Tunstall, Jeremy. *The Media Are American*. New York: Columbia University Press, 1977.

INDEX

ABC News, 166
Abel, Elie, 219
Absence of Malice, 22
Access
  right of, 65, 66, 67, 68, 133
  theory of, 56, 62, 63
Accountability, 160
Adversarial media, 21–30
Adversaries, The, 28
Advertising, 182–191
Advocacy journalism, 117–118, 123
Agenda-setting studies, 85
Ailes, Roger, 194
Alien and Sedition Acts, 27
Altschull, J. Herbert, 37
American Association of Advertising
    Agencies, 185
  creative code of, 185
American journalists, studies of, 155–156
American Marketing Association, 182
American Newspaper Publishers
    Association (ANPA), 38, 42, 49
American Press Institute, 38
American Society of Newspaper Editors
    (ASNE), 38, 129, 166
Analytical story, 121
Annual Review of Psychology, 83
Artillery of the Press, The, 25
Atkin, Charles, 98, 129
Attribution, 111
Audience research, 129, 130, 132

Bachen, Christine, 83, 85–86
Backtalk: Press Councils in America, 168

Bagdikian, Ben, 35, 41, 152
Bailey, Charles W., 167
Baker, Ray Stannard, 98
Baker, Samm S., 184, 185
Ball-Rokeach, Sandra, 85
Barrett, William, 204
Barron, Jerome, 37, 57–60, 63–64, 67
Barth, Alan, 116
BBC, 24, 174, 220
Benjamin, Burton, 156
Bernays, Edward L., 194
Berns, Walter, 14
Bernstein, Carl, 97, 103
Biagi, Shirley, 35
Bickel, Alexander, 11
Bill of Rights, 7, 8, 10, 46–47, 50–51, 54,
    58, 60, 62–63
Black, Hugo Lafayette, 7, 8, 11–12, 47
Black, Jay, 202
Blodgett, Cameron, 167–168
Blyskal, Jeff, 196
Blyskal, Mary, 196
Bogart, John, 127
Bogart, Leo, 129
Boston Globe, 97, 105
Bowman, William, 209
Brandeis, Louis, 63
Branzburg v. Hayes, 47, 48
Brinkley, David, 111, 127
British Press Council, 162
Brucker, Herbert, 116
Buber, Martin, 113
Buel, Ronald, 119–120
Bukro, Casey, 163

223

Bureau of Labor Statistics, 203
Burger, Warren, 125
Burgoon, Judee, 98, 129
Burgoon, Michael, 98, 129
Bush, George H. W., 58, 189, 194
Bush-for-President campaign, 189
Business Week, 175

Cable communication, 74–75
Carey, James W., 205
Categorical imperative, 14
CBS, 179
Censorship, 5–6, 13–14, 27–28, 49, 52, 59
Centers for media ethics, 156
Central Intelligence Agency (CIA), 26, 174
Chandler, Robert, 168
Chayefsky, Paddy, 166
Chicago Tribune, 162–163
Cleveland Press, 71
CNN, 40, 74
Colonialism, 218
Commission on Freedom of the Press, 37, 64
Committed Journalism, 156
Compaine, Ben, 72
Confucius, 13
Consequential story, 121
Cooke, Janet, 39, 153, 208
Cooley, Thomas, 6, 7
Cooper, Kent, 51
"Creative Code," 185
Cross, Harold L., 47, 51
Cutlip, Scott, 192, 196

Daily Mirror (London), 102
Dallas Times-Herald, 72
"Dark Ages of American Journalism, The" 27
DeFleur, Melvin, 85, 90, 128
DeMott, John, 115
Deontelic ethics, 141, 147
Descriptive story, 121
Des Moines Tribune, 71
Development Communication, 219
Dictionary of the Social Sciences, A, 172
Discovering the News, 111
Douglas, William O., 8, 47–48
Duties of the press, 10, 27, 35, 53

Edelstein, Alex, 66
Editor and Publisher International Yearbook, The, 208
Editorial autonomy, 12–13, 21, 25, 36, 58, 61, 64, 125–126, 128–131, 133

Electronic media networks, 40
Ellul, Jacques, 178
Emerson College, 156
Encounter, 153
Enlightenment philosophers, 7, 9
Ethical Journalism, 156
Ethics, 137–147, 150–157, 161–170, 208
Ethiopian radio, 215

Fair Play, 156
Faulkner, William, 97, 105
Federal Communications Commission (FCC), 99, 167
Federal Freedom of Information Act, 47, 54
Federal Trade Commission, 100
First Amendment, 5, 7–12, 15–16, 56–60, 63, 67, 71, 75, 87, 166, 189, 201, 207
Flexner, Abraham, 202
Forbes, 175
Fortune, 22
Founding Fathers, 12, 51, 59
"Fourth branch of government," 21, 28
Fourth Estate, 28
Fox, 40
Free and Responsible Press, A, 37
Freedom, 5–7, 10–15, 27, 53, 60
Freedom of Information, 60
Freedom of the Press for Whom?, 37
Freedom, Virtue and the First Amendment, 14
Free press clause, 48
Function of press, 21
as watchdog, 22, 25, 39

Gannett, 76
Gannett Center Journal, 196
Gannett Center for Media Studies, 38, 42
Gans, Herbert, 206
Gazette (Holland), 214
Gerald, J. Edward, 154, 155
Gitlin, Todd, 85–86
Gitlow v. New York, 8
Glasnost, 173
Global village, 220
Golden Rule, 14
Goode, William J., 203
Goodwin, Eugene, 156
Gorbachev, Mikhail, 173
Graff, Robert D., 219
Graham, Katharine, 40
Grenada Crisis, 38
Groping for Media Ethics, 156
Group-owned newspapers, 76, 77, 79
Gutiérrez, Félix, 75

INDEX

Hachten, William, 215
Hadwin, Arnold, 114, 115
Haiman, Franklyn S., 49
Hamelink, Cees, 214
"Happy talk" news, 99
Harper's, 205
Hartford Courant, 116
Harvard Law Review, 57
Harwood, Richard, 87
Hayakawa, S. I., 110
Hearst, 76
Hearst, William Randolph, 151
Hemingway, Ernest, 97, 105
Herbert v. Lando, 11
Hess, John L., 152
Hiebert, Ray, 35–36
History of the Standard Oil Company, The, 193
Hocking, William Ernest, 64
Hodges, Louis, 165
Hook, Sidney, 8, 12
Hornick, Robert C., 218, 219
Horton, Willie, 189
Hulteng, John L., 156
Hutchins, Robert, 37
Hutchins Commission, 14, 24
  report of, 37, 126
Huxley, Aldous, 183, 184

Imperative of Freedom, The, 165
Institute of Propaganda Analysis, 172
Interactive television, 66
Investigative reporting, 117
Iran-Contra, 155
Ismach, Arnold H., 121
Ivins, Molly, 72

Janowitz, Morris, 206, 209
Jaspin, Elliott, 144
Johnstone, John, 209
Journal of Mass Media Ethics, 202
Journal of Peace Research, 215
Journalism
  business of, 113
Journalism Quarterly, 85
Journalism schools, 155–156, 209–210
Journalistic conventions, 154
Journalistic ethical codes, 152, 154–155, 160–170, 197, 201, 204, 208
  voluntary, 164

Kauffman, Irving, 48
King, Cecil, 102
Kirkpatrick, Clayton, 162
Knight-Ridder, 76

Kristol, Irving, 204
Kuhn, Thomas, 85, 87

Ladies Home Journal, 189
Lambeth, Edmund, 156
Lapham, Lewis, 205
Lazarsfeld, Paul, 84, 86, 89
Lee, Ivy, 193–194
Lemert, James, 87, 90–91
Libertarian journalism, 27, 52, 61, 162
Liberty, 7, 10, 46
Lippmann, Walter, 14, 127
Loeb, William, 27
Los Angeles Herald-Examiner, 71
Los Angeles Times, 38, 111, 166
Louisville Courier Journal, 168
Lowenstein, Ralph, 153
Luedtke, Kurt, 22, 49, 50, 129, 161

McBride Commission Report, 218
McClatchy, C. K., 73
McClure's Magazine, 193
McCombs, Maxwell, 85, 90
McDonald, Donald, 113
Machiavelli, 153, 177
"Machiavellian Ethics in Journalism," 153
McLuhan, Marshall, 220
MacNeil, Robert, 39
Madison, James, 47
Madison Avenue, 185
Malcolm, Janet, 152, 154
Malice, 11
Manchester (N.H.) *Union-Leader*, 27
Mankekar, D. R., 214
Market research, 41
Marketing approach to news, 127–131, 132, 134
Marketplace theory, 37, 57
Mattelart, Armand, 115, 121, 214
Mattson, Floyd, 64
Media
  believability of, 33, 39
  competition of, 77
  concentration of, 35, 38, 40, 70, 72
  credibility of, 33, 38–39, 40–41, 145, 156
  effects of, 83–92
  ideology of, 175
  profits of, 36–41, 57, 71
  trustworthiness of, 33, 39
Media imperialism, 213–216, 219
Media issues, 1–2
Media ownership, 35, 38, 40, 71, 73–74, 76–78

Medicine, 206
Mencken, H. L., 111, 115
Merrill, John, 141, 156
Message pluralism, 77
Messenger's Motives, The, 156
Methvin, Eugene, 101
Meyer, Philip, 143, 144, 156
Miami Herald, 58
Mill, John Stuart, 15
Milwaukee Journal, 8, 168
Minneapolis Star, 71
Minnesota News Council, 167
Moon, Reverend Sun Myung, 27
Ms., 189
Muckrakers, 98, 103, 151, 193
Mungo, Raymond, 118
Munsey, Frank, 72
Murdoch, Rupert, 40, 220

Nation, The, 72
National Enquirer, 208
National Geographic, 214
National News Council, 162, 164, 167–168
Near v. Minnesota, 9
Network, 166
New England Journal of Medicine, 74
New Journalism, 117–118, 123
New World Information and Communication Order (NWICO), 215,218
New York Sun, 127
New York Times, 9–11, 36, 40, 58, 111, 126, 167, 175, 204, 208
New York Times v. Sullivan, 10
Newhouse, 76
News reporting, models of, 121
News World Corporation, 40
Newspaper Readership Project, 129
Newsweek, 214
Nieman Fellowships, 208
1984, 172
Noelle-Neumann, Elisabeth, 85–87, 90
Nordenstreng, Kaarle, 214
Novack, Michael, 112–113

Objective reporting, 109, 123, 177
Orwell, George, 172
Ostgaard, Einer, 214, 215
Other Government, The, 28
Oxford Shorter English Dictionary, 203

Parker-Plummer, Bernadette, 111
PASID, 176, 180
Pennsylvania Evening Post, 187

Pentagon Papers, 9
People's Republic of China, 173, 177, 181
People's Right to Know: Legal Access to Public Records and Proceedings, 47
Permissible Lie, The, 184
Philadelphia Bulletin, 71
Philosophy and Journalism, 163
Pluralism, 24, 37, 59, 70–79, 160, 163
Podhoretz, Norman, 103
Powell, Justice Lewis, 28
Poynter Institute, 38, 42, 156
Pratt, C. B., 214
Precision Journalism, 117, 118, 143–144
Press and the Public, The, 129
Press councils, 160–170, 204
Press coverage
  of business, 29
  of government, 29, 35, 38, 52
  of sports, 29
Press freedom, 5–16, 20–21, 27–28, 39, 48, 50, 52–53, 56, 58–61, 64–65, 67, 71, 73, 134, 142
Press performance, 161
Printer's Ink, 185
Prior restraint, 5, 9, 11, 13, 15, 57, 66
Professional standards, 206
Professionalism, 9, 12, 137, 143, 145–148, 151, 194, 201–211
Professions of America, The, 203, 207
Progressive, The, 9
Propaganda, 172–180
Providence Journal, 144
Public Agenda Foundation, 100, 166
Public communication, 1, 2, 20, 24, 39
Public interest, 41
Public Philosophy, The, 14
Public relations, 192–200
Public Relations Society of America, 192, 197
  Code of Professional Standards of, 197
Public trust, 33, 34, 63
Pulitzer, Joseph 151
Pulitzer prizes, 143, 208

Qualter, Terence H., 178
QUBE, 66
Quill, The, 101, 152

Radio and Television News Directors Association (RTNDA), 38
Ramsey, William, 197
Rand, Ayn, 58, 59, 67
Raskin, A. H., 167
Rather, Dan, 179
Redwood City press council, 162

INDEX

Reilly, Robert T., 198
Relativistic tactic of reporting, 139–147, 163, 176
Reporting Processes and Practices, Newswriting for Today's Readers, 121
Reshaping the Media, 39
Reston, James (Scotty), 25, 103, 110
Reynolds, Frank, 111
Richstad, Jim, 64
Right of privacy, 8, 63
Right of reply, 56, 66, 68
Right to communicate, 64, 65, 193
Right to Know, The, 51
Right to publish, 6
Rights, 49
  individual, 26, 46, 50, 63, 67
  institutional, 26, 46, 47, 50, 63, 67
  of the press, 10, 48
  structural, 26, 48
"Rights of man," 7
Rivers, William L., 28, 168
Roberts, Donald, 83, 85–86
Robinson, John P., 85–90
Rockefeller, John D., 193
Rogers, Will, 33
Roman Catholic Church, 172
Roshco, Bernard, 128
Rothman and Lichter, 114
Rusher, William, 114, 152

Salience information, 66
Santa Rosa press council, 162
Sartre, Jean-Paul, 113
Saxbe v. Washington Post Co., 28
Schiller, Herbert I., 214
Schramm, Wilbur, 85
Schudson, Michael, 111, 112, 185, 187
Scripps, 76
Service journalism, 117, 118
Shaw, Donald, 85, 90
Silber, John, 112
Sinclair, Upton, 41
Sixth Amendment, 8
"60 Minutes," 156
Slawski, Edward, 209
Social Responsibility of the Press, The, 154
Society of Professional Journalists, 163, 201
Staebler, Charles, 196
Steffens, Lincoln, 98, 103
Stewart, Potter, 26, 48
Stone, I. F., 30

Structural rights, 26
Structure of Scientific Revolutions, The, 85
Sulzberger, Arthur H., 40
"Supply-side" economist, 207

Tarbell, Ida, 98, 193
Teapot Dome, 155
Theories of Mass Communication, 85
Third World, 212–222
Thomson, 76
Thoreau, Henry David, 127
Tiananmen Square, 219
Tillich, Paul, 113
Time, 214
Times Mirror, 38, 114
Tobin, Richard L., 185
Topping, Seymour, 196
Tornillo, Pat, Jr., 57–58, 63
Tornillo v. The Miami Herald, 57, 62, 68
Transnational news flow, 212–222
Tribe, Lawrence, 46
Tuchman, Gaye, 117
Tunstall, Jeremy, 214
Turner, Ted, 40
TV Guide, 156

UNESCO, 213
Universal tactic of reporting, 139–141, 144–147
University of Minnesota, 156
U.S. Constitution, 5–10, 12, 15–16, 23, 45–50, 54, 63, 65, 67, 87, 207
U.S. News & World Report, 178
U.S. Office of Education, 208

Verifiable journalism, 114
Verification, 111, 114
Villard, Oswald Garrison, 41, 72
Voice of America, 220
Von Hoffman, Nicholas, 103
Vox populi, 33

Wackman, Dan, 73
Wall Street Journal, 39, 175, 196, 204
Warren, Samuel D., 63
Washington Post, 9, 39, 40, 87, 116, 126, 152, 208
Washington Star, 71, 76
Washington Times, 27, 114
Watergate, 155
Watson, George, 166
Weaver, George, 156
Weaver, Paul H., 22
West, Woody, 114

Westmoreland, General William, 156
White, Byron, 48
Wicker, Tom, 103
Wilhoit, G. Cleveland, 156
Will, George, 103
Wilson, Clint, 75
Winans, Foster, 39
Winship, Tom, 97, 105
Wiseman, Fred, 28

Wolfe, Tom, 97, 118
Woodward, Bob, 97, 103
World Media Report, 87, 202
Wright, Jim, 174
Wylie, Philip, 15

Yankelovich, Daniel, 100
Yardley, Jonathan, 152

Zenger, John Peter, 26